ROUTLEDGE LIBRARY EDITIONS:
INTERNATIONAL TRADE POLICY

Volume 14

INTERNATIONAL TRADE POLICY

INTERNATIONAL TRADE POLICY

F. V. MEYER

Routledge
Taylor & Francis Group
LONDON AND NEW YORK

First published in 1978 by Croom Helm Ltd

This edition first published in 2018
by Routledge
2 Park Square, Milton Park, Abingdon, Oxon OX14 4RN

and by Routledge
711 Third Avenue, New York, NY 10017

Routledge is an imprint of the Taylor & Francis Group, an informa business

British Library Cataloguing in Publication Data
A catalogue record for this book is available from the British Library

ISBN: 978-1-138-06323-5 (Set)
ISBN: 978-1-315-14339-2 (Set) (ebk)
ISBN: 978-1-138-09969-2 (Volume 14) (hbk)
ISBN: 978-1-315-09909-5 (Volume 14) (ebk)

Publisher's Note
The publisher has gone to great lengths to ensure the quality of this reprint but points out that some imperfections in the original copies may be apparent.

Disclaimer
The publisher has made every effort to trace copyright holders and would welcome correspondence from those they have been unable to trace.

INTERNATIONAL TRADE POLICY

F. V. MEYER

CROOM HELM LONDON

Croom Helm Ltd, 2-10 St John's Road, London SW11

British Library Cataloguing in Publication Data

Meyer, Frederick Victor
International trade policy.
1. Commercial policy
I. Title
382'.3 HF1401

ISBN 0-85664-173-1

Printed in Great Britain by
Biddles Ltd, Guildford, Surrey

CONTENTS

ACKNOWLEDGEMENTS

The author is indebted to the Social Science Research Council and the University of Exeter which financed research assistance and study trips to London and Brussels. Mr M.J.J. Macmillen read most of the typescript, Dr J.H. Coates Chapters 1 and 2 and Ms Alex Malcolm Chapter 1. Chapter 2 was seen by Professor R.H. Barback, Professor J. Black, Mr Don Moore, Mr Andrew Tessler and Mr A.J. Turner. Thanks to their help substantial improvements could be made on earlier drafts. Mr E.T. McGovern and Mr M.T. Shaw helped with the legal and constitutional issues involved in Chapter 3. Dr R. Burt and Dr R.A. Lewis advised on the historic aspects. Mr R. Rickard and Dr D. Schwarz commented on aspects of Chapter 5. On specific trading problems and information relating to various countries, discussions or correspondence with Mr S. Aberg, Ms E. Bonnier, Mr R. Chassaignon, Mr J. Daniels, Mr D. Franklin, Ms Jane E.W. Killick, Mr E.J. Mercer, Mr W. Paues and Mr M.A.G. Simpson were of value. Last but not least, the author's thanks are due to Ms Kay Beales and Mr Paul Richards for research assistance.

Exeter, November 1977

ABBREVIATIONS

CAP	Common Agricultural Policy
EC	European Communities (comprising EEC, ECSC and Euratom)
ECSC	European Coal and Steel Community
EEC	European Economic Community
EFTA	European Free Trade Association
GATT	General Agreement on Tariffs and Trade
LDCs	Less developed countries
OEEC	Organisation for European Economic Co-operation
R & D	Research and Development
UK	United Kingdom
US	United States

1 INTERNATIONAL ECONOMIC INTEGRATION

1. Introduction

A feature of the post-war scene to date has been a marked lowering of international trade barriers. Give or take a few years, this era of freer trade coincided with the third quarter of the twentieth century. The General Agreement on Tariffs and Trade (GATT) was negotiated in 1947 and implemented in 1948. The enlargement of the European Communities (EC) was agreed in 1972 and tariff-free trade in that area was made effective by 1978. At that time, negotiations were in progress for a seventh round of reductions of trade barriers under GATT. The outcome of those negotiations will largely determine whether the movement towards freer trade will continue in the final decades of the century.

To date, the freer trade movement has hinged on US trade agreements. Its main principles have been freer trade and non-discrimination. Freer trade narrowed the difference between national and non-national commercial rights in each trading country. Non-discrimination meant that all non-national commercial interests were treated alike. In other words, there were to be only two levels of commercial rights within each country, and the difference between those two levels was to be reduced through freer trade. Acceptance of those principles by other countries led to the GATT. The movement towards freer trade was put on an international contractual basis, binding on all signatories. The speed of the movement was largely determined by how far the US, the leading commercial power of the time, was willing to go. Others could go further only by forming customs unions or free trade areas. This way they conferred upon each other national commercial rights and treated third parties no worse than before. There were still only two levels of commercial rights in each of those countries.

Logically, freer trade should lead to free trade on a universal basis. There would then be only one level of commercial rights. But this goal remains elusive. Even the policy of freer trade has, in effect, been confined mainly to industrial countries with market economies and to trade in industrial goods. The reasons for the geographical limitation to date were often political and those for the product limitation largely economic.

Freer trade was negotiated. Negotiations can succeed only where the issues can be defined. That presented no unsurmountable obstacles when negotiations were about tariff rates, quotas and the rule of non-discrimination in such matters. Difficulties about definition are greater when trade is in the hands of state agencies whose decisions on quantities and prices are based on political rather than market criteria. In practice, this confined negotiations about trade barriers mainly to non-Communist countries. Again, negotiations about trade barriers have meaning only where there are protected industries in the negotiating countries. This precluded negotiations with highly specialised one-commodity economies. Some countries with such economies were bent on industrialisation as part of their desire to assert their political independence. They were unwilling to offer trade concessions unless they thought their industries well established. This further limited the possibility of successful negotiations to countries with long established industries. Effectively this meant the US, Western Europe and later on also Japan.

The freeing of trade implies restraint in the exercise of governmental powers over external trade. At the beginning of the century, a number of governments exercised self-restraint and pursued unilateral free trade or low tariff policies.

After the experiences of 1914-45, no major government was willing to exercise such self-restraint. The return to freer trade had to be negotiated and this implied contractual restraint. When two or more governments negotiated trade agreements, they had to find ways of reconciling their various powers over external trade. The reconciliation of powers over external trade also mattered where different arms of the same government had authority over different aspects of trade policy. For instance, in the US, the President has authority to negotiate trade agreements but can implement them only within limits laid down by the Congress. An effective US trade policy then depends on a reconciliation of Presidential and Congressional powers. At a time when the US was the world's leading commercial power, her domestic politics largely determined how much international freeing of trade was possible, for no other country was willing to concede more than the US.

US domestic politics also determined the product range of international trade negotiations. Agricultural protection was given priority over trade agreements legislation, and this made agricultural commodities less negotiable than industrial products. This approach was reflected in the attitude of other powers, such as the EC.

Since industrial countries were, in any case, liberal in the treatment of basic materials needed by their manufacturing industries, negotiations were largely confined to manufactured products.

If the possibility of trade negotiations depended largely on politics, the success of the resultant agreements depended largely on economics. It so happened that, during the third quarter of the century, the needs of manufacturing industries were best met by a policy of contractual reductions of trade barriers. This has not always been the case. For instance, late nineteenth century and early twentieth century manufacturing could be best served by unilateral free trade or low tariff policies on industrial inputs. Then, the chief concern was to obtain the cheapest possible supplies for price-competitive industries. Since then, manufacturing industries have become Research and Development (R & D) intensive. Products change more frequently. Their market life has become shorter. In order to recoup their R & D costs before the products become obsolete, firms have to sell the largest possible output in the shortest possible time. Access to markets for outputs has become even more important than cheap supplies of inputs. The change will be dealt with at greater length later in this chapter and also in Chapters 3 and 5. Here let it suffice to say that one country's government can through unilateral action help its industries to obtain supplies of materials as cheaply as possible. What it has to do is to admit such materials without imposts. But no one country's government can, through unilateral action, ensure market outlets in other countries. These have to be negotiated with other governments. The latter will wish to negotiate if their industries too are R & D intensive and seek access to wider markets. Successful negotiations then make existing R & D intensive activities more profitable. Once there is freer trade in R & D intensive products, firms can specialise in particular R & D intensive products and buy in the rest. The result is what has become known as intra-industry trade. A major part of post-war trade in manufactures was of this nature. This development would have been frustrated had there not been similar freeing of trade in the major industrial trading countries.

An assessment of international trade policies must take account of the structure of the trading countries' industries. Hence, export structure, and the appropriate ways of pricing such exports, provide the second theme of this book. It is given pride of place in Chapter 2, which is mainly concerned with the UK, and to a lesser extent with France and Sweden – for the simple reason that only those three countries provide the appropriate statistical information.

Subsequently the argument returns to this book's main theme of international trade policy, but the second theme will recur wherever appropriate. US tariff policy is dealt with at length. It exerted most influence on international trade policy in the third quarter of the century: not only was the US the largest single commercial power at the time; no less important was that the US had pioneered R & D intensive manufacturing, and that her foreign economic policy had developed in ways most suitable for the requirements of those industries.

Other countries responded largely according to the R & D intensities of their industries. R & D intensive activities grew markedly in the Western Europe of the third quarter of the century. This encouraged the wish to go further towards free trade than the US did. GATT seemed inadequate. A common free trade market was superimposed on it. Japan too moved towards more R & D intensive activities but somewhat later. Her response to negotiated reductions in trade barriers was also somewhat tardy. Outside North America, Western Europe and Japan, there was little or no response. There could not be. Most manufacturing industries outside the 'R & D area' were not yet ready for R & D intensive activities and specialisation in such activities. Instead, there were many attempts to do in new countries what was already done in old ones, with all the attendant risk of rivalries for the same supplies and the same markets for the same goods. But this is running ahead into later sections of the present chapter and into Chapter 5. The immediate task must be to examine the two major twentieth century attempts to integrate the world economy. These were the *Pax Britannica* which sought integration through unilateral free trade and the *Pax Americana* which seeks integration through contractual freeing of trade.

2. Two Ways of Integration

When the wars were over, in 1945, it was thought that peace could be fortified by commerce. Foreign economic policy was to promote more harmony in international relations. In order to achieve this end, there had to be less discrimination between the commercial rights of this country and that one. The policy was to treat all foreign commercial interests alike, and to minimise the difference between the rights accorded to national and foreign interests. Although this is a basic rule for any policy of peace through commerce which applies at all times, it cannot be achieved the same way at all times. If the policy is to succeed in its major aim, it must be adjusted to the political and technological opportunities of the age.

Political considerations alone precluded an effective policy of peace through commerce at almost any time between 1914 and 1945. The two periods when this could be attempted during the current century were the 1900s and the third quarter of the century. The 1900s were a late phase of the *Pax Britannica* which had reached its height in the late nineteenth century and was to be challenged in the twentieth century. It was based on unilateral British free trade. The *Pax Americana* seemed supreme in the 1950s and 1960s but came to be questioned in the 1970s. It is based on negotiated freeing of trade. The major difference in the working of the *Pax Britannica* and the *Pax Americana* may be summed up as follows. Under the *Pax Britannica*, there was economic integration of industrial countries with the primary producing world, but there appears to have been no deliberate attempt to integrate the economies of the industrial countries. Under the *Pax Americana*, there has been increasing integration of the economies of industrial countries, with primary producing interests carried along rather than directly integrated. The early twentieth-century challenge to the *Pax Britannica* came from industrial countries. The questioning of the *Pax Americana* in the 1970s was led by primary producing ones.

It could be argued that neither the *Pax Britannica* nor the *Pax Americana* have been truly universal since each concentrated on a one-sector approach and excluded large parts of the world. It could also be argued that each was the only possible approach at its time. An equalisation of commercial rights acquires economic meaning if it allows trade to grow by at least as much as industrial output grows. In the 1900s, the opportunities for increased trade seemed greatest with primary producing areas which were open to trade. In the third quarter of the century, they were greatest in industrial products of market economies. The reasons for this change, and the consequent reasons why the *Pax Americana* could not be a replay of the *Pax Britannica*, were as follows.

In so far as the contrast between the industrial world of the 1900s and the third quarter of the century can be expressed in a few words, the change was one from hard work by individuals to skilled work, from quantitative to qualitative competition between industrial firms, and from the production of similar goods in the various industrial countries to specialisation within industries on a world scale. The world of the 1900s was one of hard work, in the sense that individuals or firms or even nations could usually better themselves by putting more man-hours into familiar tasks. Methods of production did not change so often as they do now. Nor did the nature of the final products. Individual decisions determined how much there was to be. True, there was technological change then and there had been before. Eyebrows might well have been raised, had anyone suggested at the time that the 1900s were not a progressive age. They were – they saw the culmination of a long development which had changed industrial production from local production for a local market to localised production for a world market. As every student of economics knew, England specialised in cloth and Portugal in wine.

By now, 'England' specialises in some varieties of 'cloth' and 'Portugal' in others. This too is the result of a long development, and some of the pioneering stages date from the 1900s or even earlier. Now, not only markets have become world-wide, industrial production too has become world-wide (in the sense that successive stages in the chain of production of one article can take place in several countries, and in the sense that there is specialisation in the production of one or more articles within a wider product range between firms and between countries). Although food and basic materials have always had to be imported into industrial areas, now manufactured components and specialised finished goods are also imported into such areas. Often it pays to import and export manufactured goods which come under the same tariff heading. In the third quarter of the century, such imports came to equal and exceed the imports of primary commodities.

Although the appearance of finished consumer goods has always had to be changed with great frequency in order to conform with the requirements of fashion, now the nature of industrial goods and the ways of producing them have also become subject to frequent change. At the beginning of the century, new goods might have been thought of as permanent additions to the stock of human possessions or as improvements which would only gradually replace the older goods. Whatever the details, the expected market life of products was long enough that entry into industrial activities was open to anyone who had saved or was thought credit-worthy. R & D costs, if any, either had been incurred so long ago that they no longer influenced production costs or they could be spread over an expected long market life of the product. Capital costs were largely or exclusively the costs of purchasing the necessary equipment. Whether these costs were high or low, they were largely predictable. The repayment of capital could be spread over a long period of time and could be determined by purely financial considerations. Owners of money capital could decide whether there should be more steel or cotton. They would not always know of different ways of producing steel or cotton. They did not have to: where the product had a long market life, production methods were given for long periods of time.

They are no longer given. The industrial world has educated itself beyond acceptance of what there is and beyond reliance on pure chance whether there should be new goods. Deliberate attempts are made to improve industrial goods through R & D. Chance still plays its part in whether R & D leads to major breakthroughs or just minor improvements, but even chance can be helped along by continuous appraisal and reappraisal of products. If early this century products and production processes were given for a generation or longer, this is no longer the case in most industrial activities. A market life of, say, fifteen years or half a generation is now thought long. The preparatory R & D stage usually takes several years. In some of the more advanced products, that stage can take a longer period of time than the subsequent market life of the product. This change from a long market life relative to the R & D stage (which in the past could be nil for most products) to a short market life relative to the R & D stage, is a main feature of twentieth-century industrial development. It has transformed the nature of industrial activities within firms and within countries, and the relations between firms and between countries.

The *Pax Americana* cannot be the same as the *Pax Britannica* because the nature of industrial economies has changed. The implications for marketing, pricing and international economic organisation will be a recurrent theme throughout this book. But first a few words on the working of, and the challenge to, the *Pax Britannica* early this century.

3. Integration under the Pax Britannica

At the turn of the century, most manufactures and most primary commodities were standardised and gradable goods. There were numerous producers of each who could not possibly have sold direct to outlets the world over. This task was performed for them by specialist merchants who bought for and sold from stock. The merchants formed 'the market' where price was determined according to the principles of perfect competition. There were such markets for the various products. Some were markets for particular manufactures such as cotton textiles, while others were concerned with particular primary commodities, such as raw cotton. Because each of those markets worked along the lines of perfect competition, they brought buyer and seller of one product together and established a market price for each of those products. As long as these various markets acted in accordance with the same principles, there emerged free market price relationships between the various products. In this sense, there was one market economy.

Since products and methods of production remained largely unchanged for long periods of time, the ratio of primary commodities needed to produce given units of industrial output was also known for long periods of time. Where the market economy was allowed to operate freely, as in the UK, imports of primary commodities grew at about the same rate as industrial output. Since manufactures were exported mainly in order to obtain the means to buy primary commodities, exports of manufactures also grew at approximately the same rate. True, this did not hold every year. But any excess (or shortfall) of exports of manufactures was soon corrected by a movement of the terms of trade against (in favour of) manufactures; and similarly in the case of primary commodities. Over any trade cycle, the price mechanism kept the rates of growth of manufacturing and trade roughly in line.[1]

'England' could seem for ever to specialise in 'cloth' and 'Portugal' in 'wine'. With the market life of both products apparently endless, there could be no effective bar to entry into whichever activity paid comparatively best. There were numerous cloth-making firms in England, not one of whom could have satisfied more than a fraction of the national market, let alone the world market. In order to prosper, each of a large number of producers had to get the most out of the factors at his disposal. Each tried to get basic materials and labour as cheaply as possible, but competition for factors kept up prices of materials and labour. Each tried to get the most out of his factors so that production would continue until labour tired and machines creaked. Hard work continued until unit costs came to equal the market controlled price. But the tasks of production could be duplicated with more labour, more machines and more materials. There was no effective bar to entry and, therefore, no bar to more hard work.

If this applied in one country, it applied in all. Entry could not be prevented anywhere in the industrial world, but it could be encouraged. Governments of some countries tried to do so through imposing tariffs. The intention was to encourage entry into certain industrial activities by their own nationals by giving them a price advantage over foreign suppliers. Sales by former suppliers were made less profitable, so that they had to turn to third markets to maintain their sales and output. The result was that competition in third markets was intensified, prices fell in those markets and exporting to third markets became less profitable. But all industrial countries needed profitable markets for their manufactures. They needed the proceeds to purchase materials which were basic for sustained domestic economic growth.

The most rapidly growing industrial countries of the time got themselves into a vicious circle. They wanted less trade with other industrial countries in order to give their protected industries a better chance. In the process they diverted exports of older industrial countries into third markets, and this made it more difficult for each manufacturer to get the price he wanted and consequently the supplies he needed. Any latent tensions were aggravated, and this became marked by the turn of the century. By then pressure on supplies had become so great that prices of primary commodities began to rise faster than prices of manufactures. Although the change in the terms of trade was mild compared with what was to happen at some later dates in this century, it was aggravating at the time. Amongst the consequences in the UK, was a worsening of labour relations: owners of the means of production sought to compensate themselves for rising basic material prices, and workers sought to compensate themselves for a higher cost of living. Internationally, a worsening of the terms of trade of manufactures over primary commodities added a new menace to the scramble for territories which supplied, or were thought capable of supplying, such produce.

No one except perhaps an economic determinist, could seriously suggest that the pressures created by protected domestic economic growth in some of the major industrial countries were the sole cause of the conflicts to come. Nevertheless, a recent study has pointed to domestic economic growth as an ever present ingredient in exacerbating the rivalries between the great powers of the time.[2] Even if this is accepted, it still does not follow that domestic economic growth as such necessarily aggravates rivalries, though the particular form of domestic economic growth of the time may have done so. For instance, there was more domestic economic growth in the industrial countries in the third quarter of the century than in the 1900s, or even than in all the forty peace-time years of the first half of the century taken together.[3] Yet international relations between the major industrial powers improved throughout the third quarter. What characterised the economic growth of the 1900s was that the industrial economies became more alike, that their domestic economic growth equalled or exceeded the growth of their external trade, and that the unit values of manufactured goods sold at home tended to move more favourably than the unit values of such goods sold abroad. In other words, those economies became more rival, more self-confident and more bad-tempered with each other. At the same time, each become more dependent on imported primary commodities which the protectionism of their rivals, not their suppliers, had made more difficult to get. There was interdependence with primary producing countries and growing conflict of interest between industrial countries. Domestic economic growth, unaccompanied by an at least equal rate of growth of trade between industrial countries, aggravated the rivalry between such countries at the time. Nevertheless, were history just economic history, these rivalries might have been contained in the early twentieth century as they had been in the late nineteenth century.

Then, the rivalries were contained by British overseas investment and free trade. British overseas investment had facilitated an increase in the availability of primary commodities for trade in excess of British requirements. In consequence, primary commodities became more easily available to other countries as well as cheaper in terms of manufactures. This assisted industrial growth anywhere in the industrial and industrialising world. Since some of the primary commodities were sold to industrial countries other than the UK, British investors could get a return in sterling only if products from those countries could be sold freely in the UK.[4] While much of the UK's payments surplus with primary producing countries was re-invested in those countries, some of it was balanced by imports of manufactures from industrial countries. In short, domestic economic growth of industrial countries put pressure on supplies of primary commodities; protection in some of the industrial countries increased this pressure beyond levels the market economy of the time could sustain; UK overseas investment eased the pressure through making more supplies available and at more favourable prices; and UK free trade eased the pressure further by allowing other industrial countries free access to currency earnings which could be used to purchase primary commodities.

By the turn of the century, the situation began to change. Although UK overseas investment was to reach record heights in the 1900s to 1913, much of this was re-investment.[5] In any case, it was no longer sufficient to bring forth sufficient additional supplies to contain the international pressure on primary commodities. Some other industrial countries also invested in primary producing areas, but their main investment efforts were directed at domestic economic growth which was mainly industrial growth. The pressure increased and prices of primary commodities rose. The situation was no longer so well contained as in the late nineteenth century.

It will never be known whether, in the absence of wars and intensified economic nationalism, the early twentieth-century British investment effort could once more have contained the pressure on supplies. Whatever might have been, it is doubtful whether the investment effort of any one country, however strong, could indefinitely have staved off the pressure on supplies emanating from faster growing industrial rivals. As pointed out before, in the days of the *Pax Britannica*, British production and trade grew at approximately the same rate as world trade, while the production of other industrial countries grew at a faster rate than their trade. At a time when the main purpose of exporting manufactures was to pay for primary commodities, any artificial stimulation of industrial growth through protection was bound to upset the then existing trade relationships. The economic nationalism of the inter-war years precluded a return to the old order or the establishment of a new one. The world of the third quarter of the century was one where technological developments had opened up possibilities of more trade in industrial goods, and the *Pax Americana* underwrote peace between industrial countries through freer trade in industrial goods. By the mid-1970s, when there were difficulties in obtaining adequate supplies of primary commodities, the problems of integrating primary producing and industrial interests once more came to the fore. Although the *Pax Britannica* was by then past history, it still offers some lessons which may be of interest for the fourth quarter of the century.

Given that the purpose of international trade in primary commodities is to supply industrial areas, the limit to any long-term growth of trade in primary commodities is set by the growth of industrial production. Given that, in the 1900s, manufacturing and primary production were both concerned with standardised and gradable products, there could be identical market structures in both kinds of trades. Through the price mechanism, trade in primary commodities could be integrated with the economy of an industrial free trade country. This was probably the highest form of economic integration between industrial and primary producing interests to date.

A new form of integration was to emerge in the industrial world of the third quarter of the century. Although there was no complete free trade in industrial goods, the freeing of trade which took place sufficed to lead to greater growth of trade in manufactures than of production of manufactures. Seen this way, it was a higher form of industrial integration than that achieved in the 1900s. Freer trade allowed for the use of technological advances which led to specialisation within industries. The same was not open to primary production. There, technological advances in production processes led to more standardisation and gradability, and were intended to do so. The fortunes of primary producers continued to depend on the creation of maximum quantity at standardised quality. No higher form of integration has as yet become possible for primary commodities than that attained under the *Pax Britannica*. The opportunities for such integration have, however, become less. Although there are still highly organised commodity markets for basic materials and in absolute terms there has been growth and no decline in the demand for most of such materials in the third quarter of the century, the growth of manufacturing as a whole has become relatively more dependent on technological advances and relatively less dependent on imported materials. In fuels, cartelisation in various forms is widespread and the prospects for an integrated market economy seem remote. In agricultural commodities, protection became universal in the inter-war years. Since then, some of the major powers have modified their system of agricultural protection but none have abandoned protection. In short, the degree of integration between the primary producing world and the industrial countries was generally less in the third quarter of the century than it had been in the 1900s. But the degree of integration between the industrial countries was greater.

4. Basic Conditions for Integration under the Pax Americana

The *Pax Americana* to date has been an industrial *Pax*. Its political opportunity came after 1945, when there was a consensus that the over-riding need was the pacification of the industrial world. The target of policy was freer trade without discrimination. The instruments of trade policy were US trade agreements legislation and the GATT (which will be discussed at some length in Chapters 3 and 4). These were innovations in trade policy. They allowed fuller use to be made of the technological innovations of R & D based industries than would otherwise have been possible. Those industries had reached pre-eminence in the US economy by then, and were later to reach the same position in Europe and later still in Japan.

Throughout the industrial world, there was a new way of life. Motorisation made previously remote places accessible. It became possible, for instance, to live further away from work. Mechanisation of homes made the emancipation of women a reality. New products of the chemical industries made life cleaner and longer. These, and much else, are the consequences of twentieth-century technology. They are not necessarily the consequences of a particular trade policy. At times in the past, when technology was given for long periods of time, freer trade had led to more trade of the 'cloth-for-wine' variety. Looking back at the economic literature of the late 1940s and early 1950s, a further development along such lines seems to have been expected. Even where allowance was made for greater industrialisation, the expectation appears to have been that *X* industry would expand in one country and contract elsewhere, while the opposite would happen to *Y* industry. By the 1960s, it had become apparent that this did not happen. Instead, the *X* industry would expand in all the countries which participated in the freeing of trade, and the *Y* industry too would have a similar experience in those countries. Although the freeing of trade did lead to growth of trade of the cloth-for-wine (or *X* for *Y*) variety, as expected, it led to even more growth of trade of the *X* for *X* (or 'cloth-for-cloth') variety. One reason was that the 'high' cost of entering the market for technologically advanced products made it impossible for firms to do so over the whole range of their products. They specialised over a narrower range, sold that in home and export markets and bought in the rest, if necessary from abroad. This way they could have longer production runs in fewer products and so save costs and still satisfy their customers' demand for the whole range of products. The following is an attempt to explain this in more detail. It will also show why these developments would have been frustrated had international trade not become freer.

Central to the technological changes of the twentieth century is the shortening of the market life of industrial products relative to the preparatory R & D stage. R & D is costly. It also takes time. The length of the R stage remains largely unpredictable. The length of the D stage is often more predictable, but it can take several years. There is a long lead time (or D time) between the decision to go ahead with a product and having it ready for the market. The subsequent market life tends to be relatively short and also uncertain. It can never be known whether a product will be a success several years hence, nor whether and when it will be overtaken by a better one (which, at worst, could happen even before it is ready for the market). More details will be given for particular industries in Chapter 2.

In order to make any product pay, firms must sell enough units to recoup their initial outlay. If the market life of a product is long, access to international markets may be useful but not necessarily essential to the survival of existing firms. Given the choice between freer access to international markets and protection of the home market, they may be tempted to opt for the latter. In the choice between time to sell in and space to sell in, they may opt for time. Producers of goods with short and uncertain market lives have not got time. They need space. If their markets become restricted, they cannot continue with R & D intensive activities on the former scale and must disband most or all of their R & D teams.

As already mentioned, R & D intensive activities tend to lead to specialisation within industries. This is known as intra-industry specialisation. Their production range becomes narrower than that comprised in industry or tariff classifications. The work of different R & D teams leads to different results, and that alone is a reason for increasing product differentiation. As a differentiated product is sold, an increase in the number of units sold means an increase in the number of units which make a contribution to capital employed. There are increasing returns to scale. The market life of the product is seldom long enough to get into a stage of decreasing returns to scale. As shown in the previous section, at that stage past R & D costs are no longer relevant, price may be controlled by a competitive market, and individual producers do best by selling the largest possible quantity at that price. This is usually referred to as price competition, and this is the correct terminology seen from the point of view of the economy as a whole. Seen from the point of view of an individual producer, it is quantitative competition. He cannot influence price and does best if he works hard or makes his factors work hard. In the present context it may seem best to refer to this form of competition as 'quantitative competition'. Such terminology highlights the contrast with the quality competition which has become more important as increasing returns activities have become more important. Moreover it avoids the danger of giving the impression that price does not matter under quality competition or that price is not controlled by the market. Under any form of competition, price is market controlled. What has changed is the nature of the market.

The nature of the market has changed because the nature of the firms has changed. R & D is a bar to entry, partly because of the cost involved and partly because of the know-how involved. Specialised knowledge is required. In R & D intensive activities, ownership is no longer sufficient qualification to reach meaningful decisions.

Technological expertise has become just as important. Since it is virtually impossible for almost anyone to be equally expert at finance and technology, salaried managers are appointed to take the relevant decisions in their respective spheres. The function of ownership is to co-ordinate the decisions of the various managers (though even this function may actually be performed by a salaried manager). There is both devolution and integration of decision-taking. This does not stop in the board room but goes all the way down the line to the factory floor and all the way to the nature of the relations (or competition) with the firm's rivals at home or abroad. The present book is not concerned with the way decisions are, or should be, devolved or integrated as production becomes more complex within firms. Suffice it to say that the days are past when individual workers could decide by themselves whether to work harder or when owners could decide to make them work harder. For, with the increasing complexity of production, on the factory floor as well as in the boardroom, every individual is a member of a team whose actions affect other teams within the firm. Equally, a firm which produces a differentiated product is no longer just a rival of other firms but one of a team of firms within an industry. This is likely to persist as long as product differentiation persists which, in turn, is the result of increasing complexity and cost of products.

Products can only be sold where they are understood. With the most complex goods, the only ones who can understand the goods are other producers. That, by itself, does not create a market. But firms could not always hope for a sufficiently long run in time to recoup their outlay on each product, if they produced the whole possible range. In practice, they would not always know how to produce the whole range. Even if they did, they might prefer to specialise on some of that range and buy in the rest. As mentioned before, space can be an alternative to time. Firms then act as their own merchants. They are merchant-producers. In such circumstances, the market consists of actual or potential producers of the same goods. Inevitably no one will buy in what he could produce for himself if the price is not convenient. This point will be discussed at greater length in Chapter 2. Here let it suffice to say that the price can never be so high that the purchaser will prefer to produce for himself. Nor can it ever be so low as to undermine the market of the buyer's near substitutes. Internationally, and often also nationally, such attempts at price cutting would not often be tolerated. The importer would not be tempted to buy more if this undermined his own home market. He might buy the same amount as before and make additional profits. He would react strongly to attempts to sell through others and try to close market outlets or ask his government to do so. In short, here is a form of competition where the price prevailing in each market must be largely accepted. Price is market controlled, but in a different kind of market than the one prevailing under quantitative competition. Price must be accepted as it is, and only quality differentials can lead to price differences over any length of time. This is an extreme case which will be somewhat modified, but not overturned, in Chapter 2. It is a form of competition which has made international trade in industrial goods more acceptable to industrial producers in the industrial countries. It integrates their activities with those of producers in other industrial countries. The trade in manufactures could increase by more than the production of manufactures.

The technological opportunities for such trade were probably as great in the 1930s, and possibly even in the 1920s, as they were in the late 1940s and early 1950s. They were not taken in the 1920s and 1930s, since the industrial world was not yet politically ready for international economic integration. With economic nationalism rampant and unemployment widespread, technological progress in economic goods was not altogether welcome. Although it created real incomes, it all too often seemed to displace labour in existing activites. The products of foreign technology were often largely excluded by protection, and this gave domestic firms more time to sell (fewer) technologically advanced products. Displaced labour was often employed in non-economic activities. Hence economic recovery did not improve international relations. This was another instance of domestic economic growth which exacerbated already strained international relations. Although there was still a *Pax Britannica* in the Empire, it could no longer contain or even delay the economic causes of conflict elsewhere. There was not yet an effective *Pax Americana* to take its place. This does not mean to say that there is any kind of international economic organisation which could have averted the political conflicts of the time. Rather it means that at times of bad international relations, no international economic organisation is allowed to allay the tensions.

The *Pax Americana* after 1945 could however lead towards an improvément in international relations between the Western industrial countries, because this was politically wanted, because suitable instruments of trade policy were at hand, and the technological opportunities were available for a new form of competition on an international scale. This was to be different from the *Pax Britannica.*

Through its integration of industrial with primary producing interests, the *Pax Britannica* ensured supplies. Where tariffs on primary products were reduced, the competitive markets for such products ensured that price fell by about as much as the relevant tariff rate had fallen. The price reduction benefited the consumer. Although his government had to seek revenue by other means so that it is not altogether certain that the consumer was better off, what is certain is that prices were not distorted by tariffs. In relation to the goods on which tariffs had been removed, the consumer was faced by undistorted free market prices. Any government which wished to give its citizens such freedom could do so largely through unilateral action. In short, the *Pax Britannica* was a consumers' *Pax* and did best where governments did not interfere with consumers' choice. It was broken by governments which wanted to stimulate production beyond the possibilities of trade.

At the beginning of this section, the *Pax Americana* was described as an industrial *Pax* which worked largely on the relations between the industrial countries. The subsequent discussion showed that it opened up possibilities for technological specialisation and so allowed for a greater increase in the trade in manufactures than of production of manufactures. In this respect the *Pax Americana* went further than the *Pax Britannica*. The latter kept trade in line with production, but the former led to more interdependence. The subsequent discussion of the new, qualitative, competition and the marketing of high quality manufactured goods in industrial countries, revealed another difference. This is that tariff reductions on the most advanced goods do not lead so much to lower prices for consumers as to higher returns for producers. A government which wants its producers to earn more foreign exchange through exporting, cannot do so through unilateral action. It must negotiate with at least one foreign government which is unlikely to confer such benefits unless equivalent concessions are given in return. Such benefits must be negotiated. By the time a large number of negotiations have taken place, the benefits are multilateral. No government can risk a flagrant breach of its obligations to foreign producers, lest other governments retaliate and impose extra taxation on the offending country's producers. Some of the implications will be discussed elsewhere in this book. Here let it be pointed out that the *Pax Americana* is an industrial *Pax* of interest mainly to producers. Given that the major policy targets of most governments at the time were full employment and growth, trade policy was in line with the general thinking of the time.

Notes

1. W. Arthur Lewis, 'World Production, Prices and Trade', *The Manchester School*, May 1952.
2. Nazli Choucri and Robert C. North, *Nations in Conflict*, W.H. Freeman & Co., San Francisco, 1975, esp. pp.14-25, 157, 278 and 280.
3. Sir Arthur Lewis, 'World Production', Table I, and United Nations Annual Statistical Yearbooks.
4. United Nations, *International Capital Movements*, 1949, p.47.
5. Sir Alec Cairncross, *Home and Foreign Investment*, Cambridge University Press, 1963.

2 EXPORT STRUCTURE AND PRICES

1. Export Structure

(i) Concentration of Exports amongst Firms, by Value

International trade policy is the more effective, the better it fits the industrial structure of the trading countries, for trade can never be independent of production. Industrial structure influences the way goods are priced, which in turn affects the possible consequences of tariff changes. An assessment of international trade policy is thus helped if it is made against the background of the trading countries' export structure which determines, or is determined by, the sort of competition which prevails in the relevant trades.

For instance, price competition or, from an individual firm's point of view, quantitative competition is possible where there are many sellers of the same sort of product. At first sight, this condition may seem to be satisfied in export markets where firms from many countries compete on equal terms. True, national and foreign suppliers are not treated alike. National producers pay no customs duties before they can sell in their home market, while foreign producers pay profits taxes in their own countries. National industrialists need familiarity with only one set of laws, credit conditions, commercial manners and tastes, while exporters must know these things for at least two countries. In consequence, there are only few industrial countries which derive the bulk of their income from exports or spend the bulk of their incomes on imports. But foreign suppliers compete on equal terms with other foreign suppliers, at any rate in countries which abide by the letter and spirit of non-discrimination of the GATT. The number of potential foreign suppliers may always seem large even if overall domestic supplies normally outweigh foreign ones. Not surprisingly, many jump to the conclusion that international competition is price competition and advise their governments to pursue policies which make exports more price-competitive.

This conclusion is sometimes right, but not always. It is right when the products concerned are perfect substitutes for what others can supply and so compete on price. It is not right, or not right without substantial qualifications, when a product is an unique product and competes on quality rather than on price. Again, the conclusion is right when there are numerous alternative sales outlets in the importing country and numerous alternative suppliers in the exporting country or countries. The conclusion is not right when sales outlets in the importing country are tied to particular suppliers. Nor can the conclusion be right when the structure of the exporting industries is incompatible with the assumptions of the theory of price competition.

The last point is basic. In order to answer the question whether export structure is compatible with price competition, requires knowledge of the concentration of exports amongst firms. Data are available for three industrial countries: France, Sweden and the UK.[1] Inevitably, no general conclusions can be derived from the export structure of only three countries. Nevertheless, their experience cannot be ignored. They are important trading countries, ranking fourth, twelfth and fifth respectively amongst the world's exporters in 1974 and 1975.[2] Each exports mainly manufactures. But their exports met with varying success, so that any similarities in export structure cannot be taken as a key to success or failure. Such a structure is just one of the facts to be taken into account in considerations relating to exports.

In the late 1960s, it was thought that two-thirds of UK manufacturing firms never exported, or exported only intermittently, and that the exporting third numbered about 24,000.[3] More details have become available thanks to the Department of Industry inquiries into overseas transactions in 1971-4.[4] It is now known that at least 81 per cent of total UK direct exports are provided by enterprises with an annual export turnover of £1 million or more.[5] This is an understatement of concentration in trade, since it relates ex-works values to total export values and the latter also include the cost of transport from works to ports. It would seem best to read the 81 per cent as 'over four-fifths'.

The number of enterprises with an export turnover of £1 million or more was 839 in 1971. As a result of inflation, export prices rose by more than half between 1971 and 1974[6] so that it became 'easier' to exceed the £1 million mark: 1,190 firms did in 1974. Conditions in 1974 were, however, especially disturbed by a deepening world depression and industrial disputes at home, so that not too many lessons can be learned from development between those two years. In any case, the series is not long enough to allow any conclusions about trends in export concentration. It seems best to take an average for the four years as representative of the position in the first half of the 1970s. Although £1 million in 1974 was no longer the same value as in 1971, the rise in prices affected not only the value of firms' turnover but also the value of total exports. While it does not follow that the rise in prices affected firms with a certain export turnover in exactly the same way as total exports, the weight of large exporters in the total is sufficiently high that the divergence cannot substantially affect the argument. Subject to these cautions, the following results emerge. Nine hundred and thirty-three enterprises accounted for 81 per cent of exports. If the number of exporters was still about the same as in the late 1960s, less than 4 per cent of all exporting enterprises accounted for these 81 per cent.[7]

The Department of Industry Inquiry also included enterprises with an export turnover of less than £1 million a year. The average number of enterprises covered was 1,728. (This includes the top 933). Their combined contribution to exports was 84 per cent, which was only 3 per cent more than the contribution of the top 933. While it is not certain that the other 795 were the next largest, since the response amongst the smaller firms was incomplete, they were at any rate amongst the next largest. There was a high degree of concentration even amongst the top 933. Slightly more than one third of them, namely 315, had an annual export turnover of £5 million or more, and these 315 accounted for 68 per cent of exports. Those with annual export turnovers of £20 million or more numbered only 92 and they accounted for exactly half of total exports. Of these, 32 had an annual export turnover of £50 million or more and they accounted for 35 per cent of total exports.

The degree of export concentration appears to have been slightly less in France where the number of enterprises was comparable with that in the UK, and more pronounced in Sweden which has fewer enterprises.[8] 1,363 French enterprises accounted for 80 per cent of French exports in 1974. Of these 1,363 enterprises, 300 accounted for two-thirds of French exports, 120 for half and 65 for 40 per cent.[9] In Sweden, the 100 largest companies accounted for 75 per cent of exports in 1973, and the 25 largest alone for about half.[10]

It has been known for some time that the degree of concentration of industrial production amongst firms tends to be greater in smaller industrial countries than in larger ones.[11] This can now be confirmed for the export concentration of the three countries discussed here. It does not follow that the degrees of concentration in production and trade are the same. In some trades – as for instance in mechanical engineering, firms with overseas subsidiaries take orders on a 'package' basis and act as principals in buying-in from other UK manufacturers those items outside their manufacture. Thus concentration in trade is likely to be more marked than concentration in production. To turn to the three countries under review, France was the largest of the three countries in 1971-4, whether measured by value of exports or gross national product, and Sweden the smallest. While it does not follow that export concentration will always vary in direct ratio to concentration of production nor necessarily in inverse ratio to the size of the country, inevitably the smaller country has fewer producing units and fewer still which can compete effectively in international markets. In Sweden, the large exporters were the long distance exporters, while the smaller ones did not often venture further than neighbouring Nordic countries.[12]

Whatever the details, exporting was a highly concentrated activity in each of the three countries. This is compatible with the finding that the profitability of exports to firms appears to rise as export sales grow larger.[13] If so, then at any one point, the large exporters are likely to predominate. This is also compatible with the predominance of increasing returns activities in the export trades which, in turn is both cause and effect of intra-industry specialisation. But the result is not compatible with a perfect competition model and its assumption of decreasing returns to scale.

It does not necessarily follow that direct exports always increase with the size of enterprises. A survey of UK engineering exports in the late 1960s and early 1970s actually found an inverse association between the percentage of output exported and the absolute value of firms' sales.[14] What happened in those trades was that, when exports became substantial, firms tended to establish subsidiaries abroad (or were themselves subsidiaries of foreign firms).[15] The most successful still exported their technology but did not necessarily continue to be direct exporters.

The decision to establish subsidiaries was not always voluntary but a way of forestalling, or responding to import controls. For instance, a number of Commonwealth countries altered their import controls so as to be restrictive on motor cars or commercial vehicles and liberal on parts or components. Their intention was to encourage local manufacture. The UK exporters could not maintain their sales of the finished products in familiar markets. Instead they became exporters of parts or components and took a part in local assembly. Another motive for setting up subsidiaries was access to a larger market. This was especially important for technologically advanced small countries. The Netherlands, Sweden and Switzerland figure prominently as headquarters of multinational firms which would not have much outlet for their science-based technology within national markets. Their escape was the establishment of subsidiaries in other countries and especially in countries larger than their own.[16] This motive was not unimportant even for US firms. From the 1930s until the 1970s, they were attracted to Canada and the UK where they gained not only free access to local markets but also preferential access to Commonwealth markets. They were attracted to Europe, when European countries imposed quotas on imports from the dollar area in the 1950s, and created tariff-free trade for Europeans only in the 1960s. As already mentioned, UK firms were induced to set up subsidiaries abroad to maintain their traditional Commonwealth markets in the face of rising import restrictions, and they were attracted to North America and Europe in order to create new and larger markets, parallel to their home markets, for their newer goods. This applied especially before the trade barriers fell after the conclusion of the Kennedy Round of multilateral tariff negotiations in 1967 and the enlargement of the EC in the 1970s.

This treatment of the motives for the establishment of subsidiaries abroad is by no means exhaustive,[17] but it should suffice to show that typically export success came first, and the purpose of the subsidiary was to maintain or increase the firms' sales in separate markets. Initially this would reduce the rate of growth of direct exports from the parent country, while later on it could increase the direct exports from the host country. Whatever the details, the most successful exporters became multinational. This success is reflected in the multinationals' importance in direct exports.

Although sales of UK exporting firms to their own overseas affiliates were a mere 8 per cent of total UK exports in 1974,[18] the sales of UK firms with overseas affiliates came to over half of total UK exports. Their average share of total exports in 1971-4 was 53 per cent[19]. Foreign-controlled enterprises in the UK contributed 29 per cent of exports in those years. Firms without any overseas affiliates accounted for only 19 per cent of exports.[20]

Earlier it was shown that around 4 per cent of exporting enterprises accounted for over four-fifths of UK exports. Those with overseas affiliations accounted for a similar proportion of UK exports. Although the largest exporters and exporters with overseas affiliates were not always the same, there was a considerable overlap. For instance, in 1974, only 8 of the 244 establishments with an export turnover over £10 million in that year had no overseas investment links.[21] If there is doubt whether trades dominated by large firms can be conducted under rules resembling those of perfect competition, that doubt must be enhanced when the bulk of exports is also in the hands of establishments which have to consider the interests of their affiliates.

(ii) Concentration of Exports amongst Firms, by Industry Group

The degree of concentration was not the same in all industries. Details for industries are available for 1972-4[22]. The coverage is not as wide as those for the distribution of exports by value given earlier. The absence of data for 1971 makes little difference. (Had the earlier figures for concentration been given for 1972-4 instead of 1971-4, the number of firms would have averaged 1,741 instead of 1,728 and their contribution to total exports would have been 83 per cent instead of 84 per cent). More important is that the oil companies were excluded which may have the effect of understating the degree of concentration in exports of chemicals in which they play an important part. Also excluded were exports of nationalised enterprises other than the British Steel Corporation, and exports by small firms which did not respond to the Department of Industry Inquiries. In those cases, the value of exports could be derived from published sources but an allocation to particular industries was not possible.[23] The result was a survey of 1,595 firms in 1972-4 which contributed 74 per cent of total exports. If exports of fuels are excluded, their share was 77 per cent.

Table 2.1 shows annual averages of the number of enterprises and values of exports per enterprise, to the nearest £ million.[24] At a time of rapidly rising prices, this information is more usefully given in the form of an index for each group. This is shown alongside the value figures.[25] The result for all industries is made equal to 100. It will be noted that the average motor vehicle exporter contributed more than twice as much to exports as the average exporter of the second highest ranking group, nearly seven times as much as the average for all industries and eighteen times as much as the lowest ranking one.

Firms exporting transport equipment (with ranks 1 and 2) clearly head the list. Other engineering activities (3 and 4) came next, though mechanical engineering enterprises (8) made a less than proportionate contribution. But they still came higher than textiles (11) and various non-manufacturing activities which are also concerned with exports of merchandise (9, 13, 14). An above average intermediate position is held by the various processing industries (5, 6, 7). A below average intermediate position is shared by textiles and paper (11 and 12). The latter industry group is difficult to classify, since

Table 2.1: Annual Averages of the Number of Enterprises and Values of Exports per Enterprise in the UK, 1972-4

	Number of Enterprises	Average Export Value per Enterprise £ million	Index
1. Motor vehicle manufacture	28	40	668
2. Shipbuilding, marine engineering and vehicles other than motor vehicle manufacture	24	18	304
3. Metal manufacture	52	14	239
4. Electrical engineering	96	12	195
5. Food, drink and tobacco	77	9	152
6. Chemical and allied industries	131	9	150
7. Rubber manufacture	20	8	138
All manufacture[26]	*1,235*	*7*	*117*
All industries	*1,595*	*6*	*100*
8. Mechanical engineering and instrument engineering	305	5	88
9. Construction	27	3	56
10. Other manufacture	230	3	55
11. Textiles, leather, clothing and footwear	199	3	54
12. Paper, printing and publishing	74	3	52
13. Other activities	83	3	47
14. Distributive trades	251	2	37

paper-making could be classed as processing, printing as engineering, and publishing as 'other'.

It does not follow that enterprises in the same industry groups will necessarily always make the same contribution. If, in 1972-4, in the UK, groups 1-4 were the giants, groups 5-8 the intermediate groups and groups 9-14 the dwarfs, the same ranking is not necessarily to be expected at other times or in other countries. Table 2.2 is an attempt to rank French exporting firms in 1974, by calculating the same index which compares a F100 export contribution by the leading 1,363 exporters with the export contribution of firms in individual industry groups. The French data include the coal and oil exporters. Data for other French exports were rearranged to conform as far as possible to the Department of Industry classification used in Table 2.1.[27]

A comparison of this list with the UK one reveals both differences and

Table 2.2: Number of Enterprises and Value of Exports per Enterprise in France, 1974

		Number of Enterprises	Average Export Value per Enterprise F million	Index
i.	Petrol and coal	3	500	385
ii.	Transport equipment	83	364	280
iii.	Rubber manufacture	13	308	237
iv.	Metal manufacture	136	232	178
v.	Construction	32	194	149
vi.	Other activities	88	180	139
vii.	Mining products (other than i)	7	157	121
viii.	Electrical engineering	75	132	102
	All industries	*1,363*	*130*	*100*
	All manufacture[28]	*1,204*	*124*	*95*
ix.	Chemical and allied industries	159	124	95
x.	Food, drink and tobacco	261	93	71
xi.	Mechanical engineering	221	79	61
xii.	Other manufacture	38	76	59
xiii.	Distribution	29	69	53
xiv.	Paper, printing and publishing	31	68	52
xv.	Textiles, leather, clothing and and footwear	87	45	35

similarities. In most cases, the French index is lower, so that there was less divergence from the average. Thus, overall French export performance was less dependent on, say, transport equipment than overall British export performance. Overall, export concentration in 'all manufacture' appears to have been less marked in France than in all exporting activities, which is the reverse of the position shown for the UK. The inclusion of petrol and mining (i and vii) in the French data does not appreciably affect the position. Only ten enterprises were involved, with an average export of F260 million. Nevertheless, for a comparison it seems best to omit the activities which do not appear in both lists (namely petrol and mining) and also those which are not specified (namely other manufacture and other activities).

Export concentration was relatively more marked in France than in the UK in rubber manufacture, construction and distribution. It was less in every other activity. But the ranking of manufacturing activities, other than rubber manufacture, is almost the same on both lists. Transport equipment came highest, followed by metal manufacture and electrical engineering. These were the giants, as in the UK. Although the relative positions of chemicals and foods are reversed, together with mechanical engineering, they were in an intermediate position, as in the UK. Paper and textiles, though again in reverse order, were the dwarfs in both countries.

Although an equally detailed index could not be compiled for Sweden, it seems certain that it would have been particularly high in transport equipment, followed by electrical and other engineering and paper. Sweden's exports of chemicals and textiles were relatively insignificant.[29]

Export structure is one of the determinants of the sort of competition there can be, and this affects pricing. Section (i) has shown that at least four-fifths of British and French exports and at least three-quarters of Swedish exports could not have come from enterprises which operated under conditions resembling quantitative (perfect price) competition. There just were not enough exporting firms to make this possible. It has now been shown that particular trades rank high in export concentration in at least three countries. Generally, the higher up the list an activity is, the less likely it is to operate under conditions of quantitative competition. It does not follow that the ranking of industries by degree of export concentration coincides with a ranking of the same industries according to the sort of competition under which they operate. The conclusion so far is entirely negative: the higher the degree of export concentration, the less likely is quantitative (price) competition.

Even this conclusion may have to be modified for non-manufacturing activities which are concerned with the export of merchandise. Early this century, most exporting was done by enterprises whose activities fall under the heading of 'distribution'. Merchants bought goods, for eventual export, from numerous producers who could not export themselves. This still happens and distribution is still classed amongst the major British and French exporting activities, but its importance is less than it was. Only 6 per cent of the value of exports of the 1,595 top UK exporters and 1 per cent of the value of exports of the 1,363 top French exporters fall under this heading in the early 1970s. Nevertheless distribution is represented on either list, though low down. Because it is low down, the negative conclusion reached so far need not be modified for the two countries in the early 1970s. Here is an activity where the early twentieth-century rules of competition still apply, but it is no longer as important as it once was.

Construction, the other service activity listed, includes a miscellany of activities, such as building a bridge here or a hospital there. This may be 'placed' or be in response to a public tender. The export of merchandise involved would be only part of the value of such activities. They are best omitted from further consideration here, though it seems safe to say that such activities involve direct selling (and not selling through merchants) and are likely to take place under rules of competition not dissimilar to those in direct sales of manufactures.

But manufactures cannot be lumped together. Nor can it be said that to be at different ends of a list of export concentration by industry groups necessarily means that the rules of competition must be furthest apart for, say, motor vehicles and textiles. Export concentration is only one of the factors to be taken into account. Others include research intensity and prospects in intra-industry specialisation.

(iii) Export Structure and Research Intensity

Where research intensity is high, overhead costs per unit produced will tend to be high. The overheads have to be recouped soon since the end products are liable to frequent change. Overhead costs then figure high in the firms' long-run costs, and the long run cannot be longer than the products' market life. These are the cases where production takes place under conditions of increasing returns to scale. Price equals average costs and firms can enter such markets if they can meet the average costs of the nearest substitute available.

The industries with high degrees of export concentration will now be compared with the research intensities of those activities. This is done by using the Norris-Vaizey estimates of research intensities in 1968.[30] Although later figures for research expenditure are available, it seems best to use the detailed analysis provided by those two authors, especially since commercial performance in the early 1970s was most likely to have been more influenced by research in the late 1960s than by contemporaneous research. The following limitations should be noted. An industry may depend on research and yet not be research-intensive. For instance, the motor vehicle industry depends on research carried out by the engineering industries, and the food and textile industries on research in chemicals. The following relates to research-intensity and not research-dependence. There was a high degree of research expenditure in the aircraft industry, but much of this was for non-commercial purposes. But it is possible to make comparisons for the eight industry groups with similar ranking in the British and

French lists of indices of export concentration (though there has to be a different subdivision for vehicles and there are subdivisions of the engineering trades). Problems of definition make it necessary to exclude rubber and paper. The comparison is for the UK only. It is known, however, that patterns of research intensity are similar in different industrial countries. French research expenditure was somewhat higher in chemicals and the various forms of engineering, other than aircraft, than in the UK. It was somewhat lower overall, largely because of less expenditure on aircraft.[31]

Three of the Norris-Vaizey estimates will be used in the following. One, designated as NV1 in the following matrix, measures R & D expenditure in each industry group, irrespective of source of finance, as a percentage of net output. Any division is bound to be arbitrary, but there was a clear gap between industries with R & D expenditure of 3.5 per cent of net output or more, and those which spent 2.4 per cent of net output or less. The former, the high R & D spenders are shown as H, the low spenders as L. The number following the H or the L denotes the ranking of the industries concerned according to NV1. NV2 repeats this exercise on the basis of R & D expenditure, financed by the industries themselves, as a percentage of net output. The industries shown as H spent 3.2 per cent of net output or more, those shown as L 1.6 per cent of net output or less. The number following H or L denotes the ranking of the industries according to NV2. NV3 measures research intensity by the percentage of qualified scientists and engineers employed by those industries. H means 11.3 per cent or more of the total number of such scientists and engineers employed by manufacturing industry and L 6.4 per cent or less. The number following H or L denotes the ranking of those industries according to NV3.[32] The industry groups are shown according to their ranking in UK export concentration, though there are some sub-divisions which are not shown.

It will be noted that of the groups distinguished in the analysis of export concentration, only chemicals show a consistent H for research intensity. In scientific manpower (NV3), chemicals lead, occupying third place in research expenditure (NV1 and HV2) and an average intermediate position in export concentration. On grounds of research intensity and on grounds of export concentration, quality rather than quantitative competition is to be expected. Nearly consistently H is electrical engineering, though 'other electrical engineering' seems to be somewhat short of scientific manpower. But the distinction between an H and an L classification is inevitably

Table 2.3: Research Intensity of UK Industries

UK Export Concentration Rank		NV1	NV2	NV3
1.	Motor vehicle manufacture)	L6	H6	L9
2.	Other (Shipbuilding)			
	(Aircraft	H1	H2	H4
3.	Metal manufacture	L8 or 9	L9	L6
4.	Electrical engineering (electronics	H2	H1	H2
	(other	H5	H5	L5
5.	Food, drink and tobacco	L8 or 9	L8	L8
6.	Chemicals	H3	H3	H1
8.	Mechanical engineering (scientific (instruments	H4	H4)	H3
	(other	L7	L7)	
12.	Textiles, etc.	L10	L10	L7

arbitrary and other electrical engineering has the highest rank amongst the L group in scientific manpower. It seems legitimate to group electrical engineering as H on grounds of research intensity, or at least as more H than L. Quality competition would seem likely both on grounds of export concentration and research intensity. Other consistent H performers were aircraft and scientific instruments. Quality competition is to be expected on grounds of research intensity, but the information at hand relating to export concentration is not sufficiently detailed to support this conclusion.

More L than H were motor vehicles and mechanical engineering. It is not certain whether 'other' mechanical engineering rates an H in manpower since it cannot be separated from scientific instruments. But the combined manpower rank (H3) is higher than the expenditure rank (H4), so that mechanical engineering is best left as an unproven case. So it is on grounds of export concentration.

Motor vehicles should probably be classed as L on grounds of research intensity. Although on grounds of self-financed research expenditure as percentage of net output (NV2) the industry ranks H, it has the lowest ranking H in that column, and the division between the lowest H and the highest L is arbitrary. It could, however, be countered that it has the highest ranking L on grounds of total research expenditure as percentage of net output. It seems tempting to class the industry as borderline, until one looks at its poor showing in the employment of scientific manpower, where it came bottom. Thus, on grounds of research intensity, one would expect the industry to be subject to quantitative competition. But it came top on grounds of export concentration, so that the rules of quantitative competition cannot apply.

Consistent Ls were metal manufacture, despite its high ranking in export concentration; food, despite its above average intermediate ranking in export concentration; and textiles which came low in research intensity as well as in export concentration. It should be noted however, that textiles came above food and motor vehicles in the use of scientific manpower. If the comparisons made so far leave doubt about quantitative competition in motor vehicles, they must also leave some doubt about quantitative competition in textiles and food.

(iv) Export Structure and Intra-Industry Specialisation

Research intensity implies high overhead costs which have to be recouped during the market life of the product. As manufacturing became more science based, ways were sought of spreading the cost. While the division of the world into separate national economies persisted, technology could be spread in two ways. One was the use of the same technological equipment and labour force for the production of different goods. Firms became multi-product enterprises. The other was to use the same technology for the production of the same goods in different national markets. Replicas of the parent firm were set up in other countries. Firms became multinational enterprises. In either case, large firms were at an advantage. The smaller ones, which had been the mainstay of quantitative competition, found it increasingly difficult to survive.

Now it is the turn of the multi-product multinational firms to feel the winds of change. As scientific knowledge progressed and was applied to industry, the R & D costs rose further. Eventually technology became so specialised that firms had to think of the technological subdivision of activities rather than the combination of activities with the same technology. Moreover, in many cases even the largest national markets ceased to be large enough to support one production unit of viable size.

Once again, there were two escapes. One was nationalisation in open or disguised form. The other was intra-industry specialisation. Nationalisation or subsidisation by governments could ensure the survival or even the beginning of some technologically advanced activities. The cost was transferred from firms to the taxpayer. This did not lower the cost. It meant a political decision that certain technologically advanced activities should take place within national boundaries. Examples are the decisions that the first man on the moon should be an American and that US technology should be given the task of finding out whether there is life on Mars. So are the British decisions to devote much of R & D activities to nuclear energy, aircraft and computers. These were long-term projects where the pay-off has so far been elusive.

Firms which cannot do everything that is within their technological capacity because home markets are too small, have the alternative of participating in intra-industry specialisation. Each firm specialises over a narrower range of products than before. It buys in the rest of its former range from other firms at home or abroad, so that it can still satisfy its customers with the whole range. Firms abroad do the same. This is hardly a task for small firms. It involves R & D expenditure, albeit on a narrower range. It further involves merchanting for the rest of the range. Nevertheless firms are becoming smaller in two senses. Their production range narrows. This could not be done unless their market becomes wider and, to state the obvious, each firm is smaller in a world market than in a national market. Nevertheless, this is not a return to quantitative competition. Firms which had become large multi-product and multinational enterprises, are often best able to bear the initial cost. They have the brand names and domestic sales outlets and they need the sales outlets of their rivals abroad. They are the new merchants. But they are merchant-producers. They export to each other, and must do so at prices which fit in with the price relationships prevailing in the importing country. If they do not respect the national scales of values of their partners, the partners could produce the goods for themselves. Price is maintained through the importer's threat of entry into production of the exporter's range. Such entry would nullify any advantage the exporter had hoped to gain through a larger market.

The threat of entry could be reinforced by the threat of the importer's government to impose tariffs or other import controls, but as long as the importer also provides the sales outlets, this threat is not necessary. Nevertheless, intra-industry specialisation is certainly made easier by the removal of trade barriers. There were signs of intra-industry specialisation and trade in the 1900s. They were nipped in the bud by war, depression and protection. They could not develop until the third quarter of the century, when trade became freer. By the end of the 1960s, such trade was estimated to come to about half of the export trades of the major industrial countries.[33] Given the nature of such trade, competition must be by quality. There are not enough firms to allow for quantitative competition. And the merchant-producers, who are the major importers, would not tolerate price competition.

If then a new form of competition has emerged which is a form of quality competition, participation in this form of competition can provide another index of the sort of export structure a country has. Inevitably there are problems of definition. As a general principle, the higher the proportion of a country's exports which is matched by imports falling under the same heading of international trade classification the greater is the importance of intra-industry trade. But unless details of every transaction are known, the division between intra-and inter-industry trade can never be perfectly accurate. It seems best to accept the measurements of intra-industry trade used by Grubel and Lloyd in their comprehensive study of the subject.[34] They will be referred to as GL. The GL findings relate to the late 1960s and should still be largely correct. At that time, exchange rate fluctuations were not yet too frequent so that the figures are unlikely to be distorted by an alleged practice of some exporters to insure against exchange risks by matching their exports to one country by imports from the same country. Since they are experts only in their own fields, this may have swelled the exports and imports under the same tariff heading. It is a practice most likely to be indulged in by smaller traders who are unable to cover themselves otherwise. The position will be compared with UK export concentration (see Table 2.4). Since the concern is with the sort of competition to be encountered abroad, the mean for ten countries will be used.[35] The degree of disaggregation shown in GL is much greater than that in the Department of Industry Inquiry. No attempt is made to recalculate GL to fit the higher degree of aggregation. Instead the various items were listed and the most representative mean chosen for each group. The GL result for all commodities came to 50 per cent of trade. Where the most representative result was between 50 and 59, a C is shown in the column headed GL in the following matrix. Where the result was between 60 and 69, a B is awarded. Seventy and over, which would merit an A, occurred for individual items and individual countries but not overall. Below 50, a result of 40-49 is shown as D, and one below 40 as E. Again E occurred for individual items and individual countries, but not overall.

For the sake of comparison, the NV results are repeated but in accordance with the allocation to H or L suggested in the text of the preceding sections and not in detail.

Table 2.4: Research Intensity and Intra-Industry Trade

UK Export Concentration Rank		NV	GL
1.	Motor vehicle manufacture	L	C
2.	Aircraft	H	B
	Shipbuilding and other vehicles	L	D
3.	Metal manufacture	L	C
4.	Electrical engineering	H	B
5.	Food, drink and tobacco	L	D
6.	Chemical and allied industries	H	B
7.	Rubber manufacture	—	C
8.	Mechanical and instrument engineering	?	B
9.	Paper, printing and publishing	—	C
12.	Textiles, leather, clothing and footwear	L	C

It will be noted that all industries rated as H under NV are awarded B under GL. Apart from aircraft, where the Department of Industry Inquiry does not show export concentration, there are cases of above average intermediate concentration. On all three grounds, quality competition must be expected. The only other B is mechanical engineering. This was said to be an unproven case on grounds of concentration and NV. Although there is much variation amongst the various constituent items, in GL, the majority of items get a B. Thus mechanical engineering becomes a probable case of quality competition. Of the L cases under NV, motor vehicles, metal manufacture and textiles get C under GL and so improve the probability of quality competition. Other Cs are rubber and paper. There is no correlation between GL and concentration in the C cases. Shipbuilding and other vehicles, and food get D. They get L under NV. They are high and intermediate above average in concentration.

It is now possible to reach some more positive conclusions than those reached on grounds of concentration alone. Where export concentration is high, quantitative competition is unlikely because there are not enough firms. Where NV is high, qualitative competition is possible. Where GL is high, qualitative competition is almost certain to have occurred.

Before leaving this topic, a word about the relative position of countries. Only three countries could be compared for export concentration, and the likelihood of much quantitative (price) competition ruled out, at least for those three countries. On grounds of research intensity, more details are known, and the US and the UK led. But since only half of UK R & D expenditure and even less of US R & D expenditure in the 1960s was economically motivated,[36] there was no corresponding commercial pay-off. This lies in the past. R & D saving through intra-industry specialisation may alter the picture. Once the depression of the mid-1970s lifts and demand for quality revives, the countries high on the GL classification could do well.[37] Here the UK heads the list. She is the only country which could be awarded an A. Next come France, Belgium and the Netherlands with Bs. The US and Germany only get C, Canada and Italy D, Japan and Australia E. Could it be that some of the countries which were disappointed by their post-war commercial performance to date, took most to R & D saving through intra-industry specialisation and are well placed for any possible quality competition in the 1980s?

2. Export Prices

(i) Export Prices and Profitability

Quality competition implies rules of price formation in ways which differ from those to be expected under quantitative (or price) competition. The following does not try to establish any hard and fast rules of pricing under quality competition. Instead it will try to find various possible ways of pricing under such a system. The latter itself will be shown to be an extreme case, and two shades of competition between quality and quantitative competition will be distinguished, namely model competition and improvement competition. Although there are likely to be as many variations as there are products and markets, these shades or categories of competition provide some useful guidelines. They are based on some available studies of British export trades.

Before going into detail, it will be useful to consider some general points relating to export prices and profitability of exports. It is widely held that exporting is less profitable than selling in the home market. This view received support from a report issued by the Government Economic Service. The difference in profitability in the late 1960s was found to be between 4 and 8½ per cent, the result varying with the measure of profitability used.[38] But this was an overall average. Nearly one-fifth of the firms responding to the survey reported substantially higher profit rates from exporting than from home sales, while two-thirds reported similar rates of profitability.[39] The principal explanations offered for the differences in profitability were the level of export sales and price differences.[40]

On price, it was found that most exports sold abroad at prices ranging between 20 per cent below and 19 per cent above home prices. About half were within the range of 1 to 20 per cent below home prices, and nearly two-fifths within 0 and 19 per cent above.[41] Thus, two-fifths of firms reported higher export than home prices but only one-fifth reported substantially higher profitability of export than of home sales. At the same time, one half of firms reported lower export than home prices but only one-sixth reported substantially lower profitability of export than of home sales. These results are compatible with the view that, for most firms, there is less difference between the profitability of export and home sales than between export and home prices.

Since exports are sold in markets where price relations differ from those in the home market, price differences must be expected. These differences cannot be explained in terms of conditions in the exporting country alone, nor can they always be appreciably influenced by measures taken in the exporting country. Much of the remainder of this chapter will be concerned with the importance of price prevailing in the importing country. There are however other possible causes of price differences. These include additional costs of exporting which must be incurred before the goods reach their destination, and differences in timing of sales.

Exports involve additional selling costs. Some of these are a direct charge on the exporter. Examples are additional costs of merchanting and of taking legal advice in at least two countries. It may be possible to raise export price somewhat to cover these costs. But, unless these costs can be completely offset by the increased price, profitability is reduced. Another additional cost is import duty. Legally this is the importer's liability. In practice, however, importers of manufactured goods will not pay more than a price related to the prevailing domestic price of similar goods. They like to be invoiced in a way which includes all charges incurred before the goods reach their doorstep. The price charged to the importer, which includes import duty, is then higher than the price actually received by the exporter.

Exports also affect firms' production costs. With exports, firms have longer production runs in goods which can be sold both at home and abroad. This lowers unit costs in increasing returns activities and raises them in decreasing returns activities. Costs, and therefore price sought, are generally affected to the benefit or detriment of all customers. While it should always be possible to allocate costs to different levels of output, irrespective of destination, the allocation of costs according to destination is difficult unless one of two conditions is satisfied. One is that export orders are taken only after home orders are satisfied or vice versa. The other is that different labour and capital are used to meet home and export orders. In practice, it is not always possible to distinguish between the in-factory cost effects of export and home orders. Export orders are not always the first or the last to be dealt with. More usually, they are interspersed with home orders so that a precise allocation of production costs to export orders is not possible. Even in one-off products, some costs are shared with other output. Although there are special costs of exporting, these are seldom incurred within the producing factory.

Given that production costs are usually the same, whoever and wherever the customer may be, ex-factory costs cannot be the reason for charging different ex-factory prices to different customers. They would resent higher prices. They might turn elsewhere or buy through exporting agents in the exporting country. Nor would it be possible to charge consistently less to customers in other industrial countries. Established rivals there would complain of dumping and might prevail upon their governments to impose countervailing measures (under Article VI of the GATT). It may be possible to charge less to overseas customers in countries without rival manufacture. But even this cannot be carried too far. The reaction of domestic customers must be considered. They might turn elsewhere, import or even re-import the goods. In short, deliberate and persistent discrimination in the ex-factory price between overseas and home customers is largely impractical. If different prices are charged at the points of destination, the reasons tend to be post factory costs and conditions prevailing in the importing country. The latter point will be considered in subsections (ii) and (iii).

Nevertheless, there are differences between export and home prices at any one point of time, and these differences need not all be due to post-factory costs of exporting or conditions in the importing countries. Rather they may be due to the scale of operations of firms which try their new products in the home market before they export. It is thought not to be unusual for firms to sell their initial output at a higher margin above marginal costs than later sales.[42] This helps to recoup capital outlay early, which is especially important where there are uncertainties about the length of a product's market life. All that is certain is that novelty value can be exploited only during the early sales. These are usually in the home market. Later on, firms can afford to lower prices, having recouped their capital outlay earlier. If this year's models are still being tried out in the home market, while last year's are being sold both at home and abroad, aggregate data for this year suggest lower prices and profitability abroad. But this may be the result of the scale of operations and pricing strategy over time, rather than of differences between export and home markets.

One variant of this pricing strategy is to repeat it in each market when the product is first introduced there. This is a possible strategy when firms are not so nervous about whether the product will survive at all, but are unsure about its length of life in each market. They may then use the novelty value of the product to recoup quickly at least the extra post-factory selling cost incurred in each export market and, if possible, also some of the original capital cost. Whatever the detailed reasons, exports may then seem more highly priced and profitable than the home market where the novelty value has already worn off. Although the apparent difference between export and home prices is now the reverse of that in the previous case, it too is the result of differences in timing. At any one point, this may look like differences in marketing conditions and price discrimination. But it may mean identical treatment of separate markets at different points of time. Again, there may be time discrimination rather than discrimination between markets.

Price strategies over time explain some of the apparent differences between export and home prices of new goods. They would not be appropriate strategies for pricing goods which have been exported for long periods of time. For established exports (or home sales), there are no problems of recouping R & D costs. Conditions are then likely to be as close to quantitative (price) competition as can be found anywhere in industrial trade. Unfortunately detailed information is scarce. Where it is available, it applies to particular samples and industry groupings which do not coincide with the Department of Industry classifications. The first case to be looked at will be quality competition in research-intensive chemicals, to be followed by 'model competition' in motor cars, and 'improvement competition' in some traditional engineering trades. In each case there will be some modification of the points made in this section.

(ii) Quality Pricing

The chemical industries cover a wide range of products. At one end of the range are traditional products, like sulphuric acid. There competition is quantitative and price in the home market is maintained by a cartel. At the other end are the most up-to-date pharmaceuticals which sell on quality and are produced under conditions of increasing returns. But even in pharmaceuticals there are old standbys like aspirin.[43] Thus overall results for chemicals are not necessarily applicable to each product and those for individual products not necessarily overall. Subject to these cautions, it may be said that chemicals are more typically quality products than products where quantitative competition could prevail. Section 1 has already indicated a marked, though not extreme, degree of export concentration, and high degrees of research intensity and intra-industry specialisation. To this may now be added that, early in the 1970s, firms in the chemical industries claimed that half the products they sold had been newly introduced in the previous five or six years.[44]

More specifically in pharmaceuticals the average drug life has been put at five years.[45] Market life is short. Success depends upon innovation. Although major research breakthroughs are not expected more than once every ten to twenty years, lesser development results can show in about five years.[46] The R & D stage is long. Market life is often shorter than the preparatory R & D stage. Pricing strategy must allow for long-run capital outlay to be recouped in much less time.

Whatever pricing strategy is adopted, given increasing returns, there will be a tendency for price received by the producer to fall, at least relative to other prices. It does not follow that price paid by the final consumer will fall. If a product has to be split up into small lots and packaged in labour-intensive ways to suit local requirements, there may be a stage when there are falling prices for exporters and yet rising prices for consumers in the importing country.[47] Moreover, each importing market has its own price relationships and outsiders may be ill-advised to attempt a price war with established interests in the importing country. Price relationships in the importing country tend to be respected.[48] It has been argued that 'the range of prices already present in a market has a profound influence on the entry price of new products. Thus, once there is a price contrast between two markets it tends to be perpetuated'.[49] This applies even to new goods, where price in the importing country must be set in relation to the nearest home-produced substitute.

This leads to another variant of the price strategies mentioned in subsection (i). Instead of seeking to recoup R & D costs whenever and wherever the product is first introduced, it can be recouped quickest wherever the prevailing price of the nearest substitute is highest. There are different prices in different industrial markets, for reasons over which exporters have little or no influence. An exporter has to work within a range between his own in-factory costs and the price prevailing in each market. The exporter usually does not discriminate on his own volition but has to accept that importers do not normally wish to discriminate between goods from different suppliers. One consequence is as follows. Suppose the prevailing price of a particular product is higher in Germany than in the UK, but lower in France. A firm which wants to recoup its R & D costs quickly would try to sell in Germany first and France last. This assumes knowledge of markets and absence of trade barriers. If there are tariffs to start with but they are then removed, free trade with Germany helps a British exporter to recoup his R & D costs earlier (since he now gets a higher price), while removal of the French tariff still leaves him dependent on the home market to recoup such costs quickly.

This last argument does not apply where the difference in price paid by consumers is due to differences in the cost of distribution. These may be important in proprietary drugs and toiletries, where the ultimate consumer is not normally technologically well-informed. But most products of firms in the chemical industries are not sold to ultimate consumers. Most are sold to either other chemical firms for further processing or to firms which use the products as inputs for their own production of textiles, processed food, cars and almost anything else one may think of. Such buyers are well-informed. They know what it would cost them to produce the item for themselves. Often they and a firm in another country agree to specialise in particular items, so as to give each a longer production run per item. But they will not do so at any price – only at a price convenient to themselves. For entirely new products, price may have to be negotiated afresh. For others, a price may be quoted in trade journals. Such a price is seldom paid. Discounts may be negotiated for bulk, long-term contracts and whatever else may be considered relevant by the experts on either side.[50]

Thus price is set by 'the market' in qualitative competition as well as in quantitative competition. But the market is different. Instead of financially skilled merchants buying from numerous producing units and selling on price determined by competition between themselves for supplies and outlets, producing units sell direct to other producing units. They are their own merchants. Alternatively, smaller firms may let their larger rivals perform this merchanting function on their behalf.[51] In either case, there is a merchant-producer who normally sells to another merchant-producer in the importing country. The latter may or may not be the ultimate consumer. In any case, both exporter and importer are technologically as well as financially skilled. They are likely to be equally expert, and each buyer is a potential producer and seller. The exporter can succeed when he can meet the prevailing price in the importing country, as expressed in that country's currency. Since the importer is an actual or potential producer, the exporter cannot exceed the price prevailing in the importing country. For if he did, the importer could produce the goods for himself. Nor can the exporter undercut the prevailing price lest this antagonise the buyer who wants no outsider to upset the price and cost structure in his country. In short, price is set by the cost structure in the importing country at least as much as by the exporter's own costs.

Thus, even in activities where market life is short relative to the R & D stage and the product has novelty value, the exporter cannot set price any way he likes. The importer knows too much. He is an actual or potential rival. His costs are as relevant as the exporter's. These costs may be in-factory costs, or they may be legal burdens such as import duties. The removal of such burdens on the importer helps the exporter since the price the latter receives is the price prevailing in the importing country minus indirect costs of exporting. Fewer such burdens make the importing country more attractive to sell in. The export strategy of firms can be adjusted accordingly.

(iii) Price and Prejudice

Chemicals conform best with the pricing rules of quality competition, though some sectors of the chemical industries do not. For other industries, such as motor cars, the rules must be modified. The motor car industry has higher export concentration than chemicals, which makes quantitative competition even less likely. But it ranks lower in intra-industry specialisation and lower still in research intensity, which makes quality competition less likely. The sort of competition which prevails in the motor car industry may be best described as 'model competition'. This means that firms normally do not attempt to improve their market share through price cutting. Instead, they introduce new models which they sell at prices comparable with those already prevailing in the market concerned. There, price seems to be determined by the costs of the largest domestic producers. Smaller domestic producers and importers tend to accept this price. If they cannot meet it, they cannot sell. There seem to be no major and persistent price variations for similar models from different domestic and foreign firms.[52]

Here is another case where costs in the importing country tend to determine price and, for reasons to be given later, in a more one-sided way. When the UK tariff was reduced in 1968-71, after the Kennedy Round of tariff negotiations, the tariff cuts were utilised by importers to improve their returns on British sales. There were no price cuts.[53] Nor were there after the tariff reductions following UK accession to the EC in 1973. Nor do exchange rate variations seem to have had much impact on the relative prices of imported and home produced cars. Even during the oil crisis, which caused special difficulties for the motor car industry and more intense competition for markets, only one major attempt appears to have been made to compete for the UK market through price cutting. It was made by the largest home producer and did not last long.[54]

Even in countries without their own car manufacture, such as Switzerland, suppliers moved with caution. After the EFTA tariff cuts, British firms let Swiss consumers have the benefit of lower prices in order to gain a larger market share at the expense of other suppliers. They lowered unit prices they could have got for themselves after the tariff cut, but not below the levels they had received before the cut. If they risked upsetting other suppliers, there were no local ones to upset.[55]

There are similarities between the model competition in motor cars and the quality competition in advanced chemicals. But there are also differences which make model competition a less perfect form of quality competition. The differences include the lesser importance of capital costs and less direct selling methods.

It is reported that it takes between three and a half and five years to introduce a new car model, and more for specialised high performance cars.[56] This involves substantial development expenditure by an industry concerned with improving its models. It involves little or no research expenditure by an industry which seems unconcerned with discovering new means of transport. Such worries are left to the aircraft industry. In consequence, the market life of a motor car model is more predictable than that of an aeroplane or an advanced drug. Moreover, if in chemicals the preparatory R & D stage is normally of longer duration than the subsequent market life of the product, the reverse applies in motor cars. As just mentioned, the preparatory stage for most models is five years or less. This is shorter than in advanced chemicals. The subsequent market life is usually longer. In 1976, the largest British motor car producer announced a model range of which nearly half had been introduced in the preceding six or seven years.[57] By itself, this is not too far from the chemical industries' claim that half their products had been introduced within the last five or six years, especially if it is borne in mind that the 1970s included some particularly difficult years for the motor car industry. But relative to the preparatory stage, the market life is longer. It may become longer still if the tendencies towards fewer models and more variations of existing models continue. In 1976, it was claimed that there were fewer models but more choice.[58] Model competition had become somewhat less and competition through minor improvements more marked.

Whatever may happen in future, the position in the mid-1970s was one of an industry where the R & D stage was usually shorter than the subsequent market life of the model, and where the R & D stage was virtually D without the R. Hence, compared with advanced chemicals, lower capital costs can be spread over a relatively longer period. If it is still true that only about one-sixth of unit costs can be attributed to fixed costs[59] (which include not only capital costs), the tendency towards increasing returns to scale on capital employed is less marked than in advanced chemicals. Novelty pricing is less likely and so are subsequent price reductions. The lure of wider markets is also somewhat less. It still pays to sell where price is highest, but for the leading home produced models this usually seems to be the home market. There can be intra-industry specialisation but there can be no expert-to-expert selling in the finished product, though there is in motor car parts in which assembly plants buy from outside industries at home or abroad.

The number of final consumers is too large for direct selling and their technological expertise less than they may think. Although expert-to-expert selling is ruled out, the models are too differentiated for purely financial merchanting. Sales are left to dealers enfranchised by the producers. Dealers in several makes cannot afford to antagonise the suppliers of their best selling models by offering comparable ones at appreciably lower prices. Sole dealers may be free from that restraint. But they too have to act within price relationships prevailing in their country. The ultimate consumer may be more interested in credit terms than in price, unless the price difference is substantial. He or his creditor may think of price as a guide to quality, and a price out of line with prevailing differentials may arouse suspicion. For instance, he may wonder whether a low priced model will outlast the repayment period. Credit facts and local prejudice in importing countries make it unlikely that price can be related to exporters' own costs. The price leadership of the leading models in each market must be accepted by anyone who wants to enter.

While it remains unknown whether improvement competition will replace model competition in motor cars, a number of engineering products have reached that stage. Not only R but also D costs are minor considerations. Price can be related to current costs. It does not follow that prices in importing countries can be related to exporters' costs. Information on pricing in traditional engineering goods is provided in a National Institute survey.[60] Nearly all of the products covered had been exported throughout the post-war period. The survey covered twenty-nine firms in electrical and mechanical engineering, with exports of forty-one products worth about £220 million in 1970-1. (The Department of Industry Inquiry for 1972 listed 426 enterprises in those two engineering groups with export sales worth £2,134 million.) Both industry groups rank high in intra-industry specialisation, and electrical engineering also in research intensity and export concentration. That makes sole reliance on exports of traditional goods unlikely especially in electrical engineering. The survey must thus be taken as representative of exports in traditional goods rather than of exports of engineering products as such.

In their home market, firms tend to price their goods in relation to their own costs of production and their absolute profits depend on the volume of sales at that price.[61] The survey found that firms priced their exports in much the same way as their home sales, but this did not mean that the same price could be charged in all markets. True, those in highest repute abroad could adjust their export prices whenever they adjusted their home prices. But all had to take account of prices prevailing in each market. Price set within the limits of own costs and prevailing price would then be closely related to profitability.[62] This ties up with the point made before that export price must be within the limits set by exporter's costs and importer's costs or prejudice. The latter can be ignored only where there is no local production and the UK exporter is the established market leader. In all other cases, both limits must be observed. Export penetration is unlikely to make much headway against an established supplier unless the products can be differentiated. Hence even in traditional trades there is likely to be some departure from the rules of perfect quantitative (price) competition.

Under those rules the product remains unchanged. But in manufactures, not even traditional goods can remain entirely unchanged. At least minor improvements are expected in quality and design, though these may be effected in the course of day-to-day business without much D expenditure. There is improvement competition, and not quantitative competition. But the line between improvement competition and model competition may be difficult to draw. Sometimes the difference is artificial. Advertising, branding and other techniques of persuasion may be directed at consumers to make them accept an improved product as a new model. Such techniques may have different effects in different markets. Since firms can be presumed to be better at working on the prevailing prejudices in their home markets than abroad, a higher 'quality' differential may be obtained at home. While similar success in individual export markets is possible, 'the' export market as a whole will not respond in the same way, unless the firms can afford a worldwide campaign of promotion with equal effect in all markets. Techniques of persuasion may also be directed at other actual or potential producers to accept price and certain codes of conduct in marketing. With or without the aid of the law relating to restrictive practices, it is easier to persuade other home producers to conform than producers the world over. Once more this can lead to a higher home price. Last, not least, producers in each country may persuade their government to grant protection. Home prejudice is then legally enshrined in their favour. They can sell at a higher price at home than abroad and need not trouble themselves so much with improvements or developments of their products, let alone with the introduction of new ones. They cannot however force their home price on to overseas markets.

(iv) Finding Markets

The conclusion is that price obtainable in export markets for manufactures depends on conditions in the importing country. It remains valid irrespective of whether these conditions are determined by costs, prejudice or whatever else influences price in the importing country. The exporter has to meet that price.

At the risk of some oversimplification, it may be said that the classification of markets into those where quality, model, improvement or quantitative competition prevails, is a classification according to the brain intensity of production. If conditions in the importing country are decisive, it must be shown that this classification also corresponds to demand conditions. To some extent this has been covered by reference to the shortening market life of products relative to the preparatory stage. This becomes more marked the greater the R & D element. More precision is possible when it is asked whether the use and the user of a particular product can be identified.

This presents no difficulty with the most R & D intensive products.

Any such product is sold by an expert producer for a specific use by an expert user. The experts constitute the market. Use and user can also be identified in products which may not be particularly R & D intensive in themselves but are more R & D intensive than other activities in the same trade. An example would be bespoke tailoring, where there is a special element of R in measuring the customer and some special D in satisfying his or her whims. Although activities such as bespoke tailoring can only make minimal contributions to exports, the example is mentioned to indicate that R & D intensity relative to other activities in the same trade, as well as R & D intensity relative to other trades, is intended to meet specific requirements. In a study of export trades, this point helps to underline the importance of being at least as R & D intensive as others in each trade. If the point is not pursued here, the reason is that the value of international demand will tend to be greatest in products which are R & D intensive relative to other trades. In any case, demand conditions confirm quality competition in the most specialised markets. Such markets should be found *before* production takes place. Although nothing can be done to reduce uncertainties during the R & D stage, at the marketing stage there should be less uncertainty than in other products.

Model and improvement competition tend to occur in products of which the use can be identified but not the user. Examples are motor cars and off-the-peg clothing. Developments and improvements help to get closer to an identification of the user. Although individual identification is impractical, users can often be subdivided into groups with particular requirements. Advice on potential groupings may be obtained from agents and distributors, though firms may prefer to conduct or commission their own market research. Such group markets can never be as certain as the highest quality markets (where the user can be identified), but they still have to be sought in advance lest the producer have unsaleable stocks at hand.

Only in quantitative competition, can neither use or user be identified. This applies to primary commodities and some basic manufactures, such as grey cloth or metal bars, which could be put to a number of uses by numerous users. Production takes place ahead of marketing. Left to market forces, the goods are sold to and from stock at whatever price they can fetch. In practice, this works only in international trade of the 'cloth-for-wine' variety. Even then, countries with established interests in such trades which are threatened by cheaper imports, and countries with emerging interests in basic manufactures, tend to respond to low priced imports with tighter import controls. These types of manufactures have not been fully integrated in the *Pax Americana* and special protectionist arrangements were made for them.[63] Yet they share one feature with other trades in manufactures, namely that importing countries expect their scale of values to be respected. If this cannot be ensured by consent or commercial prejudice, it will be enforced by legal prejudice.

Thus, all exporters of manufactures should conform with the rule: 'accept the importing country's scale of values' – which includes price relationships. They go to the importing country as traders, and not as conquerors intent on imposing their own values. The rule presents no difficulty in quality competition which depends on co-operation and mutual respect of values. The rule should also be adhered to in model and improvement competition, where the exporter's task is to add to the choice of goods available in the importing country. He is welcome, or at least tolerated, as long as he does just that and does not upset local value relationships. At first sight, the rule does not seem to apply to quantitative competition, where the exporter simply adds to the volume of goods available in the importing country. But where there are established or emerging industrial interests in the importing country, threatened local interests tend to secure protection in one form or another. This favours local values at the expense of the exporter's receipts. In short, in all conceivable circumstances, exporters of manufactures are at best advised to accept the importing country's price relationships.

They cannot do so unless and until they have acquainted themselves with those relationships before they even attempt to export. This implies another rule: 'markets must be found'. They are not there for the taking on the basis of price set in the exporting country. Such a price is always liable to be too high for some markets and too low for others. True, it is generally recognised that exporting requires some knowledge of the importing country's laws, customs and tastes. Unfortunately it does not always seem to be recognised that the most important laws, customs and tastes of relevance to commerce reveal themselves in price relationships. An exporter who does not respect these relationships must not be surprised if he is regarded as an intruder and treated accordingly.

If this states the obvious, the 'obvious' is often obscured by ideas and traditions which worked well in another age. For instance, there was a time when the UK price of primary commodities and of some basic manufactures with a long market life was 'the' world price. In some commodities, it still is. But what applied to produce with a long market life does not necessarily hold of products with a short one. Most manufactures now fall into the latter category. It is therefore perturbing to read some of the results of a recent survey of direct marketing by 125 UK companies which, in 1973, accounted for about one quarter of UK exports.[64] Most companies in the sample insisted on price being determined in the UK.[65] They recruited to their export departments *after* an increase in production capacity in order to sell what could not be sold at home.[66] Even then they starved their export departments of manpower. In nearly one quarter of the companies, there were no full-time export specialists, and over one quarter had export departments of the 'one man and a boy' variety. Overall, the ratio of export to home trade specialists was 1:4, though even 1:70 was found in one firm which exported 60 per cent of its output.[67]

The actions of those companies were in conformity with the theory of (quantitative) price competition. Where exporters sold to all markets on identical terms, there seemed to be no need to have export specialists. Goods were sold for 'the' market and what happened to them once they were in 'the' market was no longer the producer's concern. In consequence he was not prepared, for instance, to provide after-sales service. Exporters were often exhorted to keep the London price as low as possible, in the expectation that this would increase sales. Frequently they heeded such advice.

They would have done well to do so for goods of which neither use nor user can be identified. These sell on export price. In manufactures, however, this becomes increasingly less relevant, and price in the importing country increasingly more relevant, as the technology content of the product increases. Goods have to be sold for a particular use in a particular market. It would seem that it is in this range of products, where model or improvement competition prevail, that UK salesmanship has not kept pace with UK technology. The short-run result of this disequilibrium does not necessarily reveal itself in a loss of sales below previous levels. Rather it means less growth of sales and less profitable sales. Nevertheless the loss is real and cumulative. In the long run it can be substantial. The point is now widely recognised. By the mid-1970s, the number of export specialists employed was on the increase. It was also reported that several firms gave their products a higher technology content, just in order to get away from price competition.[68]

There were of course cases of high technology quality competition where products were sold for a particular use to a particular user. In such cases expert and export department are one. The gap between technology and salesmanship applied mainly in the intermediate ranges.

Section 1 has drawn attention to the strength of British industry in research intensity and intra-industry specialisation. In other words, the technological foundations for a strong export performance were laid by the 1970s. Technological change was however accompanied by faith in immutable laws of economics. But when technology changes, economics must change with it. Marketing analysis and sales methods must be adjusted. As it happened, this was done more slowly in the UK than in countries which never had the equivalent of a London price.

Notes

1. Other countries have either never collected these data or, like the US, have ceased to do so before the 1970s. Moreover, the US data referred only to selected industries in 1963. For details see US Bureau of the Census, *Current Industrial Reports,* Series 161 (63) -1, Table 3. In the case of Japan, it is known that fourteen companies handled half of her export trade to the US in the early 1970s. See e.g. Armin H. Meyer, *Assignment Tokyo,* Bobbs-Merrill, New York, 1974, p.172.
2. *International Financial Statistics,* summary tables on World Trade: Exports (f.o.b.).
3. J.D. Gribbin, *The Profitability of UK Exports,* Government Economic Service Occasional Paper No.1, HMSO, 1971, pp.2 and 4.
4. Department of Industry, Business Monitor, M4, *Overseas Transactions, 1974,* Business Statistics Office, 1976, Table 42. Summaries can be found in *Trade and Industry:* 'Direct Exporters and the Credit Terms of Exports', e.g. 10 May 1973, pp.272-4, and 16 July 1976, pp.202-3.
5. This figure is not given in ibid. but can be derived by comparing the value of exports of enterprises answering the inquiries with the total value of exports shown in the *Monthly Digest of Statistics,* No.361, Table 125. Note that the enterprises provided information for either calendar years or their own financial years, while the total export statistics relate to calendar years. The resulting figure is then too low at a time of rising export values. For 1971-4, the figures are 80, 79, 76 and 86 respectively. If it is assumed that although the larger enterprises normally answer an official inquiry, a few just over the million mark may fail to do so, the 81 per cent are again more likely to be an understatement than an overstatement.
6. *Monthly Digest of Statistics,* No.361, Table 141.
7. Again, this is likely to understate rather than overstate the degree of concentration since a number of smaller firms were especially hard hit by the economic downturn in 1973 and 1974.
8. French census data show close on 74,000 establishments with 10 or more employees in 1962, though only somewhat over 58,000 in 1972. Swedish census data indicate a total of less than 31,000 establishments of which less than a third employed 10 or more.
9. *Moniteur du Commerce International:* 'Milliardaires et Champions' and 'Exports in the Front Lines', 15 September 1975, pp.22 and 35.
10. *Veckans Affärer:* 'The Thousand Largest Swedish Companies', 1974, p.107; and Lennard Dafgård, *New Conditions for Swedish Trade with Western Europe,* Royal Ministry for Foreign Affairs, Stockholm, 1973, pp.18-19.
11. Bela Balassa, *The Theory of Economic Integration,* Richard D. Irwin, Inc., Homewood, Illinois, 1961, pp.167-9.

12. L. Dafgård, Ibid.
13. J.D. Gribbin, *Profitability of UK Exports,* p.11.
14. P.B. Rosendale, 'The Short-run Pricing Policies of Some British Engineering Exporters', *National Institute Economic Review,* August 1973, p.45.
15. Ibid.
16. Robert Heller and Norris Willatt, *The European Revenge,* Barrie & Jenkins, London 1975, esp. Chapters V and VIII; Assar Landbeck, *Swedish Economic Policy,* Macmillan, London, 1975, pp.6 and 162; J.E.S. Parker, *The Economics of Innovation,* Longman, London, 1974, p.128.
17. For a full treatment of this subject, see J.E.S. Parker, ibid.
18. *Trade and Industry,* 'Direct Exporters', 16 July 1976, Table 3.
19. Ibid. See also Department of Industry, M4, *Overseas Transactions,* Table 44.
20. *Trade and Industry,* 'Direct Exporters', 16 July 1976, Table 3. The total comes to 101 per cent owing to rounding of fractions.
21. Ibid., p.202.
22. M4, 1972, Table 56; 1973 and 1974, Table 43.
23. *Trade and Industry,* 'Direct Exporters', 16 July 1976, p.202.
24. Derived from tables cit. in note 22.
25. Indices calculated from figures correct to the nearest £10,000.
26. Excludes groups 9, 13 and 14.
27. Derived from 'Milliardaires et Champions' (see note 9). Where data were aggregated, the headings include the following French industry classes: metal manufacture includes classes 16-19 and 28; electrical engineering 37 and 38; chemical and allied trades 22-27 and 59; food, drink and tobacco 1-13; mechanical engineering 29-36, 39-40, 46-49; paper 56 and 57; textiles 50-54; other manufacture 20-21, 55; other activities 60-66, 68.
28. Excludes i, v, vi, vii, xiii.
29. For a list of the largest Swedish exporting companies see Veckans Affārer, 'Thousand Largest Swedish Companies', and for the activities of quoted companies see 'Extel Index of Classified Companies', Extel Statistical Services, London 1975. See also Swedish Institute, *Fact Sheets on Sweden,* September 1974.
30. Keith Norris and John Vaizey, *The Economics of Research and Technology,* Geo. Allen & Unwin, London, 1973.
31. Ibid., p.50 and Table 4.3.
32. Ibid., Tables 4.2 and 4.4.
33. Herbert G. Grubel and P.J. Lloyd, *Intra-Industry Trade,* Macmillan, London, 1975, Table 3.1.
34. Ibid.
35. Canada, US, Japan, Belgium, Netherlands, Germany, France, Italy, UK, Australia, as shown in ibid.
36. K. Norris and J. Vaizey, *Economics of Research,* Table 2.4, column (2).
37. H. Grubel and P.J. Lloyd, *Intra-Industry Trade,* Table 3.1, last row.
38. J.D. Gribbin, *Profitability of UK Exports,* p.6. The largest difference shown uses return on assets as the criterion, the smallest profit on cost of sale.
39. Ibid., p.7. 'Substantially higher' means 10 per cent or more, 'similar' means within a range of ± 9.9 per cent.
40. Ibid., p.11.
41. Ibid., p.12.
42. Kenneth D. George, *Industrial Organization,* Geo. Allen and Unwin, London, 1974, p.112.
43. D.C. Corner, 'The Chemical Industries', in F.V. Meyer, D.C. Corner and J.E.S. Parker, *Problems of a Mature Economy,* Macmillan, London, 1970, pp.30-9.
44. Duncan Burn and Barbara Epstein, *Realities of Free Trade,* Geo. Allen and

Unwin, London, 1972, p.138.
45. Michael H. Cooper, *Prices and Profits in the Pharmaceutical Industry*, Pergamon Press, London, 1966, p.43.
46. Ibid., pp.175, 197-8, 200.
47. D. Burn and B. Epstein, *Realities of Free Trade*, p.178.
48. F.V. Meyer, D.C. Corner and J.E.S. Parker, *Problems of a Mature Economy*, pp.461-2.
49. Michael H. Cooper, *European Pharmaceutical Prices, 1964-74*, Croom Helm, London, 1975, p.5.
50. D. Burn and B. Epstein, *Realities of Free Trade*, pp.178, 180-1.
51. An example is the ICI depot at Europort.
52. D.G. Rhys, *The Motor Industry*, Butterworth, London, 1972, pp.151, 300, 306, 311, 328-9, 394. Note that the term 'model price' is attributed to A. Gilbertson and G. Maxcy, *The Motor Industry*, Allen and Unwin, London, 1959.
53. Rhys, ibid., p.416.
54. The Leyland 'super deal' in trade-in values in 1975. It is not clear whether the main motive was de-stocking and whether it was coincidence that it occurred at a time of US hearings of allegations that the firm had dumped its cars in the UK by selling below home prices.
55. D.G. Rhys, *Motor Industry*, attributes those events to short-run price competition 'partly due to EFTA'.
56. As measured from 'broad specification' to 'final announcement'. See Rhys, ibid., p.300.
57. 'Leyland today', Supplement to *Autocar*, 6 September 1976, p.5.
58. Ibid.
59. Estimate for 1971. See D.G. Rhys, *Motor Industry*, p.274.
60. P.B. Rosendale, 'Short-run Pricing Policies'.
61. R.H. Barback, *The Pricing of Manufactures*, Macmillan, London, 1964, esp. pp. 166 and 172.
62. P.B. Rosendale, 'Short run Pricing Policies', pp.44, 46-9.
63. See Chapter 3, section 4 (iv) (c).
64. International Trade Intelligence (ITI) Research, *Concentration on Key Markets*, A Study prepared for the Betro Trust Committee of the Royal Society of Arts, London, 1975.
65. Ibid., p.45.
66. Ibid., p.39.
67. Ibid., pp.47-8, 30 (point 3 and table).
68. Ibid., pp.29 and 46.

3 UNITED STATES TARIFF POLICY

A. THE EMERGENCE OF US FOREIGN ECONOMIC POLICY

1. Increasing Returns

The country which has exerted most influence over twentieth-century commercial development is the US. This is not just the result of the size of her economy. At least equally important is that she pioneered the new R & D intensive industries and the international trade policy which suits the needs of those industries. The combined effect of these developments has made the US the 'centre' of the twentieth-century commercial world, in the sense that she has become the world's largest producer and trader, and that her approach to international commercial relations has been the major influence over international commercial conduct in the third quarter of the century. The means through which this influence has been exercised is trade agreements. These could not have been concluded without changes in tariff policy which, in turn, coincided with or followed changes in the nature of US industries.

The tariff issue came to the fore towards the end of the nineteenth century, when the US became a net exporter of merchandise.[1] In other words, she had become able to produce more than needed to satisfy domestic requirements. The Secretary of State at the time held 'the opinion that the US has reached a point where one of its highest duties is to enlarge the area of its foreign trade', and that it would not be 'an ambitious destiny for so great a country. . .to manufacture only what we can consume, or to produce only what we can eat'.[2] Before then, the tariff had been regarded as a revenue issue or a protectionist device to secure the home market for home producers, and not much thought seems to have been given to the use of tariff rates as bargaining counters to secure export outlets. Exports were of subsidiary interest, at least until the US market had become largely independent of European supplies of industrial goods. When this stage was reached first in this industry and then in that, traditional views of the tariff issue came under scrutiny. In a way, the US had become another Europe, able to supply her own basic industrial requirements. Further growth of production in existing industries gave rise to the question of where to dispose of the surpluses. There was a fear that domestic productive resources could not be fully employed, unless there were outlets for US products in foreign markets. Not surprisingly this led to a reconsideration of the tariff issue and the first attempts to use US tariff rates as a bargaining counter in trade agreements.[3]

In the event, tariff bargaining did not become a major solution to the problems of making full use of domestic productive resources, at that time. Nevertheless, for a short time in the 1890s, the President was given power to reduce certain import duties within strictly defined limits in return for equivalent concessions from other countries. This led to a number of trade agreements which may not have been of much commercial importance at the time. But they pointed some of the way towards a trade agreements policy which was to become important forty years later.[4]

There were many political as well as economic reasons why the tariff issue died down at around the turn of the century. In the present context it must suffice to say that there were other ways of absorbing domestic productive resources without getting involved in treaty relationships with other countries. Abroad tariffs were not as high as they were to become later in the twentieth century. Most of those tariffs were non-discriminatory so that they gave the US no worse treatment than was accorded to other countries. Exports were not unduly restricted or, at least, were not unduly restricted given domestic opportunities for utilising productive resources in new ways. The new demand for these resources was created through growth of new domestic industries rather than international demand for the products of the old ones.

The US may have become more like Europe but she became so in her own way. Throughout her history, labour had been scarcer in the US than in Europe. Hence, throughout her history more use was made of the technological aids to labour available at the time. Production of the same goods was normally less labour-intensive than in Europe or, what amounts to the same, her labour was more productive.[5] These industries provided the comforts of life, such as packaged meat and clothing or the basic structural materials for homes and factories, such as steel and timber.[6] By the time there were these comforts for the mass of the population, sole reliance on these activities to provide employment would have necessitated more marked export expansion than there was. Moreover, barring colonial adventures and exclusive agreements, of which there were a few at the beginning of this century, an increase in industrial exports had to be largely in competition with Europe. This would have meant lower prices.

Since the relatively scarce US labour was accustomed to receiving relatively high wages, price competition on a worldwide scale would almost inevitably have led to serious domestic friction. But this was a labour force which was, on the whole, more productive and more used to technological advances than the labour forces in similar industries in Europe. In consequence, the US was particularly well placed to switch labour and other resources to technologically even more advanced activities. The new activities were chiefly concerned with the spread of physical and mental communications. Examples are motor cars and aircraft, electrical engineering including radio, and motion pictures.[7] They were to shape much of twentieth-century life, first in the US and then elsewhere.

Although the US market was becoming satiated with the comforts of nineteenth-century life, it was still only in its infancy for the communications goods of the new century. It was therefore possible to use relatively fewer resources in the comforts industries and more in the communications activities. The continued growth of the US economy was largely the result of structural change without excessive unemployment and without international commitments. This continued until the end of the 1920s. Moreover, in the US, as elsewhere, long-established industries work largely under conditions of decreasing returns (or increasing unit costs) as the scale of production increases.[8] For such activities a reduction in foreign tariffs may not be as valuable as it seems and protection of the home market more valuable than it seems to be at first sight. If a foreign tariff is reduced, exporters can sell at lower prices to foreign consumers without getting any less for themselves. In consequence, there should be an increase in export sales. This point is not challenged. It holds without qualification for as long as unit costs of production are constant. But if a long-established industry can sell more, it uses its plant and equipment or its labour more fully so that sooner or later unit costs of production will rise. If it can sell so much more that it pays to multiply plant and equipment, this again is not costless and the unit costs of the industry still rise, and will rise again when the new equipment is fully utilised. None of this denies that long established industries can benefit from tariff reductions. But the benefits can be partly or wholly offset or even exceeded by rising unit costs. Protection of the home market may be more valuable. It allows production with existing plant and equipment to continue for longer than would otherwise be the case. Protection raises the market price. Units which would have been too costly to produce at the old price now become saleable. Existing producers benefit.

No wonder then that representatives of decreasing returns activities often prefer the protection of the home market to freer access to foreign markets. To the present day, some activities, and especially some of the older established textile trades, could not easily survive free trade and are often given special protection despite recent trends towards freer trade.[9] By now these are exceptional cases, but at the beginning of the century the majority of activities were of this nature. They wanted protection.

For the technologically more advanced industries of the day, access to foreign markets can be more important. Especially in a technologically active age, such products may never reach the stage of decreasing returns. In contrast to cotton piece goods which can be more or less the same now as they were at the beginning of the century, a motor car or an aeroplane is an entirely different product from what it was then. Generally, where technological progress is rapid, a large number of activities have L-shaped cost curves – which means they are producing first under conditions of increasing returns (or decreasing unit costs) and then under conditions of constant returns (or constant unit costs), and never get into the stage of decreasing returns to scale. The reason for this is that, more often than not, the technologically advanced products are obsolete before decreasing returns (increasing unit costs) can set in. Because of the relatively short market life of such products, firms have to recoup the cost of capital employed at the earliest possible opportunity. Hence they seek the widest possible market in the shortest possible time. A reduction of foreign tariffs is a way of widening the market for such products and so lowers unit costs. The benefit of a foreign tariff reduction (which can be taken either in the form of charging less to foreign consumers or in the form of increased profits for the exporter) is then reinforced by falling unit costs. Protection of the home market is less valuable. While the market for the product is still expanding, protection is unnecessary. When the market approaches satiety, it is likely to be irrelevant since the market will look for new products to replace the old.

At the beginning of the century, the technologically advancing communications industries were in their infancy and still had a long way to go in the US home market. They were not yet interested in getting foreign tariffs down. With the newer industries not yet interested in foreign tariff reductions and the older industries more interested in protection of the home market, the time was not yet ripe for effective concern with foreign economic relations.

Nevertheless, foreign trade in manufactures increased in importance. A relatively small surplus in a relatively small trade had already emerged just before the turn of the century. This trade grew to substantial proportions by the 1920s and so did the surplus. In other words, the US did not keep all new things to herself. This was of advantage to the industries concerned, not least because it gave them longer production runs. In the 1920s, the American way of life no longer attracted so many immigrants as before. A major reason was the introduction of immigration control but it was not the only one. It was possible to emulate the American way of life at home by dancing the American way, by seeing American films, by copying American methods often with the aid of American capital and, last but not least, by buying American goods. This required dollars. They could be earned either by the sale of foreign goods in the US or by US lending abroad.

The sale of foreign goods to the US, was, however, made more difficult by increases in the tariff in 1922 and 1930. The difference was financed through US foreign lending.[10] This was a major involvement of the US with the outside world. But it was a one-sided and precarious relationship. It was one-sided because the US lent enough to finance any foreign dollar deficits there may have been but she did not accept enough real returns in the form of more foreign goods and services. In other words, if fewer resources were needed to satisfy domestic requirements, this did not lead to domestic unemployment problems as long as these resources could be used to satisfy foreign requirements. This helped to maintain a high level of employment and price stability in a buoyant economy from 1922 to 1929. It could not last. The saving of resources at home was translated into investments abroad, but these investments were not allowed to yield a return in actual goods and services to those who had provided them. The US economy provided real and financial savings at home for financial investment abroad but, because the tariff hindered imports, she denied herself the appropriate real returns. In real terms, such investment was unprofitable for the country. This was probably a not unimportant contributory cause of the severity of the financial crisis of 1929. Be this as it may, that crisis led to a sharp reduction of US foreign lending, while the increase in the tariff in 1930 further ensured the real unprofitability of much of past lending.

In the 1920s, the US already had the largest and perhaps the most admired economy in the world. She led the world economy but she was not yet its centre, for a centre has more two-way relationships than anyone else. If these two-way relationships are to be sustained, they must be in the trade of goods and services as well as in financial flows. There must be mutual give and take or mutual coming and going in trade as well as in the finance of trade.

Although financial facilities must always be available if trade is to flourish, the growth of trade must normally come before the growth of finance for trade. This seems to be one of the lessons of history, since financial centres have grown out of trading centres.[11] Moreover, there is no point in the growth of a new financial centre to do what an older established centre already does satisfactorily. London was, and continued to be, the major centre to finance trade which consists chiefly of an exchange of manufactures for primary commodities. When the problem was no longer just to provide markets for primary commodities but how to get more primary commodities, that need could largely be answered through lending to governments and other authorities which could create conditions suitable for the building of ports, railways and other infrastructure. This made primary commodities more accessible. But the US did not need such imports. She was, and still is, the world's largest primary producer as well as the world's largest industrial producer. Her prosperity did not so much depend on cheaper primary commodities from abroad as on the longest possible production runs for her communications industries. This required access to foreign markets and a real return for selling abroad. Lending may have helped to gain more access to foreign markets since it provided some of the means of payment for US exports. It could do no more in the circumstances of the time. Some of the lending was politically motivated and helped foreign governments and municipalities to engage in all sorts of activities which were of little or no help in providing anything of interest to the US growth sector. More of the lending was in the form of direct investment. This included investment in mining and in the setting up of branch factories in foreign countries. Investment in mining was of direct interest to US industry and would lead to an increase in imports. But investment in subsidiaries abroad was of a different nature. The main purpose there was to exploit an innovation in several separate markets all at once. This may have been of benefit to individual companies, but it did not provide the long production runs at home which could have helped to minimise costs and maximise the savings which, in turn, might have provided the basis for the finance of new and even more advanced activities. The longer production runs might have taken some factors away from other activities (though, given increasing returns, the increase in the factors used would have been less than proportionate to the increase in output). In consequence, other activities would have had to contract (though less than proportionately) and the difference made up through an increase in imports. In other words, given the starting point of the US lead in the 1920s, the US could become the centre of the world economy only through increased specialisation in industrial activities and, therefore, through increased trade in industrial goods.

The analysis leading to this conclusion has been necessarily lengthy, for it is important to understand that the US could, and did, become the world's central economy on the basis of increasing returns to her technologically advanced sector and, after 1934, through trade policies which made it easier for that sector to reap increasing returns.

2. Towards Freer Trade

The US took her opportunity through taking the lead towards freer trade in industrial goods. The instrument was the trade agreements programme which, subject to ups and downs, has been pursued from the 1930s to the 1970s. It meant that the US, which in 1934 had only one trade agreement relating to tariff rates, namely a preferential agreement with Cuba, stood at the centre of around 3,500 international trade agreement relationships by the mid-1970s.[12] This development followed the economic logic of the mid-twentieth century, since the US could increase the two-way flow of goods only through negotiated reductions of trade barriers.

Traditionally, the tariff has been seen as a purely domestic tax issue of which other countries could not complain as long as it was non-discriminatory.[13] Once tariff rates were tied in international agreements, there was some abrogation of fiscal independence. Moreover, if trade agreements were to be negotiated and implemented by the President, this was a narrowing of Congressional authority over tax rates. There was, and still is, a constitutional issue involved.[14] Even in the Trade Act of 1974,[15] the latest legislation on US trade agreement to date, the Congress only delegates to the President the power to vary tariff rates in trade agreements within strictly defined limits and for a limited period of time.

Delegated authority is not ultimate authority, for that rests in the Congress. Economically, the delegation of authority made it possible to reduce, though not altogether abandon isolationism. US tariff law continued to be US domestic law. But there had to be reconciliation of domestic and international issues. Internationally, the intention was a revival of trade on a non-discriminatory basis, yet the results include a grading of products and countries according to their fitness for freer trade. The programme moves towards freer trade but precludes free trade.

These points will have to be discussed in turn. But first the narrative must be resumed where it was left off at the end of Section 1. That section was a *post hoc* rationalisation of past events in the light of what is known to have happened afterwards. It is not suggested that arguments relating to increasing returns would have carried much weight at the time, let alone arguments relating to specialisation between and within manufacturing activities. Nor should the impression be given that there was ever a clear US design to get herself into a central position.[16] If anything, there was reluctance to assume such a role and the trade agreements programme could possibly be interpreted as an attempt to share the lead.

As mentioned in Section 1, the increase in the tariff in 1930 aggravated the real disequilibrium in the US external trade, while the deepening financial crisis of the time reduced the funds available for foreign lending. It is, of course, not unusual for protectionist sentiment to come to the fore in times of deepening depression, and this had happened before in US history[17] and was happening all over the world at the time. Nevertheless, it was accident rather than design that the increased tariff rates came into force just then. Although the exact details of the causes of the 1929 crisis remain a matter of dispute to the present day, it was preceded by increasing difficulties for primary producers, including US farmers. A special session of Congress was called to consider a limited revision of the tariff to help the farming community. As on earlier occasions when Congress set about to revise a tariff, any favours granted to one sector of the community led to demands for similar favours for others. This process of 'log-rolling' had often before meant an upward revision of the tariff even when the original intention of tariff revision had been different.[18] The 1930 Tariff Act proved to be no exception to this rule, and what was originally intended as a limited measure to raise agricultural prices finished up as a general increase in tariff rates. Although written before the financial crisis broke, it came into force afterwards.

By that time, the agricultural crisis of the late 1920s and the financial crisis of 1929 had been followed by a major slump in US production and trade. From 1929 to 1933, export prices fell by 40 per cent and the value of exports by 70 per cent.[19] This had adverse effects on domestic incomes and employment.

When the Democrats returned to power in 1933, they were committed to a national economic recovery programme which was to include measures to revive the export trades. Purely domestic measures did, however, take precedence and it was not until 1934 that the appropriate legislative measures were taken to authorise trade agreements. The relevant Bill was introduced as 'an emergency measure to deal with a dangerous and threatening emergency situation'.[20] It was not until the renewal of the trade agreements authority in 1949 that the reference to 'the present emergency' was omitted.[21] Perhaps it is only fair to add that there was always some sort of emergency between 1934 and 1949, and that it was only around 1949 that the nature of the economic post-war settlement was beginning to emerge.

Technically, the 1934 Act, which has become known as the Trade Agreements Act of 1934, was an Act to amend Section 350 of the Tariff Act of 1930.[22] That Section had authorised the President to negotiate trade agreements but given no authority to implement them. The significance of the 1934 Act was that it gave implementing authority albeit only for a limited period and within strictly defined limits. The implementing authority had to be renewed and redefined from time to time until it was allowed to lapse in 1967. It was revived in 1974. This was not quite as 'temporary' as some may have thought in 1934.

The Act was passed 'for the purpose of expanding foreign markets for the products of the United States'.[23] In more modern parlance, the intention was 'to foster the economic growth of and full employment in the United States' and this is how it is put in the Trade Act of 1974,[24] which was passed at a time when unemployment again threatened to become a major problem. If this was to lead to an increase in imports, that was a purchase price to be paid for increased export outlets. Although the then Secretary of State had wider visions and saw international trade as the life-blood of civilisation, and as a way of bringing people together, making them prosperous materially and enabling them to pool their combined civilisations,[25] such views were not universally held in the 1930s. True, these views are compatible with the more prosaic points relating to increasing returns and specialisation made in Section 1 of this chapter, but in 1934 the immediate problem was the economic depression. There was plenty of spare capacity and unemployed manpower which could be put to work with existing capacity before too much thought had to be given to further specialisation. In the circumstances, more employment was possible without a corresponding increase in investment and without even putting too much pressure on existing capacity. The assumption of constant costs was therefore applicable and this made an unqualified classical model of comparative costs applicable. Re-employment would be helped by freer trade, and re-employment would be concentrated where existing comparative advantage lay. That would be the most profitable re-employment possible at the time and so lead to a rise in incomes and then to further employment. Visions about civilisation had to wait for fulfilment in the full employment days after the Second World War. If 'civilisation' had relevance to the trade agreements programme of the 1930s, it had so in a negative way. It stemmed the tide towards further economic nationalism in Western countries and so the withdrawal from civilisation as seen by the then Secretary of State. In the circumstances of the time, this was no mean achievement.

The programme was, however, slow off the ground. The Act was not passed until June 1934, when the worst of the depression was over. Subsequently, there were procedural delays because the Tariff Commission had to investigate the possible effects of tariff concessions before any particular item could be included in the negotiations, while the other countries concerned also took time over preparing their positions. Negotiations were bilateral, although any tariff cuts made in any one agreement were automatically extended to all other countries with most-favoured-nation rights. In consequence, there were further limitations to what could be achieved. Countries were reluctant to give the maximum possible concession in any one trade agreement, lest they forfeit negotiating power in parleys with others. In consequence, most concessions would be given to principal suppliers. This made negotiations with smaller countries of relatively little importance. The most significant of the agreements concluded at the time was the agreement with the UK. But this was not concluded until August 1938, and so could have little impact before the outbreak of war. Nevertheless, thirty-two separate agreements were concluded with twenty-nine different countries before trade agreement negotiations became multilateral through the GATT in 1947.[26] Moreover, it was perhaps not unreasonable to assume that a country which was the principal supplier of a particular product was the country which had a comparative advantage in that product. True, this ignores questions of relative size and negotiating power of different countries (which, in practice, led to some modifications of the principal supplier rule).[27] Nevertheless, the method of negotiations at the time was at least in rough conformity with general principles of traditional international trade theory.

This method was modified after the Second World War, when the GATT provided a framework for multilateral tariff negotiations. Member countries came to negotiate simultaneously with several, if not all, participants. This saved time and overcame the principal supplier restraint. A series of negotiations followed. By 1951, tariff reductions had been negotiated with thirty three countries. The tariff cuts exceeded those made earlier under the trade agreements programme.[28] To the best of the authors' knowledge, more tariff cuts were made then than ever before within a span of four years.

Afterwards there was a lull in tariff negotiations. One reason was a cut in US implementing authority. In 1934 this was up to 50 per cent of Tariff Act rates and in 1945 this was widened to 50 per cent of the rates then in force. Although there were extensions of the tariff reducing authority in 1954 and 1958, they allowed for further tariff cuts of only 15 per cent and 20 per cent respectively. Since tariff reducing authority is seldom used to the full in any one negotiation, these extensions were inadequate for major negotiating achievements. Moreover, various 'safeguards' were added to trade agreements procedure. In consequence, there was little room for further effective tariff negotiations in the 1950s. The 'emergency' was over and it may have seemed reasonable to expect tariff stability for a while rather than further new initiatives.

The mass negotiations of the late 1940s and to 1951 overcame the principal supplier problem. They led to so many tariff reductions that any relevance to existing bilateral comparative advantage ceased (though there could still be relevance of the comparative advantage of each country with the rest of the world). It was a period of reconstruction and high activity where new comparative positions could emerge. Although each country still sought concessions on its principal exports at the time, the total concessions granted were sufficiently widespread that new comparative positions could develop. The result was that tariff concessions were given which allowed for potential comparative advantage and not just for actual comparative advantage. This was to pave the way for new methods of tariff negotiations in the 1960s.

By then the lull was over. As it turned out, the 1950s did not mark the end of an energetic pursuit of freer trade but no more than a pause in that endeavour. The move towards freer trade was revitalised through the emergence of the EC. Instead of the emergencies of depression and reconstruction, there was the emergence of a challenge to which the US had to address herself.

Her response was the Trade Expansion Act of 1962 which was the first (and so far last) trade agreements legislation to provide for the possibility of complete abrogation of most US tariff rates. There was a vision of a North Atlantic area of free trade in most industrial goods, with equal freedom for such goods from third countries. The condition for such free trade was to be that the US and an enlarged EC control 80 per cent of world trade in the goods concerned. Since the enlargement of the EC did not materialise until eleven years later, the vision faded. But in the following trade negotiations, the Kennedy Round, it was again possible to negotiate tariff reductions up to 50 per cent of current tariff rates. The method of negotiation between the industrial countries was no longer on an item-by-item basis but 'linear across the board'. This meant that instead of negotiating a concession on one item for another country's concession on another item, both sides made the same percentage cut in tariff rates on the same range of items. The idea has a long history in the 'contingency duties' which have for long featured in US law and were meant to ensure that foreign countries gave no worse treatment to the same goods than the US accorded them.[29] In the past, this never came to much. By the time of the Kennedy Round, conditions were ripe for the implementation of the idea. Future developments seemed to depend more on further specialisation between the industrial countries. There was growing scope for intra-industry specialisation as opposed to the inter-industry specialisation of the past.

After the Kennedy Round, Presidential authority to implement tariff cuts was allowed to lapse. It was not revived until after the enlargement of the EC in 1973, through the Trade Act of 1974. But this provides authority of tariff cutting by only 40 per cent and makes no reference to any negotiations for complete free trade except possibly with Canada.[30]

3. Towards an Effective Foreign Economic Policy

An active and effective United Stated foreign economic policy dates from 1934. In the Trade Agreements Act of that year,[31] the Congress delegated to the President basic authority to negotiate *and* implement trade agreements. This authority was not unlimited. Tariff rates could not be varied by more than 50 per cent from those laid down in the Tariff Act of 1930, and even this authority was to expire after three years. Despite these limitations, the authority given in 1934 allowed the President more latitude in the conduct of foreign economic relations than any President had before and, in some respects, more than his successors were to have in the 1950s and after 1967. In 1967, the implementing authority was allowed to lapse but it was revived in the Trade Act of 1974, though with somewhat more stringent limitations.

Under the Constitution of the United States, the President negotiates and the Congress legislates. Nothing was or could be done to change this in 1934 or at any other time. What was changed was the order in which these powers were to be exercised. The usual procedure before

1934 (and from 1967 to 1974) can be summed up as 'negotiate first, legislate later'. In 1934, and again in 1974, this became 'legislate first, negotiate later'. Under the pre-1934 procedure, the President had negotiating authority but no implementing authority. In 1934, he was given implementing authority as well, albeit implementing authority within the limits laid down by legislation passed before the commencement of negotiations. Trade agreements within those limits could then be concluded as 'executive agreements' which required no further Congressional approval.

Needless to say, there can be no trade agreements without negotiations, and negotiations must be conducted by the administrative arm of government. Equally, there can be no implementation of any tariff changes without the appropriate legislative authority. Tariff changes are tax changes, and tax law is domestic law. In countries with Parliamentary government, such as the UK, the line between negotiating and implementing authority is less clearly drawn. Disagreement on the conduct of foreign economic policy would either bring the government down or lead to a dissolution of Parliament or both. Here it does not matter so much whether negotiations precede or follow legislation. In the US, where there is a separation of powers and much of the art of government depends on reconciling the independent authorities of the President and the Congress, it does matter. There can be no certainty that a trade agreement negotiated by the President will be implemented through appropriate Congressional legislation, unless there has been prior legislation which sets out the precise limits of what the President can implement without further reference to the Congress.[32]

As long as the US followed the procedure of negotiating first and legislating later, the uncertainties of implementation were so great that tariff reductions were negotiated in only a few trade agreements and even fewer were implemented. Apart from some minor and short-lived trade agreements negotiated in the 1890s, there were only three. One, with Canada, was in force from 1855 to 1866. Another, with Hawaii, was negotiated in 1875 and turned out to be the first step towards annexation of that territory in 1900. The third one, with Cuba in 1902, was again politically motivated and remained in force until superseded by another preferential agreement concluded in 1934. These agreements were strictly reciprocal or, as we would now put it, preferential.[33] In short, foreign economic policy was isolationist and the tariff non-negotiable save in a few instances where the tariff was bent to suit special political relationships. This does not fully apply to the 1890s, when the first attempts were made to negotiate on economic grounds. The results may not have been of much commercial importance at the time. But the legislative base of those attempts can be thought of as the first tentative step in the direction of the trade agreements legislation from 1934 to 1974, even if at the time those steps were soon to be retraced.

The Tariff Acts of 1890 and 1897 authorised the President to negotiate certain tariff changes in trade agreements and to implement them without reference to the Congress. This authority was rescinded in the Tariff Acts of 1894 and 1909 respectively. Even in the 1890 and 1897 Acts, this authority was strictly limited to specified amounts and to specified commodities which were not of major importance in trade. Such concessions were to be given only in return for equivalent reciprocal favours and were not extended to third parties. Viewed in the context of the time, the authority to reduce any import duties without reference to the Congress was a departure from tradition, for it allowed the Executive an independent role in levying taxes.[34] Viewed in retrospect, that authority does not seem so startling. Since the concessions were given only in return for equivalent favours, this was an authority to grant exemptions from the full operation of individual tariff rates to some products from specified countries. It was not yet authority to lower any tariff rate as such. This was not given until 1922 and then not for negotiating purposes. That had to wait until 1934.

However ephemeral and feeble the implementing authority of the 1890s may now seem, its importance as one of the antecedents of future trade agreements legislation should not be shrugged off. There could not have been any effective trade agreements legislation without Presidential implementing authority and this was first tried in the 1890s. But a revival of this procedure alone would not have been enough to make for effective trade agreement legislation. This also needed a flexible tariff, non-discrimination between foreign countries and non-discrimination between the products on which tariff reductions could be made. At no time were all of these conditions fully met. If a flexible tariff is one which the Executive can vary without resort to new legislation, this authority has always been limited. For instance, under the Trade Act of 1974, this authority is limited to a range of 40 per cent below and 50 per cent above the rates of duty existing on 1 January 1975.[35] Such limited flexibility has its origins in the Tariff Act of 1922, although there was no intention at the time to facilitate trade agreements or even trade. There was much uncertainty about price movements in the years immediately following the First World

War and, in consequence, there was no certainty of the effectiveness of the tariff rates which came into force in 1922. In an attempt to overcome this difficulty, the President was authorised to raise or lower tariff rates by 50 per cent from Tariff Act rates if, after appropriate investigations, it was found that this would equalise the cost of production between the United States and the principal competing country.[36] In the present context, the importance of this provision is that it was a departure from the rule that only the House of Representatives can initiate tax changes, including changes in tariff rates.

This provision for flexibility was continued in the Tariff Act of 1930. The Trade Agreements Act of 1934 provided an alternative, through allowing the President to negotiate trade agreements involving 50 per cent variations in tariff rates from those laid down in the Tariff Act. As trade agreements became more numerous and involved tariff cuts, the effective flexibility of the tariff was downward flexibility. Although the possibility of upward flexibility remained, this was sparingly used. There were cases of withdrawals of trade concessions on individual products when one or the other of the various safeguards in trade agreements legislation enabled domestic interests to claim they had suffered injury from rising imports or when trade agreement concessions were withheld from countries which discriminated against the US.[37] The net result was downward flexibility with occasional reversals in special cases.

Flexibility of tariff rates implies equal treatment of imports from all foreign countries. Before 1934, other countries' interest in US tariff rates was considered irrelevant[38] and tariff rates were unilaterally determined. Before 1922, there was the possibility that other countries might negotiate exemptions from the full impact of individual tariff rates through reciprocal agreements which would not be extended to third countries unless they granted equivalent concessions. This was known as a conditional most-favoured-nation treatment. Since, in effect, this led to exclusive arrangements, negotiations were few. With the introduction of flexibility of tariff rates for purely domestic reasons in 1922, it became impossible even to contemplate special exemptions since these would have to be renegotiated every time there was a change in a tariff rate. From 1923 onwards, this was interpreted to mean that the US gave unconditional most-favoured-nation treatment to all foreign countries, since any change in US tariff rates applied to all countries irrespective of whether they gave anything in return.[39] This really was a moot point until flexibility ceased to be autonomous flexibility and become negotiated flexibility. That had to wait until the President was given authority to implement negotiated tariff cuts under the trade agreements legislation from 1934 onwards. Under that legislation, any concession the US gave to one trade agreement partner affected the relevant tariff rate or rates, so that the concession automatically applied to imports from all countries with which the US had normal commercial relations. There was provision for exclusion of countries, if they were found to discriminate against the US, but such exclusion was exceptional. Unconditional most-favoured-nation treatment became the norm.

The third condition, non-discrimination between products, simply means that the range of negotiable products must be large enough to make negotiations worthwhile. It does not mean that every negotiation must be about every product. In fact, no negotiation is likely to be so all-embracing unless it be one leading to the formation of a customs union. But the products which are non-negotiable must be the exception rather than the rule.

The trade agreements legislation from 1934 to 1974 combined implementing authority (which was first tried in the 1890s) with flexibility of all tariff rates within defined limits (which dates from 1922) and with non-discrimination between foreign countries (which is also known as unconditional most-favoured-nation treatment and, in the US, again dates from the 1920s). None of these by themselves sufficed to make trade negotiations possible. Their combination did.

B. THE RECONCILIATION OF ISSUES

4. Revenue and Constitutional Issues

(i) The Revenue Issue

A foreign economic policy can be effectively pursued as long as it reconciles the various domestic and international issues involved. Tariff policy is a domestic issue because tariff rates are a form of taxation and tax law is domestic law. Tariff policy is also an international issue because it delimits the commercial frontiers and any agreement relating to tariff rates blurs those frontiers. The least any trade agreement will do is to put a constraint on the tax laws of two or more countries. This makes trade agreements policy a revenue issue, and because it is a constraint on the way revenue is raised, it is also a constitutional issue. Further, it limits the amount of protection which can be given to domestic activities so that it is also an industrial issue. As the following discussion will show, these issues often interact.

The problem of reconciliation of such issues arises where neither the domestic issue nor the international one predominates. Where a government's revenue largely depends on customs revenue, the domestic issue predominates. A legislature which wants to control the volume and details of government activity is then unlikely to allow the administration much freedom to negotiate about tariff rates. For to do so would allow tariff rates to be tied in agreements with other countries, and that would restrain the freedom of raising more revenue through increases in tariff rates. There would be an effective limit on the expansion of government activity.

Countries where the domestic issue predominates or predominated include the less developed countries of the second half of the twentieth century and the US of the nineteenth century. Similar problems may emerge in new-style instrumentalities such as the EC which has not much in the way of 'own resources' other than customs revenue, unless new sources of revenue can be found.

At the other extreme, there are countries where the international issue predominates. These are countries whose economic activities do not stop at the political frontier but whose financial or industrial operations are worldwide. Examples are the UK in the nineteenth century and the US today.

This stage cannot be reached until domestic development has gone far enough for government to raise revenue internally and not just at the frontier. In the case of the UK and the US this meant that income tax became an alternative to customs duties as the chief source of revenue before tariff reductions became a serious issue of policy. To make this fiscal change required appropriate educational and industrial development. In the case of the US it also required appropriate constitutional development.

One educational condition is relatively easy to see. There can be no income tax or other tax which depends on form filling unless the taxpayers can read and write. Until most people can do so, the income tax base is too narrow to yield as much revenue as may be needed for the finance of government activities. A narrow tax base may have sufficed to maintain law and order in the mid-nineteenth century UK, but it would not do so now in any country where government has more widespread interests. The other educational aspect is more complex and intertwined with politics. As education advances there are more demands for equality of opportunity in jobs and choice, and commodity taxes interfere with both. Moreover, commodity taxes such as customs duties are regressive taxes and hit both rich and poor alike. The rejection of regressive taxes leads to greater reliance on a neutral or progressive system of income tax. In reliance on income tax rather than commodity taxes, the US is now most advanced, while the UK used to be at the turn of the century.

Until 1913, the US Federal Government had to depend on customs and excise taxes for its revenue. Then, the sixteenth Amendment to the Constitution was passed which made a Federal income tax constitutional. This made the Federal Government independent, or at least more independent, of customs duties for its very existence. In the early years of the century, customs revenue had contributed close on one half of total Federal revenue and that proportion had usually been higher in the nineteenth century.[40] After 1913, the importance of customs revenue declined. Although the tariff was raised in 1922 and again in 1930, customs revenue contributed only 14 per cent of Federal revenue in the 1920s and 11 per cent in the 1930s.[41] The reduced importance of customs duties in total revenue made it possible to contemplate trade agreements with foreign countries without undue impairment of Congressional control over the volume of Federal Government activity. Between 1946 and 1973, customs revenue never contributed as much as 2 per cent of total Federal revenue and averaged around 1 per cent.[42] One of the major obstacles to trade agreements had been overcome.

(ii) The Constitutional Issue

Customs duties may now be unimportant as a source of Federal revenue but they remain part of domestic tax law, and the right to initiate tax changes rests with the House of Representatives. Trade agreements impinge upon that right. Moreover, trade agreements used to be regarded as treaties with foreign countries, and so had to be ratified by the Senate. Although under the Constitution the President has the power to negotiate trade agreements with foreign countries, he cannot implement the outcome of such negotiations unless the Congress approves. Before 1934, when the procedure was to negotiate first and legislate afterwards, there were few negotiations and even fewer implementations. The significance of the trade agreement authority which the Congress delegated to the President from 1934 to 1967 and revived in 1974, is that the procedure has been reversed.

The Administration is, and always has been the agency through which trade agreements are negotiated and is also the agency through which trade agreements are implemented. But it must act within the limits of the implementing authority delegated by the Congress *before* any negotiations can even begin. Within these limits, the Administration can conclude 'executive agreements' which require no further Congressional approval. The trade agreements implemented between 1934 and 1967 came under this heading. So did the commitment to a general code of conduct of international commercial relations in the GATT.

For a long time, the Congress no more than tolerated GATT. Its attitude was expressed in the 'GATT Disclaimer' of the Trade Agreements Extension Act of 1951.[43] It reads: 'The enactment of this Act shall not be construed to determine or indicate the approval or disapproval by the Congress of the Executive Agreement known as the General Agreement on Tariffs and Trade.'[44] This remained valid under subsequent trade agreements legislation in the 1950s and the Trade Expansion Act of 1962.[45] In practice this meant that the President could commit his Administration but not the Congress, and that the Congress would take no action as long as those commitments were compatible with prior legislation and involve no new legislation.

The Trade Act of 1974 modified the Disclaimer. It now reads: 'This authorization does not apply approval or disapproval by the Congress of all articles of the General Agreements on Tariffs and Trade.'[46] It will be noted that this no longer refers to 'the Executive Agreement known as the GATT' but to 'the GATT', and that approval or disapproval is withheld from unspecified articles of GATT rather than GATT as such. The new Disclaimer does in fact follow authorisation of annual appropriations of funds to defray the US share of the expenses of GATT[47] which implies Congressional recognition of the existence of GATT. This in turn is preceded by a reaffirmation of the US policy of non-discriminatory trading[48] and a list of topics on which the President should seek a revision of GATT.[49] The revisions are sought to improve current GATT procedures, to extend the activities of GATT and to amend some of the rules. If any of those changes can be negotiated and involve new legislations, this is to be passed or rejected without amendment and within a specified period of time (so that there can be no filibuster).[50]

No new legislation would be required if GATT revisions could be obtained in conformity with the Trade Act of 1974. For instance, should it be possible to negotiate a new escape clause[51] which allows countries to withdraw trade agreements concessions where injury has resulted to domestic interests, through a substantial increase in imports, by allowing 50 per cent increases in the relevant tariff rates for five years in return for compensatory reductions of other tariff rates by 30 per cent, there would be no need for new legislation since provision for such a procedure is made elsewhere in the 1974 Act.[52]

Similarly, should it be possible to extend GATT rules so as to ensure non-discriminatory access to supplies[53] as well as to markets, the appropriate authority to include such provision is given elsewhere in the Act.[54] It may be added that such an extension of the rule of non-discrimination would avoid a repetition of the situation in 1973/4, when a number of Middle Eastern countries embargoed oil exports to the US. Even those which were members of GATT, could do so without breach of the letter of their obligations.

An amendment is sought in the balance of payments provisions of GATT[55] so that import surcharges should take the place of import quotas 'as the preferred means by which industrial countries may handle balance of payments deficits insofar as import restraint measures are required'.[56] If accepted by the other members of GATT, the rules laid down in the 1974 Act allow a temporary 15 per cent *ad valorem* import surcharge on all imports at a time of a large and serious balance of payments deficit[57] and a temporary 5 per cent *ad valorem* reduction of import duties on dutiable items when there is large and persistent balance of trade surpluses,[58] and also the imposition or relaxation of import quotas.[59]

This is by no means an exhaustive list of the GATT revisions sought or of the implementing authority conferred upon the President to meet the new trading situations of the 1970s, such as the balance of payments problems which arose for the US in 1971 and the oil embargo in 1973. It cannot be forecast whether it will be possible to renegotiate the balance of payments provisions of the GATT in conformity with the range of duty variations of the 1974 Act, though import surcharges may be acceptable. The US had, in fact, used this method in 1971 and so have other countries before or since. In the US, however, this practice was ruled invalid by the Customs Court and the surcharge had to be withdrawn earlier than the Administration may have wished. The 1974 Act legalises the procedure in the US and seeks its international acceptance through an appropriate renegotiation of GATT. This would be in line with the practice of France (1955), Canada (1962), the UK (1964-6), Denmark and the US herself (1971). Hence the request is in line with well-established practice in which other GATT members had acquiesced.[60]

Of more immediate interest in the present context, however, is the additional flexibility of the tariff through Executive action. In addition to the basic authority to lower tariff rates by 40 per cent in trade agreements and raise them by 50 per cent (or 20 per cent *ad valorem*, whichever is the higher) for purposes of threat or bargaining,[61] there is now provision for 30 per cent reductions in tariff rates in compensation to foreign countries for the 50 per cent increase in tariff rates which may be given to domestic interests injured by a rise in imports, and there is provision for temporary tariff flexibility of 15 per cent up to 5 per cent down on balance of payments grounds.

The additional flexibility of the tariff on injury and balance of payments grounds is an increase in Presidential authority over tariff rates. This is of some significance but need not rival the importance of the basic authority to cut tariff rates in trade agreements. Here Congressional influence was increased in 1962 through the appointment of Congressional delegates to trade negotiations and the number of such delegates was increased in 1974.[62] These changes, together with the modification of the GATT Disclaimer indicate an intention to exercise Presidential and Congressional powers over foreign trade more in tandem. This may become of increasing importance as tariffs are further reduced in trade agreements and attention shifts to non-tariff barriers to trade as well as GATT revisions to meet new trading situations. Any agreement relating to non-tariff barriers will have to be submitted for Congressional approval after negotiation. The procedure is the same as that laid down for GATT revisions, namely approval or disapproval without amendment and without long-drawn-out debates.[63]

Should it be possible to extend the scope of trade agreements so as to involve the US in more than tariff cutting, it will once more be 'negotiate first, legislate later' albeit in a modified form. The modifications include the procedural ones mentioned, the inclusion of Congressional delegates in the US negotiating team, and the expression of the sense of the Congress of the sort of GATT revision desired and of the kind of non-tariff barriers which are negotiable. Reference has been made to some of the GATT revisions that are desired. In the case of non-tariff barriers, the expressed aim is to seek their 'harmonization, reduction, or elimination'.[64] The non-tariff barriers mentioned are subsidies and the American selling price basis of customs evaluation.[65]

The listing of desirable objectives for inclusion in the agenda of possible future international negotiation means that some sections of the Trade Act are not actual law but wished for law.[66] In effect this means that there is now less of a distinction between trade agreements legislation as domestic law enacted by the Congress, and the Administration's objectives in international negotiations. While this may tie the hands of the US negotiators, it also makes it more likely that agreements will be approved if their outcome is within the sense of the Act than if their outcome creates a new situation.

An example of the risk involved in entering into negotiations, on matters where the sense of the Congress had not been formulated in trade agreements legislation, was provided by the negotiation of a bilateral trade agreement between the US and the Soviet Union in the early 1970s. This agreement would have extended most-favoured-nation treatment to a country which had been barred from such treatment by prior legislation. The Trade Agreements Extension Act of 1951 prescribed a discriminatory import prohibition on certain furs and skins originating in the Soviet Union or Communist China[67] and the Trade Expansion Act of 1962 denied most-favoured-nation rights to all Communist countries.[68] The relevant clauses had not been repealed at the time the Administration negotiated the Soviet agreement as part of a policy of *détente*. Consequently new legislation was involved and the Trade Act was meant to provide it. The Act makes no reference to Communist countries and provides authority to extend most-favoured-nation treatment to 'countries not currently receiving non-discriminatory treatment'.[69] During its passage through the Congress, this was amended so that most-favoured-nation treatment would be denied to countries which impede the emigration of its citizens in general and to the US in particular.[70] This, together with a limitation of credit which government agencies could extend to the Soviet Union without prior Congressional approval,[71] proved unacceptable to the Soviet Union.[72]

It may seem curious that other sections of the Trade Act try to prevent the sort of situation which these amendments have created, namely that President and Congress have different aims in their dealings with foreign countries which, in this instance and often before 1934, led to Congressional frustration of Presidential foreign economic policy. The new procedures may overcome the difficulties involved wherever negotiations precede legislation. As already mentioned, the general statements of negotiating aims in the Act, the presence of Congressional delegates at the negotiations, the preclusion of amendments and filibusters, means a new way of exercising Presidential and Congressional powers in tandem. 'Negotiate first, legislate later' made trade negotiations difficult or impossible before 1934 and the more recent experience with the Soviet trade agreement suggests that the independent exercise of Presidential and Congressional powers can still result in frustrating an effective foreign economic policy. 'Legislate first, negotiate later' is suitable for tariff cutting where it is possible to give a clear definition in precise figures of what authority is delegated. Such precision becomes impossible when it comes to revise GATT so that it should become more than a negotiating forum for countries which accord most-favoured-nation treatment to each other's exports (or a renegotiating forum whenever difficulties arise from tariff cuts previously negotiated), as it has been from the time of its inception in 1947 to the time of writing. It is equally impossible to be so precise about non-tariff barriers or rules for extension of most-favoured-nation treatment to non-market economies. The solution foreshadowed by the 1974 Act seems to be: 'first legislate in general terms, then negotiate, and finally give unqualified approval or disapproval of the specific results of the negotiations'.

For tariff rates, however, 'legislate first, negotiate later' continues. This order of procedure which was evolved to reconcile the constitutional separation of powers with the trade agreements policy from 1934 onwards, has effectively set the international timetable for tariff negotiations. Any major increase in Presidential tariff reducing authority from 1934 to date, has been followed by major negotiations leading to marked reductions in trade barriers. Lesser increases or mere extensions of this authority were followed by negotiations leading to only minor results. The reason is that other countries prepared their positions in response to the offer of the leading trading power of the age.

Since Presidential implementing authority is limited in time, as well as in extent, no major negotiation could start when Presidential authority was nearing its end. Nor could negotiations start immediately upon enactment of the relevant legislation, sinces its implications had to be studied and consultations with affected interests had to take place in each of the countries willing to negotiate. In consequence, major negotiations were most likely to start in earnest not earlier than a year or two after the grant of Presidential implementing authority and not later than a year or two before its expiry.[73] This did not preclude the negotiations from dragging on. Knowledge of the time limit concentrated the negotiators' minds on the end of that period. This was especially important during the Kennedy Round of tariff negotiations under the 1962 Act, when there was implementing authority for five years. Although the negotiations dragged on for over three years, it was reported that serious negotiations did not really get under way until about five months before the expiry of the US Presidential implementing authority (in June 1967).[74] Agreement was reached only shortly before the expiry of that authority in 1967. Each delegation held out for the most advantageous terms for as long as possible, in the hope that the other delegates would concede more rather than go home empty-handed. While this was not the only reason why the Kennedy Round was so protracted, it was not an unimportant one.

Thus the limitation of the time during which the President has implementing authority had its effects on delaying the start of negotiations and on protracting negotiations. But on completion of a negotiation, implementation in the US was virtually automatic as long as the US negotiators kept within the limits of the President's implementing authority. Should the results of tariff negotiations under the 1974 Act be kept separate from the outcome of negotiations towards the other objectives of the Act, there will be no change. If, however, the negotiations lead to an agreement which involves a package of tariff and other trade concessions by the US, implementation will not be so automatic and the tandem will be put to the test.

5. Protection versus Freer Trade

(i) The Protectionist Issue: Pre-Agreement Relief

The way the US resolves her constitutional issues in relation to trade agreements policy will continue to have a major influence over the extent and timing of international trade concessions. But the direction in which the US wishes to go, be it towards further tariff concessions or further control of trade, or be it through multilateral agreements or unilateral action, will depend on the state of her economy in relation to the world economy. Economic considerations are never clear-cut. Although in the forty years following 1934 trade became freer, this was not achieved without a protectionist rearguard action which sometimes scored some successes.

That trade agreements legislation has been a compromise between freer trade and protection is evidenced by the limitations on the Presidential implementing authority in extent and time. The tariff reducing authority and the limitations on tariff rate increases are balanced by the limitation on tariff reducing authority and provision for tariff rate increases. Trade agreements are possible, but their validity is limited to three years and thereafter subject to six months' notice.[75] In practice, tariff rates were reduced substantially and only sparing use was made of the tariff-raising authority, while most trade agreements continue in operation after the initial three years. Nevertheless, although trade agreements legislation was used to make trade freer, the legal authority to do so was balanced by authority to make it less free. It still remains theoretically possible to denounce all trade agreements and so restore the tariff rates of the Tariff Act of 1930.

Such an extreme course of action would have been contrary to the declared aims and actions of successive US governments since 1934 and can probably be regarded as a legal curiosum. It was, however, politically important to reconcile protected interests to the policy of freer trade and this was done through the various safeguards written into trade agreements legislation and prior laws as well as the safeguards implied in the administrative provisions of trade agreements legislation. Some of these safeguards can be applied before a trade agreement can be negotiated, others can be used after an agreement has come in to force, and yet others at any time. A detailed account of all the relevant laws and administrative provisions would be beyond the scope of this study. Here it must suffice to give some indications of the legal restraints which can prevent the full use of tariff-cutting authority, the administrative procedures which delay the commencement of trade negotiations and may even protract the negotiations, and the legal facilities for reversing trade liberalisation.

The following gives two examples of how prior laws could frustrate or override trade agreements legislation in respect of certain chemicals and agricultural products. The Tariff Acts of 1922 and 1930 had given special protection to certain products, including chemicals, by prescribing customs evaluation in accordance with the American selling price of equivalent domestic products, instead of the usual evaluation on the basis of actual value. This was protection but not tariff protection, and so it remained unaffected by trade agreements legislation before 1974. It is not unusual for countries to give special protection to selected products and so exempt them from the normal process of tariff bargaining. But when the US sought substantial tariff reductions in the 1960s, other countries made some of their concessions on chemicals contingent upon a repeal of the American selling price regulations.[76] They were not repealed at the time and one part of the negotiations was frustrated. The 'American selling price' is one of the non-tariff barriers named in the Trade Act of 1974 which provides for the possibility of negotiations on non-tariff barriers.[77]

Perhaps more important in the present context is legislation relating to agriculture. Section 22 of the Agricultural Adjustment Act authorised the President 'to restrict imports when they tend to render ineffective the program of the Department of Agriculture'.[78] In consequence, quotas were imposed unilaterally on a number of raw products, including wheat and raw cotton, and on final products made from agricultural raw products, such as flour and certain textiles.[79] At first, Section 22 protection and the trade agreements programme were administered side by side but, in 1951, priority was given to Section 22 protection. The result was that some trade agreement commitments were negated.[80] This priority was confirmed in subsequent trade agreements legislation, including the Trade Expansion Act of 1962 which exempts from that Act all import restrictions imposed under Section 22 of the Agricultural Adjustment Act 'heretofore and thereafter'.[81] This continues under the Trade Act of 1974.[82] In consequence, there can still be no tariff bargaining on products accorded Section 22 protection.[83] But an alternative to Section 22 was provided by Section 204 of the Agricultural Act of 1956. This authorised the President to negotiate with foreign countries the level of their exports of agricultural products to the US. Under this authority, quotas for textiles were negotiated from 1961 onwards.[84] These were quota arrangements and not tariff concessions, but they were negotiated quotas and not unilaterally imposed ones. Provision for such 'orderly marketing agreements' was incorporated in the Trade Expansion Act of 1962[85] and continued in the Trade Act of 1974,[86] so that trade agreements legislation now applies to some 'agricultural' protection and Section 22 protection is effectively confined to agricultural raw products.

These are special cases, where other laws have led to the exclusion of some items from effective negotiations. Of wider applicability are the administrative provisions, written into trade agreements legislation itself, which cannot prevent negotiations but delay the start of negotiations and can limit the extent of possible concessions below the full legal tariff cutting authority. The details of the administrative provisions have been changed but the essential features have not. There are official investigations of each item on which a concession is contemplated in a forthcoming negotiation and there are consultations with all interested parties. A brief outline of the procedure under the 1974 Act is as follows.

To start with, the appropriate procedure cannot be set into

motion until the appropriate tariff changing authority is enacted. (In the case of the 1974 Act, this was in January 1975.) The President then prepares and publishes a list of articles on which customs and excise duties might be modified in forthcoming trade agreements.[87] This list is then studied by the International Trade Commission, (until the 1974 Act known as the Tariff Commission), a six-member bi-partisan commission charged with investigating tariff matters and giving advice to the President.[88] The Commission is to advise, within six months, with respect to each article on the list, on the probable economic effects of modifications of duties on affected domestic interests, and also on such effects of modifications of non-tariff barriers. Before tendering its advice, the Commission must hold public hearings.[89]

The Commission's task is wide and vague. It is wide because the probable economic effects include profits and employment at home, and also involves consideration of production conditions, including real wages, abroad.[90] It is vague since there is no indication of the degree of modification envisaged other than the legal maximum laid down in the Act. Greater precision was attempted in the 1950s, when the Tariff Commission had to lay down 'peril points' below which no duty should be reduced.[91] This interposed an administrative barrier between current rates of duty and the maximum legal reduction. Although the peril points could be breached as long as this was reported to the Congress, negotiations were made more difficult since US offers were that much less than the legal maximum and by different amounts for each item. Peril points were effectively abandoned during trade negotiations in 1960-62 and legally abandoned in the Trade Expansion Act of 1962.[92]

While the International Trade Commission makes its independent inquiries, the President must seek advice from interested Departments of the Administration. In addition to such intra-governmental consultations, arrangements must be made for a special agency to hold public hearings where any interested person can present his views concerning any article on the President's list for possible modification of duties in a trade agreement.[93] These investigations, consultations and hearings relate to possible modifications of duty on individual items. Advice on the general objectives and bargaining positions is to be sought from representative elements of the private sector. There is an Advisory Committee for Trade Negotiations, composed of representatives of government, the private sector and the general public. It meets under the Chairmanship of the Special

Representative for Trade Negotiations, an official of Ambassadorial rank whose main task is to be chief US representative at trade negotiations. There are sub-committees to deal with individual sectors. The Committee gives both policy advice and technical advice, or on any other factor relevant to positions of the US in trade negotiations.[94] The Committee is also charged with commenting on trade agreements when concluded, as well as reporting on the general working of the Trade Act when the current implementing authority expires five years after enactment. Although this Committee's tasks are not at an end when a trade agreement is concluded, it has to be heard before conclusion of an agreement.[95]

In short, trade negotiations cannot start immediately upon enactment of trade agreements legislation. It is not enough to reconcile Presidential and Congressional powers in the appropriate legislation to be able to enter into meaningful negotiations with foreign countries. In between legislation and negotiation come these administrative procedures for consultation. They cause delay and limit the possible range of negotiations but they are also a way of ensuring acquiescence of affected interests.

The administrative provisions can delay or limit the progress towards negotiated freer trade. They cannot halt it. They are part of a law enacted to promote freer trade. While those who fear injury are given hearings, the onus of proof is upon them. Moreover, they cannot now seek so much shelter under prior law. The early trade agreements legislation was concerned mainly with tariff-cutting authority and its administration. The relevant Acts were short. Law relating to other aspects of trade had to be found elsewhere and this sometimes gave special protection. The 1962 and 1974 Acts range more widely and are more likely to impinge on other legislation than be in need of supplementation by other legislation. There will be less shelter to be found elsewhere.

(ii) The Protectionist Issue: Post-Agreement Relief for Special Cases

(a) The Escape Clause and Tariff Relief. Pre-agreement relief was in any case bound to become less important with the passage of time. In the early days of the trade agreements programme, it may have seemed plausible to think of a particular reduction in a tariff rate as the cause of an increase in imports of an item which had become less protected. Even to the present day, preparations for trade negotiations include attempts to forecast the effects of particular changes in tariff rates. In the US, these preparations are prescribed by law, in the form

of the various administrative procedures outlined in the preceding sub-section of this chapter. Were perfect forecasting possible, such procedures would ensure that no tariff cut can be made in any trade agreement which subsequently causes, or threatens to cause, injury to domestic interests. It was soon realised, however, that even the best possible forecasts cannot allow for unforeseen contingencies. If there was to be effective relief for protected domestic interests, provision had to be made for post-agreement relief to meet unforeseen injury.

At first, post-agreement relief was entirely by means of tariff rate increases. There was, and still is, an escape clause in every trade agreement. This provides for renegotiation or withdrawal of tariff reductions in force as a result of a particular trade agreement. The theory behind such post-agreement relief is the same as that behind pre-agreement relief: a tariff cut is 'the' cause of increased imports. The difference between pre- and post-agreement relief was that the former was concerned with predictable, and the latter with unpredicted, increases in imports. The former prevented a tariff cut, the latter undid it.

After forty years of trade agreements, with more than one tariff rate reduction on most items and some of those reductions made decades ago, the distinction between pre- and post-agreement relief has become impractical. The effects of hypothetical future tariff cuts can no longer be disentangled from those made in the past. Nor can a particular increase in imports be attributed to any one particular tariff cut. As time went on, the underlying theory that particular tariff reductions were 'the' cause of increased imports and, therefore of potential injury, gave way to thinking that increased imports could be a substantial cause of injury irrespective of what tariff cuts may have been made in the past.

Those injured by a substantial increase in imports can obtain relief through tariff action. But, since particular tariff rate reductions are no longer seen as 'the' cause, under US law tariff relief is no longer tied to the extent of earlier tariff cuts[96] – though it is still so tied under GATT rules, unless and until these rules can be revised.[97] Moreover, once the theory of a causal connection between changes in individual tariff rates and changes in relevant imports was abandoned, post-agreement relief no longer had to be confined to tariff action. It became supplemented by 'orderly marketing agreements' which are a form of import control by quotas, and by 'adjustment assistance' which is a form of subsidising injured domestic interests. These non-tariff reliefs were first implemented in the 1960s. It is not impossible that one day they will be used, or misused, as major forms of protection in place of the tariff, but this has not been the case to date. On the whole, they have been sparingly used and, like the pre-agreement administrative safeguards, the post-agreement reliefs provided for special cases have been a means of ensuring domestic acquiescence with the move towards freer trade.

As mentioned, the first post-agreement relief was the escape clause. This was evolved gradually and, by 1947, assumed a form suitable for escape from negotiated tariff concessions but not suitable for escape from an increase in imports due to other causes. Right from the start of the trade agreements programme in 1934, its administrators sought to guard against the unexpected. Initially they tried to avoid injury through detailed pre-agreement investigations into possible effects of individual tariff concessions, through the subdivision of tariff items so that the concession concerned would benefit only one or few suppliers, through willingness to renegotiate concessions which had led to unforeseen results, and through excluding special risks.[98] In so far as the search for safeguards led to pre-agreement relief, this has already been discussed. But the search for safeguards against special risks was to lead to the escape clause and other post-agreement relief.

In its earliest form, the escape clause provided for withdrawal or renegotiation of a tariff concession which benefited mainly third countries. In those days, trade negotiations were bilateral. But negotiations were about tariff rates, so that any negotiated reduction benefited all third countries which had most-favoured-nation rights in the two negotiating countries. The escape clause first appeared in the trade agreement between the US and Belgium, of 1935. This allowed for withdrawal or renegotiation of a concession, should its major benefit accrue to third countries so that 'an unduly large increase in importation will take place'.[99] The same provision was made in the trade agreement with the UK of 1938, if imports of the article concerned from any third country 'increase to such an extent as to threaten serious injury to producers' in the importing country.[100] It may be noted that, in its early form, the escape clause did not refer to injury caused by trade with the other agreement partner. Nor was any specific reference made to imports from the agreement partner in any of the later trade agreements. But such imports became effectively covered, when the reference to third countries was omitted from the US trade agreement with Mexico of 1942. An escape clause covering imports from any source has been incorporated in all US trade agreements ever since, and is also provided for under GATT.[101]

Under these rules, the ultimate remedy for injury resulting from imports was a unilateral withdrawal or modification of a concession given in a trade agreement. But unilateral action could be taken only after adequate notice had been given and the possibilities of renegotiation explored. If renegotiation failed and unilateral action was taken, the trade agreement partner could withdraw an equivalent concession, but the rest of the agreement was left unimpaired.[102] It remains to be seen whether these rules will continue, or whether the US will secure international acceptance of an escape clause which allows for an increase in tariff rates by a fixed percentage amount, as provided for in the Trade Act of 1974,[103] instead of the restoration of a former tariff rate.

Curiously, Mexico was the first country to invoke the escape clause in its Mexican form, in 1947. Although the US demanded compensation where the nature of protection was changed, she accepted straight increases in tariff rates without compensation.[104] She could hardly have done anything else at the time. For in that year, an Executive Order was issued which provided for the inclusion of a Mexican-style escape clause in all future trade agreements and established machinery for domestic interests to apply to the Tariff Commission for an investigation and hearings, and for the Commission to report to the President for possible action.[105] In the same year, the GATT came into force and included provision for an escape clause in essentially the same terms as in the Mexican agreement. Since GATT agreements were negotiated between several pairs of countries at one and the same time, a reference to third countries would have been confusing. If there was to be an escape clause in multilateral trade agreements, it had to be in the Mexican form. In 1951, this US executive and GATT practice became part of trade agreement legislation.[106]

An increase in imports, to which injury could be attributed, was defined as either an actual increase in quantities or as an increase relative to domestic production. The latter definition was to be a special safeguard for declining industries. From 1955 onwards, any actual or relative rise in imports was to be taken as a cause of injury. The possibilities of relief seemed further strengthened when National Security provisions were written into trade agreements legislation. These were to be applied irrespective of trade agreements obligations, whenever imports were thought to impair the national security. For a time, the 'economic welfare' of any industry was thought to be relevant.[107] In practice, little use was made of the National Security provisions. They were mainly applied to oil[108] and were otherwise largely unworkable as instruments of trade policy. Although still part of trade agreements legislation,[109] they need not be considered further in this study. Even the escape clause was fiercer in wording than in fact. During the whole period from 1947 to 1962, it succeeded only in fifteen cases[110] and in none on grounds of relative increase in imports.[111]

Renamed 'tariff adjustment', the escape clause reappeared in the Trade Expansion Act of 1962, though confined to cases where there was an actual increase in imports and where the Tariff Commission found that this increase in imports was 'a result in major part of concessions granted in trade agreements'.[112] In other words, it was no longer assumed that there was a causal connection between a tariff cut, a rise in imports and injury. The connection had to be established.[113] Thus, the 1962 Act tightened the escape route through tariff adjustment. In the following years, no more than four cases were pending in any one year and often less. Few succeeded. For instance, in 1974 no new action was initiated. Only one tariff rate was increased as a result of an earlier action, while a 1970 duty increase on pianos was rescinded.[114]

The escape clause, on which protectionists had pinned much hope in the 1940s and 1950s had indeed become rather *piano*. The attempt to counter the general trend towards freer trade, through countervailing action in special cases, had largely failed. Moreover, the 1962 Act provided for alternative forms of protection for special cases through orderly marketing agreements and adjustment assistance. It may be added that there also was some inconsistency between escape clause legislation and practical policy. Thus, the 1962 Act authorised tariff rate increases, for four years, up to 50 per cent above the Tariff Act rates in force before the commencement of the trade agreements programme in 1934.[115] But it also made tariff adjustment contingent upon a proven link between tariff cut and injury.[116] Since a tariff cut could only have been made from a rate in force in 1934 and after, almost any adjustment to a higher rate would have overcompensated the injured interest. In any case, no more than a restoration of a former tariff rate would have been compatible with the Mexican-style escape clause in the US's trade agreements. At the time, this inconsistency was probably no more than a legal curiosum. It prolonged the life of the lingering escape clause. But it also reaffirmed the latent theory that the US tariff is flexible in either direction. This was to become more important in 1974.

The 1974 Act provided for flexibility in other ways. It re-introduced escape clause action under the name of 'import relief' through tariff action. It removed the inconsistency of the 1962 Act in relation to the escape clause, by allowing tariff increases of only 50 per cent above rates currently in force.[117] Since most tariff rates on industrial goods, other than textiles, in force in the mid-1970s were well below two-thirds of the 1934 rates, a 50 per cent increase in a current rate would normally lead to a rate below that in force in 1934. That the period of escape was lengthened to five years, does not affect the argument since GATT permits a permanent restoration of a former rate in escape clause cases. A new situation was created, however, by the complete severance of the connection between tariff rate reductions and injury.

Instead of investigating the effects of past tariff cuts, as the Tariff Commission used to do, the International Trade Commission is to determine 'whether an article is being imported into the United States in such increased quantities as to be a substantial cause of serious injury, or threat thereof, to the domestic industry producing an article like or directly competitive with the imported article'.[118] As before 1962, an increase in imports can be an actual increase or an increase relative to domestic production.[119] 'Substantial cause' is defined as 'a cause which is important and not less than any other cause'[120] and explained as one which involves idling of productive facilities, lack of profitability and unemployment.[121] In other words, given substantial unemployment, there may be a return to higher tariff rates. It does not follow that this will necessarily happen, especially since the 1974 Act provides for such tariff action mainly as a last resort, when other forms of relief cannot be obtained in adequate measure.

The least important of these changes seems to be the restoration of a relative rise in imports as a cause of injury. Of no effect when part of trade agreements legislation in the late 1950s, it is not likely to be significant now, when a rise in imports has to be established as a substantial cause of a decline in domestic industry.

The most important change is the final severance of the link with past tariff reductions. Once a rise in imports, as such, is recognised as a possible substantial cause of injury, the way may be open to a return to an autonomous flexible tariff. As mentioned in section 3 of this chapter, this was last tried between 1922 and 1934. Then there had to be comparisons of costs of production in the US and elsewhere.

There is no such restraint now, but there are others.

There is an international restraint through GATT. Escape from rising imports, rather than from trade agreement concessions, would require a revision of Article XIX of GATT. Should international agreement be possible on this point, one wonders whether GATT would not have to be transformed. So far GATT has been a code of conduct. Its organisation has been minimal, and the tasks of its Secretariat have been the preparation of trade negotiations and the monitoring of their observance. If there is to be escape from imports, would that organisation not have to be strengthened to supervise trade flows, if it is not to break up?

Whatever the outcome of any international renegotiation of GATT, the Trade Act itself limits the use of tariff or quota action to cases where adjustment assistance cannot be relied upon to remedy an injury.[122] Since adjustment assistance can be given to individual firms, groups of workers or regions, while tariff action applies to an industry as a whole, it should normally be difficult to prove an injury to an industry which cannot also be proved for constituent parts of that industry. Even if such proof is forthcoming, there still has to be an investigation whether this injury is caused by dumping. Should this be established, restrictive measures can be taken against the offending country. These can, but need not necessarily, take the form of special import duties. If so, the most-favoured-nation tariff rate continues to apply to other countries.[123] Until 1975, such tariff action could be taken only in respect of articles subject to import duty. Amending legislation passed in that year has made such anti-dumping action possible even for articles on the free list.[124]

Yet another alternative to tariff relief is the negotiation of an orderly marketing agreement with foreign countries, limiting the exports from those countries and the imports into the US of relevant articles. Tariff relief can be given when such agreements cannot be negotiated or cease to apply.[125]

When these alternatives have been explored and found impracticable, the President still has to consider whether tariff relief would be effective, the consequences for consumers, the reaction of foreign countries and their impact on exporters, and several other factors before he gives import relief.[126] As mentioned before, this is then limited to five years. Moreover, it is to be phased down after three years.[127] In short, tariff relief has been made the least eligible form of import relief.

(b) Adjustment Assistance. Of the preferred reliefs, adjustment assistance may become the most widely used, simply because it does not depend upon negotiations with foreign countries. Escape clause action is by industries and affects the appropriate tariff rates. Adjustment assistance is given to segments of industries and leaves tariff rates unchanged. It can be given to groups of workers, individual firms and 'trade impacted areas'.[128] The idea was that changes in Federal trade policy could cause local unemployment pockets, so that Federal aid should be made available beyond the assistance already provided by State insurance schemes.[129] Such aid could take the form of higher unemployment benefits than would otherwise be available, assistance with job search, relocation and training. Similarly, individual firms may suffer from market disruption resulting from changes in Federal trade policy. They could be compensated financially or through counselling or with technical assistance. The 1974 Act added communities suffering from heavy unemployment as a result of imports. Private borrowers, with qualified projects in such trade impacted areas, can get special loan guarantees. The intention here is to bring work to the workers, since factors militating against the mobility of labour had turned out to be so strong that hardly any use had been made of relocation benefits.[130]

The 1962 Act had already given preference to adjustment assistance over tariff adjustment. The procedure was quicker, applications for such assistance were allowed to continue even though a parallel case for tariff adjustment had been dismissed, and the benefit was given in a form more tangible to the recipient.[131] Nevertheless, relatively little use was made of adjustment assistance between 1962, when it was first introduced, until 1974, when it was revised. The first worker assistance was not given until 1969. In the following five years, around one in 100 of the unemployed qualified.[132] If this is thought to be a small proportion of the unemployed, it should be recalled that adjustment assistance did not replace unemployment benefits but was supplementary to such benefits. Nor was it for all the unemployed but only for those whose unemployment was attributed to tariff reductions. Similarly, only limited use could be made of adjustment assistance to firms. Between 1962 and 1974, only thirty-five firms qualified. Fewer than twenty actually received assistance pursuant to certified adjustment proposals.[133] The main reason why not more use had been made of adjustment assistance, was thought to be the requirement to establish a causal link between tariff concessions and increased imports.[134] This requirement was abandoned in the 1974 Act.

Like tariff relief, adjustment assistance can now be claimed on grounds of injury caused by increased imports, and it no longer matters why imports have increased. This causal requirement is less strict for adjustment assistance than for tariff relief. For the latter, increased imports must be a substantial cause and *not less* than any other cause.[135] For adjustment assistance, increased imports need only be an important cause, and this is defined as 'a cause which is important but *not necessarily more* important than any other cause'.[136] Even if the relaxation of the causal requirement should lead to greater use being made of adjustment assistance, this form of protection is essentially a form of subsidisation to tide over localised difficulties due to one particular cause. It is not a means of assisting whole industries. Moreover, it is limited by budgetary considerations and international obligations. During the deliberations preceding the enactment of the Trade Act of 1974, the budgetary cost was thought 'not to be unreasonable', especially since loan guarantees are the first choice in assistance to firms and communities.[137] Trade agreement obligations do not allow subsidies which interfere with trade to any marked degree. The Trade Act itself provides for countervailing duties on subsidised imports from other countries.[138] Effectively this limits adjustment assistance to import-competing activities with no major export interests. Particularly favoured were applications from interests in the footwear industries.[139] Given inter-industry specialisation between countries, this approach is suitable.

Intra-industry specialisation may seem to complicate the issue.[140] But this need not be a major limitation, for a simultaneous increase in imports and exports of similar goods is most likely to occur in the growth sector. That sector tends to be in the increasing returns stage. It does not normally need assistance. There may yet be isolated and localised problems of transition and, in such cases, adjustment assistance may smooth over such difficulties. The budgetary limitation will probably ensure that such assistance is never carried so far as to convert an activity from one injured by imports into a successful exporting one. Thus, adjustment assistance is unlikely to come up against trade agreement obligations.

It does not follow that adjustment assistance can be used on a larger scale for the more traditional activities which are in the decreasing returns stage. Although this would conform to the general rule of thumb that protection is most beneficial to decreasing returns activities, decreasing returns are not so much a localised problem as a technically determined one which can affect whole industries. Assistance to industries can be given by means of tariff relief.

The definition of industries for tariff purposes is, however, largely a consumers' definition. Tariff schedules often distinguish several hundreds of items, although large numbers of them may be produced under similar or identical technological conditions. But protection is for producers. If producers can get increased protection solely through adjustment assistance or tariff relief, post-agreement relief is bound to be no more than a minor protectionist rearguard action. The somewhat wearisome case-by-case procedure laid down for adjustment assistance, and the even more wearisome item-by-item procedure for tariff relief, will probably ensure that. It remains to be seen whether the same applies to orderly marketing agreements.

(c) Orderly Marketing Agreements. Orderly marketing agreements are a way of forcing other countries to limit their exports of specified product to the US. They have been applied to a number of products, but chiefly to a range of textile products. In effect this came closer to industry protection than the protection of segments of industries under adjustment assistance, or the protection of individual items under tariff relief. It is a form of protection which has been decried as a new mercantilism.[141] Nevertheless, the procedure for a claim to protection through orderly marketing agreements is the same as that for tariff relief.[142] Although such agreements can replace unilateral tariff or quota action by the US, and so are a method of protection preferred to tariff relief under the terms of the 1974 Act,[143] they have to be internationally negotiated. In consequence, they depend on foreign governments as well as on the US Administration. Inevitably, this limits the range of possible application of this form of protection.

Nevertheless, this form of protection, or any form of protection, is disproportionately useful to producers in decreasing returns activities. These are more common in the traditional basic comfort-providing industries than in the more innovation-minded communications industries. Two of the traditional industries, textiles and steel, began to emerge as problem cases when post-war reconstruction was over in the mid-1950s. Although output was rising by about one half, imports of some textiles and steel trebled in the 1960s.[144] Since there seems to be less scope for intra-industry specialisation in textiles and steel than in some of the newer industries, the increase in imports meant more inter-industry specialisation. This implies displacement of some domestic production by imports which, in turn, arouses protectionist sentiment. The US textile and steel interests were no exception. Since they were substantial interests, it would have been difficult for politicians to ignore them. A special form of protection was sought for them.

The point must not be exaggerated, since the share of imports in the US market for steel did not come to more than one-sixth even towards the end of the 1960s, and that of textiles to less.[145] Nor should the protectionist response be exaggerated. Its most widely publicised result, the Long Term Textile Agreement, did not in effect protect all sectors of the textile industry but only individual categories. Although these categories comprise several tariff items, quota restraint remained an alternative to tariff relief. What had changed was the manner in which such protection was given. Details were as follows.

The special treatment of textiles amongst industrial goods, dates from the days when textiles were accorded agricultural protection and so could be protected by the unilateral imposition of quotas. Such protection was pre-agreement relief and effectively precluded tariff bargaining on most textiles in trade agreements. By the mid-1950s, this was out of line with the general foreign economic policy of the US in relation to industrial goods. By that time, the first attempt was made to negotiate quota protection for textiles. In 1955 and 1956, Japan was prevailed upon to impose voluntary restraint on her textile exports to the US. In this context, 'voluntary' meant that the exporting country administered the agreed quota. This procedure was legalised under Section 204 of the Agricultural Adjustment Act of 1956 which authorised the President to negotiate bilateral agreements to restrain the export to the US of agricultural products and textiles. An amendment, dating from 1962, authorised multilateral negotiations for the same purpose and also allowed for the unilateral imposition of quotas on similar goods from countries not parties to the agreement.[146] Under these provisions, orderly marketing agreements were negotiated first for cotton textiles, in 1962, and then for most textiles, in 1974.[147]

In the meantime, such arrangements had become part of trade agreements legislation. The 1962 Act made orderly marketing agreements an alternative to tariff adjustment, and this was continued in the 1974 Act.[148] This widens the application of orderly marketing agreements to all products which are eligible for tariff relief. In consequence, orderly marketing agreements became a form of post-agreement relief. By 1970, such agreements were applied to 67 different kinds of products, and not only to textiles,[149] though the latter continued to be the largest single group of products covered.

A series of agreements relating to cotton textiles was in force from 1962 to 1974, then to be replaced by the multi-fibre textile agreement which covered woollen and man-made fibre textiles as well. The agreements were between the major textile importing and exporting countries. The US divided cotton textiles into 64 categories, while other countries used broader categories. Any member government which considered its domestic industry threatened by market disruption through rising quantities or falling prices of imports, could request any other member to restrain the export of that category to specified levels, though not below actual levels of trade. If the restraint were agreed and in force for more than one year, the quota had to be increased for the second and subsequent years, normally by 5 per cent. But if the exporting country refused to comply within sixty days of such a request, the importing country could prohibit imports beyond specified levels and would not be under an obligation to increase the quota in subsequent years. These agreements were negotiated under the auspices of GATT, but not all requests for restraint had to go through the multilateral machinery of GATT. Countries continued to have the right to negotiate bilaterally and, as time went on, more use was made of bilateral negotiations than of restraint through the multilateral agreements.[150] One reason for this was that, under bilateral agreements, the coverage of products could be widened beyond cotton textiles and the provisions for quota increases could be varied.[151] Such bilateral agreements were to pave the way towards the multi-fibre agreement of 1974. Under that agreement, the US negotiated a three-fibre arrangement with Japan. This provided for an overall textile quota, with flexibility between the limits set for cotton, woollen and man-made fibre textiles, and between the various categories of those groups.[152] In effect, the multilateral agreements came to be occasional consolidations of bilateral arrangements.

Since nothing but a change in fashion or technology can revive the fortunes of the American and European cotton textile industries, these agreements may have had less effect on trade than on the manners of international commercial conduct. Exporting countries are faced with the choice of either 'voluntary' restraint and some increase in trade later on, or mandatory restraint with a standstill in the volume of trade. If they elect some increase in future trade, they have to bear the administrative burden. Governments of less developed countries may be unable to do so, and all governments may find it odious to have to restrict their own nationals' trade. Industrialists in all countries may find it difficult to alter their marketing plans at only sixty days' notice. Moreover, requests for restraint were almost exclusively addressed to Japan and Asian developing countries. Some of the latter are reported to have been bewildered when, having received aid for development, the donor country then cut off some of the fruits of development through restrictive trade policies.[153]

However valid this point may be, it is all too easily forgotten that the labels of countries as 'developed' and 'developing' does not necessarily apply to all sectors of such countries' economies. In some categories of textiles, there has been more progress in the developing countries than in the developed ones. In other words, some textile producers in advanced countries have been less able to adjust themselves to changing trading conditions than their rivals in developing countries. Such activities may yield decreasing returns in advanced countries and increasing returns in developing ones. Perhaps the developed countries should leave such activities to the developing ones. Nevertheless, there may be a case for temporary protection of some products in which otherwise advanced countries have fallen behind.

The emphasis must, however, be on 'some products' and the case cannot be generalised. In the actual working of the textile agreements, this limitation was observed. There was no request for restraint on all of the 64 categories of cotton textiles, while such protection was confined to cotton textiles, and there was flexibility between the various textiles under the multi-fibre agreements. Although there was potential protection for the whole of that industry, this was not given. It can thus be claimed that the way the agreements were worked made protection of textiles through agreed quotas an alternative to tariff relief on individual items. What was avoided was an increase in tariff rates on textiles. Owing to the origin of textile protection as agricultural protection, many categories of textiles had been effectively reserved from tariff rate reductions in trade agreements. Import relief through tariff action could thus have raised import duties on some textiles above the rates in force when the trade agreements programme began in 1934.[154] Because import relief was given by means of an orderly marketing agreement, there was no increase in tariff rates.

There could be no reduction in tariff rates either, while import relief was given in any form – and this provision was continued under the 1974 Act.[155] It so happened, however, that the long-term textile agreement of 1962 was due to expire in 1967, and that negotiations for renewal became part of the Kennedy Round of tariff negotiations which were completed in 1967. The textile agreement was extended, subject to a bonus quota increase, and what matters more in this context, subject to tariff rate reductions. The tariff reductions on cotton textiles averaged around one-fifth, compared with overall tariff reductions in the Kennedy Round of over one-third.[156] Whatever the details, not only was a tariff increase on textiles avoided, but cotton textiles ceased to be reserved from tariff negotiations.

By the time of the conclusion of the Kennedy Round of tariff negotiations, the US made little use of the multilateral long-term textile agreement. Only seventeen categories, involving imports from three countries, were so restrained. More use was made of bilateral agreements which involved restraint of forty-five categories from four countries.[157] In the early 1970s, bilateral agreements relating to other textiles became more important and, by 1973, US textile imports from thirty-seven countries were subject to restraint. Another twenty-five arrangements were concluded in 1974, under the multi-fibre agreement.[158] It remains to be seen whether this is really a new mercantilism or whether these are temporary palliatives to smooth the way towards further tariff reductions.

Whatever the outcome, orderly marketing arrangements have not yet, and may never, become a method of industry protection, with industry defined from a producers' point of view. Although the categories are wider than individual tariff items, they are categories defined by final use rather than methods of production. It remains to be seen whether an orderly marketing arrangement for footwear will fulfil this requirement. At the time of writing, it was only part of the wished-for law of the 1974 Act,[159] still to be negotiated.

The textile agreements, and any potential footwear agreements, are agreements between governments and within the authority conferred by trade agreements legislation. This was not so in the case of steel. In 1968, British, EC and Japanese steel producers agreed to a 'voluntary export restraint program' and 'offered' this scheme to the State Department.[160] They observed the 'self-imposed' overall restraint on their steel exports, but not any limitations on speciality steels within the overall restraint.[161] The foreign producers entered this scheme on the understanding that it was compatible with US domestic law. When it was challenged in the Federal courts under US anti-trust legislation, it was withdrawn in 1974. A special clause was inserted in the 1974 Act to indemnify the foreign producers from any legal consequences.[162] Quota arrangements remain a prerogative of government and cannot be supplemented by industrial arrangements even with the connivance of an agency of government.

Textiles and steel are not the whole of the US economy, but they comprise substantial sectors of decreasing returns activities. Next only to agriculture, they are less adaptable to changing trading conditions than most other activities in advanced industrial countries. If there is a case for protection in such countries, textiles and steel are high on the list. Nevertheless, the special problems of steel were not allowed for long to be an excuse for flouting other laws; and the special problems of textiles were not allowed to divert the Administration from its major long-term objective of freeing international trade. That objective was actually brought closer when the reserved status of textiles ended. All US tariff rates on industrial goods are now negotiable.

(iii) The Protectionist Issue: General Relief through Staging

Post-agreement relief is not confined to special cases. There are general limitations on the tariff reductions which can be implemented. Again, initially this was done through pre-agreement relief. All trade agreements legislation has limited the President's implementing authority and this continues. Tariff cuts were limited to 50 per cent in 1934, another 50 per cent in 1945, 15 per cent in 1955, 20 per cent in 1958, 50 per cent in 1962, and 40 per cent in 1974. Since full tariff-reducing authority is not often utilised in trade agreements, the move towards freer trade was more gradual than these limits suggest.

An even more gradual approach was prescribed in the 1950s, when tariff reductions agreed in trade agreements were no longer allowed to be introduced at once. Instead they were to be carried out in stages. This is a form of post-agreement relief which applies to all negotiated tariff reductions. At that time, there was reluctance to cut tariffs further than they had already been cut in the immediate post-war tariff negotiations. Some further tariff-reducing authority was however needed in 1955 in order to negotiate the accession of Japan to GATT, and some more in 1958 as a first response to the emergence of the EC. But these were follow-up operations rather than new initiatives towards further universal tariff reductions. If some tariff rates had to be cut in order to achieve these more limited aims, the impact on domestic industries was to be softened. The method chosen was staging.

The 15 per cent tariff reductions allowed in 1955 were to be made effective in three stages of not more than 5 per cent each. The first one was to come into force immediately upon the proclamation of an agreement, the second one a year later, and the final one two years after proclamation. The 20 per cent tariff reductions authorised in 1958, were to be effected in two stages of not more than 10 per cent in any one year. On both occasions, an alternative was provided for tariff rates over 50 per cent. These could be reduced in three stages down to 50 per cent. Since less than one-third of the tariff-reducing authority conferred in 1955 and only about half of that conferred in 1958 was actually utilised in the subsequent trade negotiations, this was not of too much importance at the time.[163] But it was to become important in the 1962 and 1974 Acts.

Although the Trade Expansion Act was intended to revive and speed up the move towards freer trade and gave substantial tariff reducing authority, it also accepted and refined staging. The actual introduction of negotiated tariff reductions was to be in stages of not more than one-fifth of the negotiated reduction in any one year, with the first stage effective immediately upon proclamation and the fifth four years later.[164] Since the negotiations following the 1962 Act were not concluded until shortly before the expiry of the implementing authority in 1967, there was a nine-year gap between legislation in 1962 and full effectiveness of the tariff reductions in 1971.

One implication was that the final effectiveness of the tariff reductions came after the lapse of implementing authority. This presented no problem in the implementation of the negotiated tariff reductions. The proclamation of implementation was made within the legal time limit and this made it law. Only the execution was delayed. But there was less urgency to renew the implementing authority when it lapsed in 1967 than there had been on earlier occasions. For there was a provision that a year must elapse between the actual reduction of a tariff rate under the terms of one trade agreement and its further reduction under the terms of a subsequent trade agreement.[165] Since the tariff reductions agreed in 1967 were wide-ranging, there was then no scope for further major tariff negotiations until 1972. For the first time since 1934, the implementing authority was allowed to lapse until it was renewed in the 1974 Act. In the meantime, no new trade agreement could be implemented without Congressional approval after the conclusion of negotiations. None was implemented.

When Presidential implementing authority was revived in 1974, it was again qualified by a staging requirement. Tariff rates in excess of 5 per cent *ad valorem* can be reduced by only 40 per cent; and staging is required for all tariff rate reductions of more than 10 per cent of the duty in force before the reduction.[166] In other words, while low tariff rates can be abolished and small tariff reductions can be made fully effective immediately upon proclamation, medium and high tariff rates cannot be abolished and their reduction can be effected only in stages.

There are two alternative rules for staging. Upon proclamation, a tariff rate can be reduced by either 3 per cent *ad valorem* or one-tenth of the total negotiated reduction, whichever is greater. This is to be followed by equal reductions, at one-year intervals, until the total reduction is fully effective.[167] The 3 per cent *ad valorem* rule will apply for all reductions where the initial tariff rate was over 5 per cent *ad valorem* and less than 75 per cent *ad valorem*. For when, as under the 1974 Act, the maximum possible reduction of a tariff rate is 40 per cent (irrespective of its *ad valorem* equivalent), one-tenth of the total reduction is greater than 3 per cent *ad valorem* only if the initial rate was over 75 per cent *ad valorem* and the maximum reduction is made. If the tariff rate is reduced by less than 40 per cent, the initial rate would have to be correspondingly higher before the one-tenth rule would apply.

Very high tariff rates are however rare and, even where they persist, do not necessarily amount to 75 per cent *ad valorem* or the equivalent of 75 per cent *ad valorem*. For instance, on certain dyes and intermediate chemicals, where the American Selling Price regulations apply, the *ad valorem* equivalent was estimated at about 70 per cent in the late 1960s.[168] Peak rates also persist on some alcoholic beverages, tobacco, certain textiles and clothing.[169] These are products on which it has been particularly difficult to negotiate substantial tariff cuts in the past, so that it would require a fundamental change in attitudes before the maximum permissible reductions could be expected on these items. True, a fall in import prices would raise the *ad valorem* equivalent of current specific duties. But the average *ad valorem* equivalent of even the peak duties was well below half of 75 per cent before the 1974 Act,[170] so that import prices would have to fall drastically before the one-tenth rule can become important. Where it applies, there will always be ten stages and, with the first stage effective immediately upon proclamation, this means nine years and a day.

Normally the 3 per cent *ad valorem* rule applies. The break-even point between the one-tenth and the 3 per cent rules is when the tariff rate is cut by 30 per cent *ad valorem*. Either would require ten stages or the nine years and a day just mentioned. Since most tariff rates in force on 1 January 1975 were well below 30 per cent *ad valorem*, fewer stages will be required in most cases. Thus, the median *ad valorem* equivalent of the US tariff on dutiable industrial imports, in 1972, was estimated at 8.6 per cent.[171] If this can be taken as representative, tariff reductions of 35 per cent would bring the median tariff down to 5.6 per cent and this could be effected in one stage of 3 per cent *ad valorem*, while a full 40 per cent cut would require two stages (or a year and a day). For most industrial products one or two stages will suffice, though for textiles and clothing four stages would be the average for full 40 per cent tariff cuts.[172]

Since full tariff-reducing authority is seldom utilised in trade negotiations, it can be presumed that most tariff reductions negotiated under the 1974 Act will be immediately effective or effective within a year and a day. Final effectiveness may however be deferred if there is a tariff increase under US legislation in the intervening period.[173] For instance, should tariff relief be given on an article on which a duty reduction has been proclaimed and at least one stage made effective, the clock could be stopped for the period during which such relief is given. Under the terms of the 1974 Act, this could be up to five years.[174]

Thus staging has not reversed the movement towards freer trade, but has delayed it somewhat, especially under the terms of the 1962 Act. The rigid five-stage requirement under that Act broke the continuity of implementing authority. Although the 1962 Act remained in force until it was replaced by new legislation twelve-and-a-half years later, it provided implementing authority for only five years. Without implementing authority, trade agreements legislation is lame legislation. It remains to be seen whether the alternative staging requirements under the 1974 Act will avoid a repetition of this situation.

Suppose that tariff negotiations under the 1974 Act are concluded so late that they cannot be proclaimed until the last day of the implementing authority under the Act, namely 2 January 1980. Then the one-tenth rule could delay final effectiveness until 2 January 1989. Tariff relief could delay it further until 2 January 1994. The difficulties in the way of obtaining tariff relief, rather than other relief, make 1994 unlikely but not impossible. The improbability of full tariff concessions on the most highly protected goods, make a delay until 1989 unlikely but not impossible. There is now no provision that a year must elapse between a tariff rate reduction under one trade agreement and a further reduction under another agreement,[175] so that there can be no further delays. But 1994 is far enough from 1974 for most purposes. The point must not be exaggerated. As already mentioned, under price relationships prevailing in the early 1970s, some of the highest duties just fell short of the *ad valorem* equivalent of 75 per cent which would make the one-tenth rule applicable. It would need a drastic fall in import prices, before the *ad valorem* equivalent of specific duties would rise so much as to make the one-tenth rule widely applicable.

Nevertheless, trade negotiators will be presented with a dilemma. The later they agree and the larger the tariff reductions sought, the greater is the risk that staging will delay final effectiveness beyond the date when the current implementing authority expires in the US. If 1967 is any guide, such delay would reduce the urgency of renewal of that authority and that would delay the next round of tariff negotiations.

True, the Tokyo Round of multilateral trade negotiations started in 1973, when a Trade Reform Bill was before the Congress. That Bill would have given the Administration wider authority than the Trade Act eventually did. While the Congress deliberated, the negotiations could not go beyond preparatory stages. When the Act became law in January 1975, all concerned needed time to study the implications and then to conduct the appropriate hearings at national levels before any international bargaining could commence in earnest. Even if no other problems had arisen, no actual tariff bargaining could have been executed until 1976. In the event, the economic difficulties of the industrial countries, at that time, delayed matters further. Whatever the eventual outcome may be, there was no departure from past experience in so far as there had to be a lapse of time between US legislation and actual tariff bargaining. To this traditional pre-agreement delay, staging has added post-agreement delays in making negotiated tariff reductions effective.

Here the 1974 Act looks both ways. It increased the number of stages from a mandatory five to a possible ten. But the ten stages provided for are applicable only in exceptional cases and, for most likely tariff reductions, less than five stages will actually be needed. But while there are any staging requirements, it is possible that any trade agreement concluded late during the currency of the present implementing authority may become fully effective only after the expiry of that authority. In 1967, this was a factor in breaking the continuity of implementing authority.

C. CREATING A MACRO-ECONOMIC TARIFF POLICY

6. The Fall in Tariff Rates

In general, the 1974 Act may turn out to be either an instrument towards further freeing of trade or an instrument towards a new form of protection. It restored the President's implementing authority which has been the core of all trade agreements legislation. It did so within limits. Its 40 per cent tariff reducing authority may be less than the 50 per cent given in 1934, 1945 and 1962, but more than conferred in other extensions of this authority. In the event, the major rounds of multilateral tariff negotiations in the 1940s and 1960s cut the US tariff by about one-third, so that the 40 per cent authority encompasses the most that had been achieved in any one round of negotiations in the past. Seen this way, the 1974 Act is the heir of the trade agreements Acts from 1934 to 1962 and an instrument to carry this policy further.

Nevertheless, trade agreements legislation in 1974 could not have the same meaning as that of 1934. The legislation of 1934 was the first move towards the lowering of a high tariff. That of 1974 was one more move towards a further lowering of an already much reduced tariff. In the early 1930s, before trade agreements legislation, the *ad valorem* equivalent of duties levied on all imports came to about 19 per cent and on dutiable imports to 55 per cent.[176] In 1972, after the implementation of the reductions agreed in the Kennedy Round in 1967, the corresponding figures were 6 per cent on all imports and 9 per cent on dutiable imports.[177]

This marked reduction in the *ad valorem* equivalent of the US tariff was not solely due to reductions in tariff rates. Price movements too played their part and so did changes in the composition of imports. Prices rose almost incessantly during those forty years. By the early 1970s, US import prices were three times as high as they had been in the early 1930s.[178] This affects the *ad valorem* equivalent of a tariff to the extent to which it consists of specific duties (of so and so many dollars or cents per unit imported). Since the US Tariff Act was written at a time when protection was sought especially from low priced imports, specific duties are numerous. They accounted for somewhat over three-quarters of US tariff rates in most of this period. There were also compound duties (consisting of a specific duty plus an *ad valorem* duty). Altogether, about 80 per cent of US tariff rates were specific or had a specific element.[179] The preponderance of specific duties implied a fall in the *ad valorem* equivalent of the tariff at a time of rising prices.

Unfortunately, no precise estimate of the effects of price movements are possible. Price movements were not uniform. There were changes in the commodity composition of imports and even in the nature of products falling under any one tariff item. There was a reclassification of tariff items in the 1960s. Could all these difficulties be ignored, it might be said that price movements alone would have lowered the *ad valorem* equivalent of the tariff from the 19 per cent on all imports recorded in the early 1930s to a hypothetical 9 per cent in the early 1970s. This would have been more than three-quarters of the actual reduction from 19 to 6 per cent. Similarly, price movements would have lowered the *ad valorem* equivalent of the tariff from the 55 per cent on dutiable imports recorded in the 1930s to a hypothetical 27 per cent in the early 1970s. This would have been almost three-fifths of the actual reduction from 55 per cent to 9 per cent.[180] Although these are crude approximations rather than precise estimates, they suffice to show that the fall in the *ad valorem* equivalent of the US tariff overstates any possible effects of tariff rate reductions during those forty years. It does not necessarily follow that the rise in import prices was more important than the fall in tariff rates, for the fall in tariff rates allowed for the importation of more valuable imports. The foreign suppliers were not taxed as much as before. They could charge more and the US market became more attractive to them. Consequently, more dutiable items were imported. In the early 1930s, when the US tariff was at its height and prices particularly low, only one-third of US imports were dutiable. By the early 1970s, when the US tariff was much reduced and prices high and rising, two-thirds of US imports were dutiable.[181] This meant a major change in the composition of imports from free to dutiable items. Had this composition of trade remained the same throughout, the *ad valorem* equivalent of the tariff on all imports would have been only half of what it actually was in the early 1970s, namely 3 per cent instead of the actual 6 per cent. Thus the change in the composition of trade means that the fall in the actual *ad valorem* equivalent of the tariff on all imports understates the effects of tariff changes. If the rise in import prices means that the fall in the *ad valorem* equivalent overstates the effects of tariff reductions on all imports by three-quarters, but the change in the composition of trade means an understatement of one half, only one-quarter of the fall in the *ad valorem* equivalent can be attributed to price changes. This result should be taken as indicative rather than as precise. It is based on aggregates alone. Moreover, changes in tariff rates, import prices and the composition of trade interact. No more can be said than that tariff rate reductions played a major part in the lowering of the *ad valorem* equivalent of the US tariff, and probably the major part. The effects of past tariff reductions cannot be explained away. Because they were substantial, there is now less scope for further reductions.

Further tariff reductions could yet have a major impact on trade. A reduction in the average *ad valorem* equivalent of rates on dutiable items from 9 per cent to, say, 6 per cent could make a substantial difference to the profitability of trade. After every reduction in tariff rates in the past, trade in dutiable goods grew. Presumably this will continue until all tariff rates are zero. But the ultimate prize of free trade remains elusive under US trade agreements legislation.

Two circumscribed offers of free trade were actually made in the 1962 Act. One concerned the possibility of negotiating complete free trade in most industrial goods with an enlarged EC. This offer was abortive since the EC was not enlarged until 1973, by which time the implementing authority under the 1962 Act had expired. The 1974 Act did not repeat this offer. The second offer of free trade concerned items on which tariff rates were already low. Where the *ad valorem* equivalent was 5 per cent or less, the complete abolition of such duties could be negotiated. Such a transfer of dutiable items to the free list had been ruled out under earlier trade agreements legislation. This offer, first made in the 1962 Act, was repeated in the 1974 Act.[182] So far, however, this has been important mainly in establishing the principle that reductions in tariff rates could ultimately lead to their elimination. The 1974 Act was written at a time when the average *ad valorem* equivalent of the tariff on dutiable items was still 9 per cent, so that the limitation of tariff reducing authority to 40 per cent meant that most tariff rates would remain above 5 per cent. Price increases between the time of preparation of the Act and 1 January 1975 somewhat reduced the *ad valorem* equivalent, and tariff reductions can be negotiated from their level at that date. But it does not follow that the full 40 per cent reduction will actually be conceded on the relevant items. Were they to be conceded, it would then take only one more major increase in tariff reducing authority to make a repetition of this offer important. But that depends on the success of the negotiations under the 1974 Act and on whether, and in what form, implementing authority will be renewed in the 1980s. In the meantime, there is no major break with the tradition which seeks negotiated reductions in tariff rates rather than their elimination.

This one target of policy can be pursued within the framework of one law. Trade agreements legislation originated with an amendment to one section of the Tariff Act of 1930, which delegated to the President certain implementing authority for negotiated changes in tariff rates. Trade agreements legislation could then be brief and to that one point. Although all sorts of safeguards were added in the various Extension Acts, these were qualifications still relating to that one point and did not range beyond it. Congress could ignore the details of tariff rate reductions and even the GATT, as long as the tariff rate reductions were within the prescribed limits and GATT rules not incompatible with US law. If tariff rate reductions were an end in themselves, this would still suffice. But as time went on and tariff reductions became marked, both domestic and international implications came to the fore which led to the extension of trade agreements legislation beyond the scope of tariff rate changes.

7. Towards a New Tariff Policy?

From the outset, trade agreements legislation was meant to serve the twin objectives of trade expansion and fuller employment in the US. Freer access to foreign markets would lead to a higher level of employment in the US. Discriminatory practices abroad impeded US trading opportunities. The US technological lead was marked and wider markets lowered the unit costs of her increasing returns activities. The two objectives were truly twin objectives. Both were attainable through trade agreements. But, as time went on, discriminatory trading practices abroad were negotiated away or into more acceptable forms. Other countries' economic progress narrowed the technological gap. This led to more intra-industry specialisation between the US and other industrial countries which, in itself, was a sign of success of the freer trade policy. It also led to rising fears that some US interests would be injured. There are always some who cannot easily adjust themselves to changing circumstances which, in the present context, means there are some who cannot participate in intra-industry specialisation. They are usually to be found amongst the older, decreasing returns activities. They cannot produce more with existing equipment and see their home sales threatened by rising imports. To date, the fearful amongst US industrial interests have been in the minority. Yet they were not ignored and some were given special treatment. At first they got this through the administrative provisions, the escape clause and peril point provisions in trade agreements legislation which was effectively confined to the law as it relates to tariff rates. The 1962 and 1974 Acts went further. They provided that those who cannot adjust themselves could be given adjustment assistance. That made one form of unemployment relief part of trade agreements legislation.

As far as domestic legislation was concerned, the 1962 Act was already a lengthy document which devoted more space to the provision of Federal relief for injury resulting from trade agreements than to trade agreements authority and procedure. Nevertheless, it confined its concern for the injured to those injured by tariff rate reductions. There was an extension of the scope of trade agreements legislation into domestic employment policy, but it was a sphere of employment policy which was still strictly relevant to tariff rate policy.

The 1974 Act, an even more voluminous document, severed the link of relief to trade agreements concessions. Instead it provided relief from rising imports. This was trade legislation and no longer just trade agreements legislation. The central point of this part of the 1974 Act is not tariff rates but whether there is enough protection from imports. The link between tariff rates and tariff policy having thus been broken, the tariff ceased to be the sum total of protection given to individual items. It could become an instrument of macro-economic policy.

Once a rise in certain imports, as such, was thought of as a threat to the solvency of individual firms and a cause of localised unemployment, the sum total of rising imports could be considered a threat to the balance of the economy as a whole. The micro-economic adjustment assistance was given its macro-economic counterpart in the balance of payments authority. This allows the President to vary all tariff rates simultaneously, for a limited period of time, in order to counter balance of payments deficits or surpluses. Since the authority to raise the tariff in times of deficit is greater than that to lower it in times of surplus, this authority is more protectionist than liberalising. Since all rates can be moved together, irrespective of the needs of individual sectors, the intention is to provide temporary protection for the economy as a whole rather than for individual sectors. This is a form of tariff policy. But it is not tariff rate policy as all US tariff policy had been before 1974.

In some ways, this new authority is a return to an autonomous flexible tariff. There had been such a tariff in the 1920s. But then autonomous flexibility was intended to negate relative cost changes in the US and elsewhere in so far as this affected individual sectors. The remedy then was a permanent change in individual tariff rates. By contrast, the flexibility of the 1974 Act is all-embracing and intended to negate temporary cost changes in the US economy as a whole relative to the rest of the world. Normally, this kind of problem is thought of as one of monetary policy. But there was much uncertainty about exchange rates in the early 1970s, and the dollar was left to float. A general rise in the tariff is often thought of as an alternative to a depreciation of the exchange rate, and a lowering of the tariff as an alternative to appreciation. The balance of payments authority was in line with the thinking of the time.

Whether this could become autonomous flexibility depends on whether the other members of GATT are willing to accept this tariff flexibility as a means of combating balance of payments difficulties. If they do, such flexibility would become automatic rather than autonomous. If they do not, the balance of payments authority would become autonomous unless it remains a dead letter.

Should the balance of payments authority be used, the tariff will become a different form of protection from what it had been before. The idea is not new. The authority legalised what had actually been done in 1971. Moreover, protection of the balance of payments has been the concern of mercantilists throughout the ages, but it had never before been part of US tariff policy. Did the success of the trade agreements programme mean that the traditional tariff rate policy could no longer be used as an effective instrument of protection for most items, so that the choice became one between abandoning the tariff or using it for new purposes? The success of the trade agreements programme lay in the reduction of US tariff rates and the lessening of discriminatory practices elsewhere. Although most trade agreements included tariff rate reductions both ways, often the US gave more by way of tariff rate reductions and others more by way of less discriminatory or non-discriminatory trading practices. By the early 1970s, the US tariff was lower than the tariffs of her major industrial competitors, so that the US could no longer expect to obtain so many concessions from others by offering lower tariff rates. She had two choices. Either she had to offer law, other than the law of tariff rates, for international negotiation. Or she had to accept discrimination as part of the international order. The Trade Act offers a bit of both.

US law, other than the law relating to tariff rates, is offered for negotiations through the provisions to negotiate GATT revisions and on non-tariff barriers. The wished-for law relating to GATT revisions has already meant a somewhat grudging Congressional recognition of GATT. This is more than the mere toleration of GATT under former legislation, though still limited to the unspecified parts of GATT which the Congress approves of. The offer of negotiations on non-tariff barriers is an offer to negotiate about practices which are unlikely to be based on trade agreements legislation. Hence some other laws have become negotiable. US law and international law may become more closely intertwined.

Concern with individual tariff rates was already on the wane during the multilateral tariff negotiations of the 1960s. Efforts were made to lower tariffs as a whole rather than to strike bargains over individual rates. The major industrial countries, including the US, negotiated 'across the board'. This method of negotiation will be dealt with at greater length in Chapter 4. Here it must suffice to point out that those countries' concern was to get tariffs down and individual tariff rates were a secondary consideration. Any reductions they agreed amongst themselves were automatically extended to all countries with most-favoured-nation rights. Not all countries negotiated on this basis. Some were mere by-standers. Thus the less developed countries negotiated little or not at all, and this was generally accepted. But there were also intermediate countries, such as Canada. They claimed that their export trades were mainly in a few products. Across-the-board concessions by others would give them little of interest to themselves, while they would give much of interest to others. They continued to negotiate item by item. Although this claim was accepted at the time of the tariff negotiations in the 1960s, there was some feeling afterwards that some of the intermediate countries had, in fact, been largely 'free riders' at those negotiations.[183]

The US reaction was that future negotiations should seek 'reciprocal non-discrimination' from all industrial countries. The Trade Act specifically names Canada, the EC and Japan, but allows for the possibility that the President may designate other countries as 'industrial'. At the conclusion of negotiations under the 1974 Act or before the expiry of the Act, whichever is earlier, there is to be a review of whether each of those countries has given the US concessions 'substantially equivalent' to the concessions received from the US. Any major industrial country which does not conform may find itself excluded from any concessions given by the US. Such exclusion would, however, require special legislation.[184]

Countries have been excluded from most-favoured-nation treatment before. Most notably, the majority of Communist countries were excluded for most of the post-war period. Their exclusion was on grounds of discrimination against US exports or on security grounds, and further political reasons for their exclusion were found in the Trade Act. In their case, the rates of the Tariff Act of 1930 were applied and no trade agreements concessions extended to them. These were special exclusions. Other countries received most-favoured-nation treatment, either by virtue of trade agreements or because they were not specially excluded. 'Reciprocal non-discrimination' would however imply the creation of two different types of most-favoured-nation countries. Those who will not pass muster, under the review of the working of the 1974 Act, will still receive all concessions given before the Act but none of the concessions negotiated under the Act. Other countries will receive both the pre-1974 and the post-1974 concessions. Will this be a step towards a return to the pre-1934 ideas of reciprocity?

The US, the EC and Japan are bound to be the principal negotiators on tariffs in the 1970s. They may be expected to negotiate 'across the board', as in the Kennedy Round. No one supposes that any of those three will give or receive concessions without an adequate *quid pro quo.* The provisions for review of the working of the Act thus seem to be addressed to Canada. Her status as an 'intermediate' country in trade negotiations is called into question. It does not follow that Canada is likely to be singled out for less favourable treatment than either the EC or Japan. More likely is that a special regional arrangement with Canada will be sought if multilateral negotiations cannot be expected to lead to reciprocity in concessions. This is indicated in one of the final sections of the Act which envisages negotiations for a free trade area between the US and Canada, though there is no commitment to ratify such an agreement.[185]

The US and Canada have for long been each other's major trading partners. Before international tariff negotiations became multilateral, there were more trade agreements between the US and Canada than between the US and any other independent country. Both countries were founder members of GATT. Even if they did not always negotiate directly, most concessions they granted to any third countries in item-by-item negotiations were of reciprocal interest. No special difficulties arose until the 1960s, when the US altered her negotiating method from item-by-item to across-the-board while Canada did not. Since the negotiations of the 1960s concerned largely the trade relations between the US and the EC, and the change in negotiating method largely suited that purpose, the question of trade relations with Canada was not to the fore in the multilateral negotiations at the time.

Nevertheless a special relationship with Canada had been considered on several occasions before. For instance, the original version of Article XXIV of GATT allowed customs unions as an exception from non-discrimination. This was soon amended to embrace free trade areas as well.[186] A major reason for this amendment was to allow Canada and the US to form a free trade area without consolidating their tariffs.[187] Although this amendment was to be widely used as the basis for the formation of free trade areas in several parts of the world, in relation to US-Canadian trade the only attempt at regional free trade to date has been an agreement relating to automotive products, which has been in force since 1965.[188]

This agreement related to only one group of products and, since it provided for complete free trade in those products, exceeded the President's tariff-reducing authority. Because it related to only one group of products, it was not covered by Article XXIV of GATT. Canada solved this problem by making free trade in those products applicable to all most-favoured-nation countries. The US applied it only to Canada. She had to obtain a GATT waiver from her most-favoured-nation obligations to other countries.[189] Since the agreement provided that US tariff rates on automotive products would not be levied on such imports from Canada, special legislation was required in the US.[190]

The agreement was to foster the development of the motor car industry on either side of the frontier. For the US, this was largely a question of unimpeded trade between sectors of US-owned companies, and the saleability of the final products of such companies. This purpose could be served through free admission of such products into the US, irrespective of who in the US purchased those products. For Canada, it was more of a question of how much value US companies added on her side of the frontier. She restricted free trade in such products to purchases by manufacturers. Moreover, she obtained undertakings from those manufacturers that the value added in Canada would increase by an amount correlated with the growth of the Canadian home market in motor vehicles.[191] In other words, the Automotive Products Agreement was a way of fostering the expansion of US-owned activities on Canadian territory. The US sought profits, Canada an equivalent of rent. It is therefore not altogether surprising that even marked growth of trade in such products did not assuage feelings that this was not a reciprocal two-way free trade agreement, and that a new approach should be tried.[192]

Thus, in relation to Canada, the 1974 Act provides for various possibilities. At one extreme, there is the offer to negotiate a free trade area, though no guarantee that such an agreement would be implemented. At the other extreme, there is an implied threat to withhold from her any concessions negotiated under the 1974 Act, though again without any certainty that such a threat could be implemented. In between, there is the possibility that a rapprochement between the US and Canadian negotiating methods would lead to enough 'reciprocal non-discrimination' as to give Canada neither more nor less than unconditional most-favoured-nation treatment.

While the 1974 Act contains an implied threat to Canada and other major industrial countries, it shows forbearance to Less Developed Countries (LDCs). In the past, the US had frowned upon preferential tariff agreements between other countries. Her own preferences to Cuba had ceased in 1962. Her preferences to the Philippines ceased in 1974. The full preferences to that country had already come to an end in 1956. In the following years, duties on Philippine goods were raised gradually until most-favoured-nation rates were reached in 1974.[193] Just when the US tariff had been cleared of such preferential arrangements, provision was made for a Generalised System of Preferences.[194]

The Generalised System of Preferences does, however, differ from the preferential arrangements the US and other countries once had with dependent territories, since it specifically excludes countries which give reverse preferences to other countries.[195] Moreover, the preferences are not given on specific items. Instead there is a blanket provision for preferences, if the value of such imports from any country is less than half of the total imports of such item into the US and if the value of such imports does not exceed $25 million. The latter figure is adjustable in proportion to the rise in the US gross national product.[196] Excluded are products from industrial countries, products of Communist countries which do not receive most-favoured-nation treatment, and products from countries which deny the US non-discriminatory access to supplies. The latter group of countries includes all members of the Organisation of Petroleum Exporting Countries (OPEC), including those which did not embargo exports to the US in 1973.[197] An amendment was proposed to allow for the grant of preferences to OPEC countries which do not discriminate against the US.[198] Excluded are also certain sensitive articles, such as textiles and footwear.[199]

The blanket grant of preferences, subject to exceptions, is in line with the attitude that the tariff is to be viewed as a macro-economic instrument of policy, where reductions are given across the board, subject only to exceptions for import-sensitive items. The more favourable treatment of LDCs than of industrial countries is, however, a new form of differential protection. The exception list apart, this is not differentiation between items as in the past when the emphasis was on different tariff rates for different items. Instead there is differentiation between countries according to their stage of development. Moreover, there is no request for 'reciprocal non-discrimination' in trade concessions. LDCs made few or no concessions in the Kennedy Round and the same is to be expected in the Tokyo Round. Reverse preferences to other developed countries are banned and none asked for in respect of US trade.

There is thus a new form of grading countries. The LDCs are to be subsidised to export to the US. The result is ensured by the limitation of the value of exports which can benefit. It means that different tariff rates are to apply to preferred and other imports. The preferred supplier then gets not only the price other suppliers get but also the margin of preference. Were it not for this limitation, the preferred supplier might eventually supply total US import requirements which would make further price discrimination impossible and the only result would be trade diversion. Thus the LDCs will be subsidised as long as they supply less than half of US import requirements. In return they need grant no favours to US exports but must not discriminate against the US in the determination of the destination of their exports. Industrial countries cannot expect such favours. They are to treat the US, and be treated by her, on the principle of non-discriminatory reciprocity. Any advanced industrial country that does not conform may be excluded from concessions negotiated under the 1974 Act. Should that country be Canada, it is offered the alternative of regional free trade.

In short, tariff rate policy may be replaced by macro-economic tariff policy, the differentiation between items by different treatment of various classes of countries, and protection of individual sectors of the US economy by a neo-mercantilist protection of the balance of payments. The 1974 Act provides a legislative basis for such changes. But it also provides for the possibility of a further move towards freer trade along the path followed since 1934.

Notes

1. US Department of Commerce, *Historical Statistics of the United States, Colonial Times to 1957,* US Government Printing Office, Washington, D.C., 1961, series U1-20.
2. Secretary of State James G. Blaine in 1890, quoted by Tom E. Terrill, *The Tariff, Politics and American Foreign Policy, 1874-1901,* Greenwood Press, Westport, Connecticut and London, 1973, p.170.
3. For details see: H.U. Faulkner, *American Economic History,* 8th ed., Harper & Rowe, London, 1960, esp. pp.165-8, 239-40, 545-52; A.S. Link, *American Epoch*, Vol.I, Alfred Knopf, New York, 1938, esp. p.21; and T.E. Terrill, *ibid.*, esp. pp.170-1, 182, 187.
4. H.J. Tasca, *The Reciprocal Trade Policy of the United States*, University of Pennsylvania Press, Philadelphia, 1938, p.39; and T.E. Terrill, *ibid.*, p.173.
5. For details see e.g. H.J. Habakkuk, *American and British Technology in the 19th Century,* Cambridge University Press, 1967; and S.B. Saul, *Technological Change: The United States and Britain in the 19th Century,* Methuen, London, 1970.
6. A.S. Link, *American Epoch.*
7. Ibid., Vol.II, pp.261-5.
8. These are the sort of industries which work along the lines described and analysed in A. Marshall, *Principles of Economics*, 8th ed., Macmillan, London, 1920.
9. For instance, the Long Term Textile Agreement of 1962 and the Multi-fibre Textile Agreement of 1974. A short summary of these and other special protectionist measures can be found in the 25th Report of the US Tariff Commission, *Operation of the Trade Agreements Program,* T.C. Publication 708, Washington, DC, 1974, pp.14-19. See also Thomas B. Curtis and John Robert Vasentine, Jr., *The Kennedy Round and the Future of American Trade,* Praeger Publishers, New York and London 1971, Chapter 12; and Gerald M. Meier, *Problems of Trade Policy*, Oxford University Press, 1973, Problem II.
10. H.B. Larry and Associates, *The United States in the World Economy*, US Department of Commerce, Bureau of Foreign and Domestic Commerce, Economic Series No.23, US Government and Printing Office, Washington, 1943.
11. See e.g. J.E. Nash, *The Future of Financial Centres in a European Monetary Union,* SUERF Series 4A, 1972, p.3.
12. US Tariff Commission, *Operations of the Trade Agreements Program,* 25th Report, 1973, TC Publication 708, Washington, DC, 1974, p.48 shows that there were 83 members of GATT and two applicants for membership in 1973. Since any agreement tied each to every other member, the number of bilateral relationships came to 3,403 with 83 members and 3,570 with 85 (on the formula of $\frac{n(n-1)}{2}$). The number of trade agreement relationships is larger than the number of trade agreements since not every country negotiated directly with every other.
13. President Hoover, and Secretary of State Stimson, quoted by William B. Kelly, Jr. (ed.), *Studies in United States Commerical Policy*, Chapel Hill. The University of North Carolina Press, 1963, p.29.
14. See Section 4 (ii) of this chapter.
15. United States, *Trade Act of 1974*, Public Law 93-618, 93rd Congress H.R. 10710, 3 January 1975.
16. H.J. Tasca, *Reciprocal Trade Policy,* p.10.

17. Ibid., p.11.
18. William B. Kelly, *United States Commercial Policy*, p.11 and H.J. Tasca, *Reciprocal Trade Policy*, p.72.
19. William B. Kelly, ibid., p.13.
20. Secretary of State Cordell Hull, US Congress, Senate Committee on Finance Hearings on H.R. 8687, 73rd Congress, 2nd Session, 1934, p.5, quoted by Harry C. Hawkins and Janet L. Norwood, 'The Legislative Basis of United States Commerical Policy', in William B. Kelly (ed.), ibid., p.84.
21. William B. Kelly, ibid., p.85.
22. US Tariff Commission, *Trade Agreements Program*, 25th Report p.1.
23. Statutes of the United States, Session Laws, 73rd Congress, 2nd Session, 1934, Washington, D.C., 1934, p.943, quoted by H.J. Tasca, *Reciprocal Trade Policy*, p.39.
24. Trade Act 1974, Sec. 2 (1).
25. Secretary of State Cordell Hull, quoted by H.J. Tasca, *Reciprocal Trade Policy*, p.84.
26. US Tariff Commission, *Trade Agreements Program*, p.10. The number of agreements is not the same as the number of countries, because there were three agreements each with Canada and Cuba, while Belgium and Luxembourg were joined in a customs union and acted as one negotiating unit.
27. H.J. Tasca, *Reciprocal Trade Policy*, p.136.
28. U S Tariff Commission, *Trade Agreements Program*, p.43.
29. William B. Kelly, *United States Commerical Policy*, p.36.
30. Trade Act of 1974, Section 612.
31. United States: An Act to Amend Section 350 of the Tariff Act of 1930, Public Law 316, 73rd Congress, 48 Stat. 943, 12 June 1934.
32. For a brief discussion of these issues at the time when the Trade Bill was before the Congress in 1973, see: Paul W. McCracken (Moderator), *Foreign Trade Policy*, An AEI Round Table held on 10 September 1973, American Enterprise Institute for Public Policy Research, Washington, D.C., 1974. See also Section 4 (ii) below.
33. William B. Kelly, 'Antecedents of Present Commercial Policy, 1922-34,' in William B. Kelly, Jr., *United States Commercial Policy*, pp.25-6, including footnotes.
34. Tom E. Terrill, *The Tariff, Politics and American Foreign Policy, 1874-1901*, Contributions in American History No.31, Greenwood Press, Westport (Connecticut) and London, 1973, p.173.
35. Trade Act of 1974, Section 101(b) (1) and (c) (1).
36. William B. Kelly, *United States Commercial Policy*, p.14.
37. For details on withdrawal of tariff concessions see relevant sections in the Reports of the Tariff Commission and John M. Leddy and Janet Norwood, 'The Escape Clause and Peril Points under the Trade Agreements Program', in William B. Kelly, ibid, Chapter 3. On the withholding of tariff concessions in the 1930s, see H.J. Tasca, *Reciprocal Trade Policy*, pp.156-8. Post-war, tariff concessions were withheld from Communist countries.
38. See note 13.
39. For details of the history of the most-favoured-nation clause in US tariff history, see R.C. Snyder, *The Most-Favored Nation Clause*, King's Crown Press, Columbia University, New York, 1948, esp. pp.197-236.
40. US Department of Commerce, Bureau of the Census, *Historical Statistics of the United States, Colonial Times to 1957*, Series Y 258-263.
41. Ibid.
42. Ibid., and *Annual Statistical Abstract of the United States*, 1973, Tables 620 and 624, and corresponding tables in earlier issues.
43. *Trade Agreements Extension Act of 1951 As Amended*, Public Law 50, 82nd

Congress, 65 Stat. 72, 16 June 1951, as amended by the The Trade Agreements Act of 1958, Public Law 85-686, 72 Stat 675, 20 August 1958, and The Trade Expansion Act of 1962, Public Law 87-794, 76 Stat. 882, 11 October 1962, reprinted in Stanley D. Metzger, *Trade Agreements and the Kennedy Round*, Coiner Publications, Fairfax, Virginia, 1964, pp.A7-9.
44. Trade Agreements Extension Act of 1951, Sec.10.
45. The Trade Expansion Act of 1962 does not refer to GATT but Sec.10 of the 1951 Act was not repealed.
46. Trade Act of 1974, Sec 121 (d), last sentence.
47. Sec. 121 (d), first sentence.
48. Sec. 121 (a).
49. Sec. 121 (a) (1)-(12).
50. Sec. 121 (c) and Sec. 151.
51. Revised Text in 'Review of the General Agreement on Tariffs and Trade', Cmd 9413, 1955, Article XIX. Revision sought in Trade Act of 1974, Sec.121 (2).
52. Sec. 203 (a), (b) and (d) (1) and Sec. 123 (b).
53. Sought in Sec. 121 (a) (7) and (8).
54. Sec. 108.
55. Article XII of GATT.
56. Trade Act of 1974, Sec. 121 (a) (6).
57. Sec. 122 (a) (3) (A).
58. Sec. 122 (c) (2) (A).
59. Sec. 122 (a) (3) (B) and (c) (2) (B).
60. See note 57 and Report of the Committee on Finance, US Senate, on the Trade Reform Act of 1974, 93rd Congress, 2nd Session, Report No. 93-1298, p.88.
61. Sec.101 (b) (1), and (c) (1) and (2).
62. Trade Expansion Act of 1962, Sec. 243, and Trade Act of 1974, Sec. 161.
63. Trade Act of 1974, Secs. 102, 121 (c), 151.
64. Sec. 102 (b).
65. Sec. 102 (g).
66. Notably Secs. 102, 104, 121 and much of Title IV.
67. Trade Agreements Extension Act of 1951, Sec. 11.
68. Trade Expansion Act of 1962, Sec. 231.
69. Trade Act of 1974, Title IV.
70. Secs. 402 and 409 (a).
71. Sec. 613.
72. Press reports.
73. H.J. Tasca, *Reciprocal Trade Policy*, p.78; Harry C. Hawkins and Janet Norwood, 'Legislative Basis', p.81.
74. Edward L. Morse, *Foreign Policy and Interdependence in Gaullist France*, Princeton University Press, Princeton, New Jersey, 1973, pp.269-70.
75. Trade Act of 1974, Sec. 125(a) and corresponding clauses in earlier Acts.
76. US Tariff Commission, *Operation of the Trade Agreements Program, 19th Report,* 1967, Tariff Commission Publication No. 287, Washington, D.C. 1969, p.186.
77. Trade Act of 1974, Sec. 102(g) (1).
78. US Tariff Commission, *Operation of the Trade Agreements Program, 2nd Report,* April 1948-March 1949, T.C. Report No.163, Washington, D.C., 1949, p.79.
79. See the US Tariff Commission Reports on the Operation of the Trade Agreements Program for the extent of Section 22 protection in each year. For instance, 1st Report, p.22; 2nd Report, p.79 and appropriate sections in later reports.

80. John M. Leddy 'United States' Commercial Policy and the Domestic Farm Program' in William B. Kelly, *United States Commercial Policy*, p.208.
81. Trade Expansion Act of 1962, Sec. 257 (h).
82. Trade Act of 1974, Sec. 602 does *not* repeal Sec. 257 (h) of the Trade Expansion Act.
83. Stanley D. Metzger, *Trade Agreements and the Kennedy Round,* p.85.
84. US Tariff Commission, *2nd Report*, p.14. See also 14th Report, pp.76-8.
85. Trade Expansion Act of 1962, Sec. 352.
86. i.e. not repealed by Sec. 602.
87. Trade Act of 1974, Sec. 131 (a).
88. Sec. 172.
89. Sec. 131 (b), (c), and (e).
90. Sec. 131 (b) and (d) (4).
91. Trade Agreements Extension Act of 1951, Sec. 3.
92. Trade Expansion Act of 1962, Sec. 221.
93. Trade Act of 1974, Secs. 132 and 133.
94. Secs. 135 and 141.
95. Sec. 135.
96. Trade Act of 1974, Title II, Chapter 1. See also Trade Expansion Act of 1962, Secs. 301 and 351.
97. See note 51.
98. John M. Leddy and Janet Norwood, 'The Escape Clause', p.124.
99. R.C. Snyder, *Most-Favored Nation Clause,* p.104.
100. Trade Agreement between the United Kingdom and the United States, 1938, Cmd. 5882, Article 18.
101. John M. Leddy and Janet Norwood, 'The Escape Clause', p.125.
102. Cmd. 9413, 1955, Article XIX; or *Report on the Geneva Tariff Negotiations with the Text of the GATT,* Cmd. 7258, 1947 Article XIX.
103. See notes 51 and 52.
104. US Tariff Commission, *Operation of the Trade Agreements Program,* 2nd Report, April 1948 – March 1949, T.C. Report No.163, Washington, D.C., 1949, p.5. The change in the nature of protection refers to the introduction of compound duties (consisting of a specific and an *ad valorem* component), where the US did not accept the claim that the *ad valorem* incidence was unchanged.
105. John M. Leddy and Janet Norwood, 'The Escape Clause', pp.126 and 134.
106. Trade Agreements Extension Act, 1951, Sec. 7.
107. John M. Leddy and Janet Norwood, 'The Escape Clause', pp.141 and 143.
108. U.S. Tariff Commission, *Operation of the Trade Agreements Program,* 25th Report, p.5.
109. Trade Act of 1974, Sec. 127.
110. John M. Leddy and Janet Norwood, 'The Escape Clause', p.146.
111. Stanley D. Metzger, *Trade Agreements and the Kennedy Round,* p.48.
112. Trade Expansion Act of 1962, Sec. 301 (b) (1). See also Sec. 301 (c) on eligibility and Sec. 351 on implementing provisions.
113. Stanley D. Metzger, *Trade Agreements and the Kennedy Round,* p.48.
114. US Tariff Commission and US International Trade Commission, *Operation of the Trade Agreements Program,* 15th Report, p.81; 17th Report, pp.23 and 25; 23rd Report, p.3; 25th Report, p.5; 26th Report, p.4.
115. Trade Expansion Act of 1962, Sec. 351 (b) (1) and (2), and (c) (1) (B).
116. Sec. 301 (b) (1).
117. Trade Act of 1974, Sec. 203 (d) (1).
118. Sec. 201 (b) (1).

119. Sec. 201 (b) (2) (C).
120. Sec. 201 (b) (4).
121. Sec. 201 (b) (2) (A).
122. Sec. 201 (d) (1) (B).
123. Sec. 201 (b) (6) and Sec. 301 (a) (4) (A) and (B).
124. US International Trade Commission, *Annual Report*, 1975, Washington, 1976, p.4.
125. Trade Act of 1974, Sec. 203 (a) 4 and (e) (3).
126. Sec. 202 (c).
127. Sec. 203 (h) (1) and (2).
128. Title II, Chapters 2-4.
129. Report of the Committee on Finance, US Senate, on the Trade Reform Act of 1974, 93rd Congress, 2nd Session, Report No.93-1298, pp.131 and 143.
130. Ibid., pp.151-2.
131. Stanléy D. Metzger, *Trade Agreements and the Kennedy Round*, p.59.
132. Senate Committee on Finance, op.cit., p.131, gives the number certified as eligible as 47,000. The average number for total unemployment, according to *Survey of Current Business* was about 4¼ million a year between 1969 and 1973.
133. Senate Committee on Finance, ibid., p.144.
134. Ibid.
135. Trade Act of 1974, Sec. 201 (b) (4), italics mine.
136. Sec. 222(3), Sec. 251 (c) (3). Sec. 271 (c) (3), italics mine.
137. Senate Committee on Finance, op.cit., pp.144 and 155-60.
138. GATT article XV1 and Trade Act of 1974, Title III.
139. US International Trade Commission, *Operation of the Trade Agreements Program*, 26th Report, p.5.
140. Herbert J. Grubel and P.J. Lloyd, *Intra-Industry Trade,* Macmillan, London, 1975, p.144.
141. E.g. by T.B. Curtis and J.R. Vasentine Jr., *The Kennedy Round*, Chapter 12 and G.M. Meier, *Problems of Trade Policy*, Problem II.
142. Trade Act of 1974, Sec. 203 (a).
143. Sec. 203 (e) (2).
144. T.B. Curtis and J.R. Vasentine Jr., *The Kennedy Round,* pp.129 and 162-3.
145. Ibid.
146. Ibid., pp.166-7.
147. US Tariff Commission, *Operation of the Trade Agreements Program,* 25th Report, pp.15-18.
148. Trade Expansion Act of 1962, Sec. 352 and Trade Act of 1974, Sec. 203 (a) (4) and (5), and (e) (2) and (3).
149. C.F. Bergson, 'Crisis in United States Trade Policy', *Foreign Affairs*, July 1971, p.619. For a list of some of those products, see Curtis and Vasentine, *The Kennedy Round*, pp.232-3.
150. U.S. Tariff Commission, *Operation of the Trade Agreements Program,* 16th Report, p.87 and 19th Report, pp.192-8.
151. 17th Report, p.19 and 18th Report, pp.18-19, and G.M. Meier, *Problems of Trade Policy*, pp.155-6.
152. US International Trade Commission, op.cit., p.20.
153. C.B. Curtis and J.R. Vasentine Jr., *The Kennedy Round*, p.172 and G.M. Meier, *Problems of Trade Policy*, e.g. p.165.
154. See notes 115 and 117.
155. Trade Act of 1974, Sec. 127 (b).
156. C.B. Curtis and J.R. Vasentine Jr, *The Kennedy Round,* p.175.
157. US Tariff Commission, *Operation of Trade Agreements Program*, 18th Report,

p.19, and 19th Report, pp.195-8.
158. 25th Report, p.16; 26th Report, pp.18-20.
159. Trade Act of 1974, Sec. 121 (a) (12).
160. C.B. Curtis and J.R. Vasentine Jr., *The Kennedy Round*, pp.127 and 154.
161. US International Trade Commission, *Operation of the Trade Agreements Program*, 26th Report, p.29.
162. Senate Committee on Finance, op.cit., p.232, and Trade Act of 1974, Sec. 607.
163. US Tariff Commission, *Operation of the Trade Agreements Program*, 8th Report, p.5 and 14th Report, p.19; S.D. Metzger, *Trade Agreements and the Kennedy Round*, p.17.
164. Trade Expansion Act of 1962, Sec. 253 (a).
165. Sec. 253 (c).
166. Trade Act of 1974, Sec. 101 (b) and Sec. 109 (a).
167. Sec. 109 (a).
168. According to an investigation by the US Tariff Commission quoted by C.B. Curtis and J.R. Vasentine, p.106.
169. US Tariff Commission, *Operation of the Trade Agreements Program*, 19th Report, p.236 and Fig.4.
170. Ibid.
171. Senate Committee on Finance, op.cit., p.72. Note that this does not include alcoholic beverages and tobacco.
172. Derived from ibid., Table 7 on p.71. An average of three stages would be required for the sector 'mineral products and fertilisers, ceramic products and glass'.
173. Trade Act of 1974, Sec. 109 (c) (2).
174. Sec. 203 (a).
175. Trade Act of 1974, Sec. 602 (d) repeals Sec. 253 of the Trade Expansion Act of 1962.
176. Averages for 1931-3. Cf. US Department of Commerce, *Historical Statistics of the US, Colonial Times to 1957*, Series U 19-20.
177. US Department of Commerce, *Statistical Abstract of the US, 1974*, Table 1334. The appropriate figures for 1971 are the same although the last stage prescribed for the implementation of the Kennedy Round reductions came during that year. The figures for 1973 were 5 and 8 per cent respectively but may have been influenced by the political and economic difficulties of that year.
178. The average of 1971-3 was exactly three times the average of 1932-4, linked to a 1970 base, with 1955 and 1962 as link years. Derived from *Historical Statistics,* Series U 34; *Statistical Abstract, 1974,* Table 1323 and *Statistical Abstract 1965,* Table 1246.
179. US Tariff Commission, *Operation of the Trade Agreements Program*, 5th Report, p.13. This relates to 1949. But there were no transfers from the dutiable to the free list before 1967, so this can be taken as representative.
180. 20 per cent of the tariff rates were *ad valorem* and unaffected by price changes. 80 per cent of tariff rates were specific or had a specific element. If the initial *ad valorem* equivalent was 19 per cent and the *ad valorem* equivalent on 80 per cent was reduced by one-third, then $[1(19) + 4(6.33)] \div 5$ gives 8.86. If the compound duties are assumed unchanged and only three-quarters of duties were affected, the result comes to 9.5. For dutiable items, the results are 26.7 and 27.5 respectively. Hence the 9 per cent and 27 per cent given in the text.
181. *Historical Statistics,* Series U 15-17; *Statistical Abstract,* 1974, Table 1334, and corresponding tables in other years.

182. Trade Expansion Act of 1962, Sec. 202, and Trade Act of 1974 Sec. 101 (b) (2).
183. Senate Committee on Finance, op.cit., pp.94-5.
184. Trade Act 1974, Sec. 126.
185. Sec. 612
186. Cmd. 7258 and Cmd. 9413.
187. US Tariff Commission, *Operation of the Trade Agreements Program*, 2nd Report, pp.21-2.
188. Agreement concerning Automotive Products between the Government of Canada and the Government of the US, 16 January 1965.
189. U.S. Tariff Commission, *Operation of the Trade Agreements Program*, 25th Report, p.10.
190. Automotive Products Act of 1965.
191. US Tariff Commission, *Operation of the Trade Agreements Program*, 17th Report, p.9; 19th Report, p.10; 23rd Report, p.12; 25th Report, pp.10 and 108.
192. Senate Committee on Finance, op.cit., p.235.
193. US Tariff Commission, *Operation of the Trade Agreements Program*, 25th Report, p.9.
194. Trade Act of 1974, Title V.
195. Sec. 502 (b) (3).
196. Sec. 504 (c).
197. Sec. 502 (b).
198. Secretary of State Kissinger, *US Trade Policy.* Excerpts from a Review in Testimony before the Senate Finance Committee, 30.1.1976. Official Text, US Embassy in London, 2.2.1976.
199. Trade Act of 1974, Sec. 503 (c) (1).

4 THE GENERAL AGREEMENT ON TARIFFS AND TRADE

1. The Nature of GATT

GATT is the international counterpart to US tariff policy. When the GATT agreement was signed, in 1947, the most recent experiences with trade agreements amongst countries with market economies were those concluded under the trade agreements programme of the US since 1934 and the preferential trading agreements amongst the countries of the British empire which were concluded in 1932. In so far as GATT provided for non-discrimination in countries' external trade, the US view prevailed. In so far as GATT negotiations were simultaneous negotiations between several pairs of countries, GATT drew on British experience.

In the actual working of GATT, the chief influences were the increases in tariff reducing authority in the US and the response of other industrial countries, and especially the industrial countries of Western Europe. The result was substantial tariff reductions on industrial goods, and more can still be done along those lines. But when it came to trade in agricultural products or to commercial relations with less developed countries or Communist countries, tariff policy was either not thought appropriate or was inadequate to lead to major results.[1] Recognition of these limitations does not belittle the achievements of GATT. Tariff disarmament amongst the major industrial countries was a major factor in the prosperity of the post-war world, and in this GATT played its part. But it could not go beyond its assigned role, and even in this role it could go no further than the US was willing to go.

The GATT agreement provided a code of conduct for international commercial relations. The principal rules are that there should be no discrimination between foreign countries which are members of the agreement, that protection should be mainly by tariff, and that tariff rates be negotiable. The code committed the Executive branches of member governments from the time of implementation. But it did so only to the extent to which it was 'not inconsistent with existing legislation'.[2] In other words, neither the founder members nor acceding members were obliged to abandon at once all practices which were not strictly compatible with GATT, but they were obliged to refrain from new initiatives which were incompatible with GATT. For instance, Imperial preference continued until the 1970s, although the Commonwealth countries were founder members of GATT and tariff discrimination was against the rules of GATT. But no new initiatives could be taken without the consent of the other members of GATT, and such consent could not be taken for granted. Moreover, the existing preferences between the UK and Canada ceased to be contractual so that they could be freely varied without the consent of the other. If the UK and Canada continued to consult each other on preferences, this was done out of courtesy and not because of any legal obligation.[3] US agricultural protection still continued to be mainly by quotas and not tariffs, although GATT prefers tariffs. GATT did not make countries alter their ways at once. What it did instead, was to sketch out the route along which they could move.

The code of conduct came to life in the non-discriminatory application of negotiated tariff reductions. These reductions were agreed at the major 'Rounds' of tariff and trade negotiations which followed the changes in US trade agreements legislation. Between 1947 and 1967, there were six such Rounds, and a seventh is in progress in the mid-1970s. The agreed tariff rates are put together in schedules for each country. For instance, all UK concessions are in Schedule XIX and those of the US in Schedule XX. All this made GATT a forum for negotiations and also an archive of negotiated tariff rates.

GATT is also a forum for renegotiations. Besides the major Rounds, there are regular sessions of GATT members concerned with the working of GATT agreements. Amongst the problems which arise at the regular sessions are renegotiations of scheduled concessions and requests for waivers from general GATT obligations. GATT agreements are valid for three years at a time. Until 1955, all concessions had to be revalidated before renewal. Since then, they have been extended automatically, unless a member government gave notice of modification of tariff rates in its schedule. This resulted in triennial 'open seasons' for renegotiations of any GATT concessions which had given rise to difficulties.[4] The government concerned had either to negotiate an alternative concession or agree to the withdrawal of an equivalent concession by interested countries. A similar procedure could be used at any time, under the escape clause, when a government felt that injury to its domestic interests was such that it could not wait for the open season.[5] Waivers are needed when a government wants to take a new initiative which is not compatible with the general GATT rules. As mentioned in Chapter 3, the US obtained such a waiver to grant free trade in automotive products to Canada but not to other GATT members. Since renegotiations and waivers are the exceptions which are allowed in order to ensure the overall observance of the code, they will not be dealt with at length here. Their availability must nevertheless be borne in mind, since they are the counterparts of the various reliefs member governments provide to ensure the acquiescence of protected interests in the freer trade policy.

To return to the main theme, GATT is a code of conduct and a forum for negotiations and renegotiations. Yet it has no life of its own. Originally intended to be a provisional forerunner of an International Trade Organisation, which would have done for tariffs and trade what the International Monetary Fund did for money and exchange rates, GATT survived when the US Congress refused to approve such formal organisation for tariffs and trade. Ever since, GATT has been tolerated as long as it did not involve legislation in member countries. The only organisation it ever had is a Secretariat. This acts as a channel of communications between governments, prepares and hosts negotiations and renegotiations, and sometimes promotes studies into problems of trade and trade policy. All this makes the Secretariat a storehouse of knowledge, and enables it to advise and conciliate. But it has neither legislative nor judicial nor executive authority.

By the time these pages are read, it may be known whether a more formal structure will be imposed on GATT, following the US Trade Act of 1974 and the Seventh Round of major GATT negotiations. Whatever the outcome, GATT has so far survived its successes in the major tariff reductions of the late 1940s and 1960s, as well as the failure to achieve major results in between. So far, it could always be activated when new US Presidential tariff reducing authority breathed new life into it. Then it was there to be used. In between it could be a forum for renegotiations, and this ensured the continuance of earlier major negotiating achievements.

2. The Bilateral Phase before GATT

Initially, GATT drew on the experiences of the US trade agreements programme since 1934 and British negotiating methods in dealings with Commonwealth countries. The target of US policy was freer trade through lowering tariff rates towards levels permitted under US legislation, the elimination of other trade barriers, and the non-discriminatory application of concessions to all countries with most-favoured-nation rights. The British negotiating method was simultaneous negotiations of bilateral agreements with several countries.

Between 1934 and 1947, that is between the time US trade agreements became possible and the First Round of major GATT negotiations, the US concluded trade agreements with twenty-nine countries. But it was not possible to negotiate quickly. The trade agreements with Canada and France were not effective until 1936, and that with the UK not until 1939. Those three countries were the three largest trading partners of the US at that time.[6]

The delays were due to the need to prepare negotiations and inexperience in how to negotiate. Negotiations were with one country at a time, and each negotiation had to be prepared and conducted separately. This followed tradition. US trade negotiations had always been bilateral. The difference between the pre-1934 and the post-1934 negotiations was that the pre-1934 negotiations concerned the exemption of one country from the full impact of the relevant US tariff rates, while the post-1934 negotiations concerned the reduction in tariff rates themselves. In other words, the post-1934 negotiations led to concessions which were automatically extended to all countries with unconditional most-favoured-nation rights. The concessions were bilaterally negotiated and applied multilaterally.[7] Although an innovation for the US, this had been a European practice of long standing which has been traced back to the twelfth century.[8] Independent countries have normally been reluctant to negotiate on any other terms. For any trade agreement which is applied only bilaterally is liable to lead to the subordination of one partner to the other.

The unconditional most-favoured-nation principle has not had an unchequered history. There were lapses and long periods when there were few negotiations. But only after the slump of 1929 did all Europe seem to abandon the rule of multilateral application of bilaterally negotiated concessions. Just then the US adopted it.[9]

This was one of several ways in which the US became, for a time, the custodian of traditional European standards of behaviour when Europe seemed to abandon them. Eventually this was to enable her to reintroduce the unconditional most-favoured-nation principle to Europe via GATT. Non-discrimination in trade agreements is possible only for as long as the major commercial powers abide by it. At the beginning of 1934, the US did not discriminate but she had not negotiated any trade agreements since the 1900s (and these were discriminatory).[10] Europe continued to negotiate but, by the 1930s, mainly in order to discriminate. Only the US could break the impasse, through offering a trade agreement with the world's largest commercial power as an alternative to the drift into discriminatory practices.

In the trade agreements which followed 1934, the US bargained reductions in her tariff rates for guarantees against further discrimination as well as reductions in other countries' tariff rates. To this end, the trade agreements always included schedules of agreed US tariff rates, known as 'scheduled concessions'. Most trade agreements also included scheduled concessions by the other country though, on balance, the US gave more by way of scheduled concessions than she received that way. She sought and received more by way of 'general concessions' which brought the overall commercial conduct of other countries more into line with the rule of non-discrimination.

For instance, what the US wanted most from Canada, in 1936, was most-favoured-nation treatment. The Canadian tariff was a three-column tariff with general, intermediate and preferential rates. The preferential rates were reserved for Commonwealth countries with most-favoured-nation rights, chiefly the UK. The intermediate rates applied to foreign countries with most-favoured-nation rights. The general rates applied to all other countries, including the US. The grant of most-favoured-nation treatment alone affected over two-fifths of Canada's dutiable imports from the US on which the general rates had been higher than the intermediate rates.[11] Once reciprocal most-favoured-nation treatment was agreed, the further concessions negotiated in two more US-Canada trade agreements during the bilateral phase contained mainly scheduled concessions both ways. It may be noted, however, that some of the scheduled concessions the US made to Canada in 1938, were in compensation for Canada's loss of some preferences in the UK market resulting from the US-UK trade agreement of that year. The US 'paid' scheduled concessions to one country in order to reduce discrimination in that country's favour in another.

In France, the problem for the US was quota discrimination rather than tariff discrimination. During the depression, France had erected an elaborate system of import controls, and this had unfavourable discriminatory effects on US exports. The 1936 trade agreement made French quotas non-discriminatory as far as US exports were concerned, and also provided for equality of treatment for US and French goods for revenue tax purposes.[12]

Although the Canadian and French agreements were important steps towards the elimination of discriminatory trading practices, the principal general target for negotiation appears to have been Imperial preference.[13] This does not mean that Imperial preference was the worst form of discrimination practised at any time between the 1930s and 1970s. Even from a US point of view, there were worse offenders, such as Germany in the 1930s and the Communist countries in the post-war era. From them most-favoured-nation treatment was withheld altogether. But Imperial preference covered a wide part of the trading world, and was practised by countries with whom negotiations were thought possible. Moreover, it embraced Canada and the Caribbean dependencies, which have always been sensitive areas in US-UK relations.

Throughout, the US attitude towards Imperial preference was somewhat ambivalent. When the Ottawa agreements were concluded in 1932 and led to the widespread application of preferential tariffs throughout the empire, the US was in no position to comment. Only two years earlier had she contributed to the drift into economic nationalism by raising her tariff, and she did not yet negotiate. When she began to negotiate in 1934, one of the first studies ordered by the Administration was one into the feasibility of free trade between the US and the British empire. But when it came to prepare for the trade agreement with the UK, a study was made into how to undermine Imperial preference.[14]

This is not the place to go into much detail about the misunderstandings or half-understandings that arise when governments take major foreign policy decisions, without the sort of consultations which became customary in the post-war world through, for instance, GATT. Suffice it to say that to the UK authorities, at that time, Imperial preference seemed an alternative to greater all-round tariff protection. Having been driven off gold and free trade, the UK could contain her own return to protection only through negotiations with other countries. Since neither the US nor any one other major foreign commercial power was willing to negotiate at the time, her only negotiating opportunity was within the empire.[15] Within the empire, preferential tariff rates in favour of the UK had a tradition dating back in some instances to the late nineteenth century. In her revenue duties, and in the relatively small number of protective duties the UK imposed before 1931, the UK gave preferences in return. When UK protection was generalised, provision was made for preferential as well as general tariff rates. The preferential rates were negotiated at Ottawa in 1932.

Those were bilateral negotiations. They were conducted on an item-by-item basis where each country sought concessions for its major exports. This was in line with traditional trade negotiating procedure, which was later adopted by the US and continued to be generally used until the 1960s. The application of the Ottawa concessions was, however, confined to empire countries with most-favoured-nation rights. Where agreements were concluded, as between the UK and each of the dominions, the UK concessions were extended to all empire countries. This was known as 'most-favoured-empire-nation treatment'. But the concessions the dominions gave to the UK were given only to the UK, or such other empire country to which they were tied under separate agreements, unless and until the dominions concerned negotiated reciprocal most-favoured-nation treatment. This was done only gradually and did not become general until all the Commonwealth countries accorded each other most-favoured-nation treatment under GATT. Even then, Canada reserved some preferences she gave to other Commonwealth countries, but not to the UK, though she then undertook not to increase such special preferences.[16]

All this was in conformity with past and future negotiating practices between independent countries, though the application of the Ottawa agreements was limited to empire countries. What was new was the fact that the Ottawa negotiations were simultaneous bilateral negotiations. To the best of the writer's knowledge, this was the first series of simultaneous bilateral tariff negotiations which actually led to agreements and their implementation. One result was that the number of products covered in these agreements was larger than could be expected in a single bilateral agreement. Inevitably this tied the hands of the UK in further major tariff negotiations. There had to be prior consultation between Commonwealth countries before negotiations with foreign countries could be concluded. If this meant delay in reaching agreement between the UK and the US, it also meant that a number of governments got used to mutual consultations on tariff rates even when there were no direct negotiations between them. Since simultaneous negotiations and mutual consultations were to be of the essence of GATT, it is worth noting that this had a forerunner. In the event, this was to be as important in making GATT work as US trade agreements legislation was in making it possible.

In the meantime, the US had begun to negotiate. Her negotiations were with one country at a time, and proceeded item-by-item. Inevitably this made negotiations with a larger trading partner more far-ranging than negotiations with a smaller one. Moreover, since bilaterally negotiated concessions had to be multilaterally applied. negotiators were wary of giving full concessions to any country other than the principal supplier of the item under negotiation. Otherwise they would have reduced negotiating strength in parleys with the principal supplier. Although the principal supplier rule could not always be strictly adhered to, if agreements with smaller countries were not to be ruled out, it often acted as a restraint on giving full concessions. The US trade agreements programme could then not become really meaningful unless agreement could be reached with the UK, her largest trading partner at the time.

The principal supplier restraint was not only a restraint on the giving of concessions. It was just as much of a restraint on the asking for concessions. When countries sought increased outlets for their exports in order to increase domestic employment, they were more interested in concessions on major than on minor exports and on items of interest mainly to themselves rather than to others. The smaller and medium sized countries did not ask for so much by way of scheduled concessions and were not given more than necessary to make an agreement possible. Nor were they asked for so much by the US, who was often content to receive mainly general concessions.

Negotiations for concessions to principal suppliers are, in effect, negotiations to allow for better utilisation of apparent comparative advantage. The assumption is that a country has a comparative advantage in the products of which it is the principal supplier to another. No consideration is given to products which are not supplied because trade barriers are prohibitive before the negotiations. At a time when the chief consideration of economic policy was fuller employment in existing activities, this approach could none the less be thought to lead towards the intended goal. But it took no account of potential comparative advantage. Moreover, the procedure was slow as long as negotiations were with one country at a time and each negotiation required elaborate preparations. These difficulties could not be overcome until there was agreement between the two largest trading countries of the time, namely the US and the UK. The principal supplier restraint mattered less in those negotiations than in any other, since the US and the UK were each other's principal suppliers in more products than any other two countries at the time. The major difficulties which had to be overcome to make that agreement possible were Imperial preference and consultations with third countries.

As mentioned before, for the UK Imperial preference had been a way of salvaging some of her former world role from the great depression, at a time when neither the US nor any other major power was willing to negotiate. The conversion of the US to negotiating, two years later, could not be expected to lead the UK to abandon the

Ottawa policy so soon. It had struck a chord of Imperial sentiment which alone would have made abandonment politically impractical. The US offer was only half of an offer, since tariff reductions could not exceed 50 per cent and had yet to be negotiated item by item, which in most cases meant reductions of less than 50 per cent. Moreover, the Ottawa agreements were valid for five years. They were renewed in 1937. This was after some renegotiation which somewhat reduced the number of items on which preference was given but left most of the agreements intact.

To the US, these preferences seemed a cause of trade diversion at her expense. A major bone of contention was the preference the UK had conceded to Canada on wheat. This had diverted Canadian wheat sales from the continent of Europe to the UK and forced the US to intensify competition elsewhere, with adverse effects on prices. Since Canada had to sell any surpluses in excess of UK requirements in world markets and could not charge more to the UK than to other buyers, her gain of a more secure market in the UK was 'bought' at the expense of a lower export price, though those were times when security of outlets may have mattered more than price. Although Canada, and not the US, was the principal supplier of wheat to the UK, the two countries together were the main sources of supply, and the US insisted on the inclusion of wheat in the negotiations. The UK was unable to concede the removal of the wheat preference without Canadian consent which, in turn, depended on US concessions to Canada. Wheat was not the only item involved, and there were problems relating to preferences the UK received in Canada as well as the preferences Canada received in the UK. But it illustrates the point at issue.

Canada was not, however, party to the US-UK negotiations in 1938. She had concluded an agreement with the US in 1936. On bilateral grounds, there seemed no urgency for renewed US-Canadian negotiations. But the only way to reduce both British and Canadian preferences was for the US to offer tariff reductions to Canada in exchange for the loss of some preferences in the UK, and to the UK in exchange for the loss of some preferences in Canada. In effect, this meant trilateral negotiations. Formally, however, there were only two bilateral negotiations leading to the US-UK and the US-Canada agreements of 1938. The UK and Canada did not negotiate a new agreement but released each other from some of their Ottawa obligations in order to make agreement with the US possible. In effect, the UK-Canada agreement was renegotiated. Although some of the changes affected the trade of other Commonwealth countries as well, they could claim no compensation as long as the only preferences at issue were the preferences in the UK-Canada agreement. Other Commonwealth countries were, however, consulted and agreed to some modification of their rights.[17]

In later years, GATT was to be worked by way of simultaneous bilateral negotiations and renegotiations. By then more than two or three countries were to be involved, partly because more countries had become willing to negotiate, and partly because progress along the lines of the US-UK agreement would have been limited. As mentioned before, when countries negotiated two by two, the result of trade agreements was most likely to be more trade in products where bilateral comparative advantage had been apparent before the negotiations. As long as agreements were between countries of which one had a small and specialised economy, or as long as concessions were mainly general concessions, there were no further problems. But when both partners to the agreement had versatile industrial economies and there was a large number of scheduled concessions, the question arose as to who would be the chief beneficiary.

To repeat yet one other point – in bilateral negotiations concessions were sought and given to principal or substantial suppliers of individual items. Bilateral agreements enhanced bilateral apparent comparative advantage, irrespective of who the partners were. But since the concessions were automatically extended to all countries with most-favoured-nation rights, it was possible that a main effect of a concession could be that a potential comparative advantage of another industrial country be enhanced. For instance, most of what is produced in the UK and Belgium, either is or could be produced in both. The initial response to this possibility was an escape clause which allowed for withdrawal of a concession which benefited mostly third countries. Although this was compatible with the principle of negotiating for bilateral benefit, its widespread use would have negated the ideal of freer trade between the industrial countries. The problem could not be solved just by making the escape clause more comprehensive, which was done. Nor could it be solved by an increase in US tariff-reducing authority, which was given. The only way to reconcile these targets of policy was to negotiate scheduled concessions with several industrial countries at one and the same time. After the US-UK agreement, there were too many scheduled concessions to allow for any other course.

The list of scheduled concessions in that agreement was particularly long because of the substantial volume and variety of trades involved. It was longer still through a *de facto* compromise on Imperial preference. Although the elimination of preferential tariffs was a major target of US foreign economic policy, at that time it would have been no more possible for UK negotiators to make such a general concession than it would have been for US negotiators to concede scheduled tariff reductions in excess of Congressional authorisation. The compromise was that, in the general Articles of the agreement the two countries guaranteed each other most-favoured-nation rights, and expressly excluded from this any preferential arrangements between the US and Cuba or within the British empire and, to make doubly sure, also excluded any existing treaty obligation.[18] But this did not mean that Imperial preference was left unscathed. The long list of scheduled concessions by the UK affected only the tariff rates applicable to foreign countries and there was no overt reference to reductions in margins of preference.[19] But the limitations put on the tariff rates applicable to foreign countries effectively limited possible preferential margins on the items concerned. The UK also negotiated on behalf of dependent territories. In all but one of those schedules, there was no reference to actual tariff rates but there were limitations on the margins of preference allowed.[20] Although the US did not obtain a general concession to limit Imperial preference, the large number of scheduled concessions she obtained had virtually the same result. Imperial preference was not abandoned, but for most practical purposes it was frozen.

In this, as well as in its general negotiating aims and procedures, the US-UK agreement prepared the way for GATT. It did so in other respects as well. The agreement was to be no bar to either country joining a customs union with a third country. Non-discrimination was to be the rule in state trading. There were safeguards against dumping. Quotas were to be allowed to regulate markets which presaged the orderly marketing agreements of the 1960s. There were even undertakings to ensure access to supplies, which were to surface again in the 1970s.[21]

Since the agreement did not become operative until 1939, and war broke out in that year, its effects on trade remains unknown. None the less, the agreement was no dead letter. It represented the thinking and compromises acceptable to the two powers which were to have most influence in shaping the trading rules for the West after the war. It was the culmination of the bilateral phase of the US trade agreements programme, through which the US abandoned the increases in tariff rates she had unilaterally imposed in 1930. The *ad valorem* equivalent of US import duties on dutiable articles had been 39 per cent before the 1930 Tariff Act, 53 per cent in 1930-33 when there were no trade agreements, and 37 per cent in 1939. On all imports, free and dutiable, the relevant figures came to 14, 18 and 14 per cent.[22] For the UK it meant the end of Imperial preference as an active instrument of policy. The UK did not abandon Imperial preference, nor did the US abandon her tariff. But in and after the 1938 agreement, both could only go down.

3. The First Multilateral Phase

The GATT of 1947 was the US-UK trade agreement writ large. The general concessions largely resembled those of the earlier agreement. This time, however, the text had to be agreed between twenty negotiating partners[23] and not just two at a time. The rules of non-discrimination became truly general. No longer could there be problems of changes in those rules from one agreement to the next.[24] In this sense, there was *one* agreement. It was multilaterally negotiated, agreed and applied.

The scheduled concessions too were multilaterally applied. But they continued to be bilaterally negotiated and agreed. Nor was there a general approach towards tariffs, within the bilateral negotiations of 1947. The negotiations were still item by item. The innovation was that several negotiations were conducted simultaneously. No less than 123 bilateral agreements were concluded during the seven months of the Geneva (1947) negotiations.[25] This was a record. The record of the number of agreements concluded in one Round of negotiations was broken two years later, when 147 bilateral agreements were concluded at the Second Round of simultaneous negotiations at Annecy.[26] But as far as the volume of trade covered and the extent of tariff reductions were concerned, the first Geneva (1947) negotiations were to remain unrivaled until the conclusion of the Sixth (Kennedy) Round twenty years later.

One reason why the First and Sixth Rounds stood out is that they followed the new US tariff-halving authorities of 1945 and 1962 respectively. On both occasions, the negotiations led to US tariff reductions on dutiable items averaging somewhat over one-third.[27] The US had already abandoned her 1930 tariff increases during the bilateral phase of the trade agreements programme. In 1947, she was to reduce the *ad valorem* equivalent of her tariff to lower levels than any known since the mid-nineteenth century.[28] At that time, other countries 'paid' for the US scheduled concessions with either general or scheduled concessions. Overall, the US gave about two scheduled concessions for every one received. By 1967, when the US no longer had to 'buy' general concessions, the amount of scheduled concessions received and given was about equal.[29] By then, however, negotiating procedure had changed.

This leads to the second reason why the First and Sixth Rounds were especially important. Apparently it is not possible to achieve the same results by using the same procedure on too many occasions. As shown in the preceding section, the possibilities of purely bilateral negotiations were nearing exhaustion with the US-UK agreement of 1938. The pre-war agreements had set out to enhance any apparent bilateral comparative advantage. But the large number of products covered by the 1938 agreement effectively opened the door wide to potential comparative advantage of other countries. The simultaneous negotiations of 1947 overcame the divergence between bilateral and multilateral negotiating aims.

GATT then came to be an extension of the US-UK agreement in its scheduled concessions as well as in the general ones. That agreement had come into force so shortly before the war that it had never been put to the test. New negotiations could only have covered the same ground. The solution was that the 1938 agreement was repeated and somewhat improved upon. The UK's new reductions in tariff rates in agreements with the US and eight other negotiating units affected a mere 3½ per cent of her imports, and bindings of existing tariff rates about twice as much. The UK also agreed to some further reductions in preferential tariffs in the Commonwealth. In return she received concessions affecting somewhat over 10 per cent of her exports, and the total concessions received from the US were almost as important as those received from all her other negotiating partners combined.[30]

Although for the US the GATT of 1947 was more than a minor extension of the 1938 agreement, that agreement remained the core of tariff reductions. There were completely new reductions in tariff rates on items accounting for 18 per cent of US imports. But further reductions of previously reduced rates affected 36 per cent of her imports, and amongst the previous reductions those in the 1938 agreement were prominent. If bindings are included, 70 per cent of US imports were affected by concessions made in 1947.[31] This was more than a minor extension of the 1938 agreement, though that and other past bilateral agreements were the starting point.

Further development depended on simultaneous negotiations. They overcame the principal supplier restraint, and they reconciled the bilateral negotiating target of fostering apparent comparative advantage between two countries with the multilateral freer trade target of releasing potential comparative advantage between industrial countries. One result was that trade in industrial goods began to pay better. In most industrial countries, there was marked growth of trade in both imports and exports of goods which fall under the same tariff classification. Rapid technological change required quick pay offs on capital employed, and this was facilitated when access to wider markets became easier. Firms specialised in a few ranges of potential output and imported the rest. This intra-industry specialisation could not have come about without technological innovations. But these would have been frustrated had there not been freer trade. The simultaneous bilateral agreements released much potential comparative advantage. Eventually, this led to a situation where countries were more interested in the reduction of tariff rates on the goods they both imported and exported, and not just on the goods of which they were exporters. The item-by-item negotiations then gave way to linear across-the-board tariff reductions in the Sixth (Kennedy) Round, at least in the negotiations between the industrial countries. Item-by-item negotiations continued for other countries. This was to lead to a new division of the world into industrial and non-industrial countries, with special problems in the 1970s. But this is running ahead of the narrative. The next task must be to deal with the progress of GATT in the early Rounds.

The first three Rounds of GATT negotiations (at Geneva in 1947, Annecy 1949 and Torquay 1951) were conducted under the terms of the US tariff-halving authority of 1945. The First Round was the major negotiation. The Second and Third Rounds were concerned mainly with the accession of new members. As mentioned before, in 1947 the US gave about twice as much as she received by way of scheduled concessions because she wanted to 'buy' the adherence of others to the general principles of her trade agreements programme. In the Second and Third Rounds, she gave only half as much by way of scheduled concessions as she received. It was the turn of the acceding members to 'buy' admission to the general agreement. None of the countries that gained admission at the time was comparable in size with the US. The largest to join in 1949 was Italy, and in 1951 Germany which was then in a relatively weak position. The proportion of US imports affected by new concessions in the Second and Third Rounds taken together came to no more than 10 per cent. The acceding countries' concessions varied from virtually all-round concessions (Finland, 1949) to virtually none (Brazil, 1951). Italy and Germany made concessions on about three-quarters of their imports from the US which also benefited the other founder members.[32] The latter negotiated some improvements in their agreements as well as with the new members. But no substantial new tariff reductions were conceded by the UK[33] and other founder members. But even if each of the founder members conceded only a little more than in 1947, or in the case of the UK in 1938, in the absence of simultaneous negotiations most of them would probably have conceded nothing in 1949 and 1951. Trade agreements would have continued to be mainly bilateral agreements of the US, and the principal-supplier restraint would have made it difficult to go much beyond the 1938 agreement, even in 1947.

To allow for the progress made in 1947, and its extension to new members in 1949 and 1951, required a new negotiating procedure. Initially, this took the form of simultaneous use of established procedures. At national level, negotiations were prepared with much the same sort of hearings and investigations there had always been before negotiations could begin. But when negotiations were prepared with several countries and not just one, emphasis inevitably shifted from investigations into items which figured predominantly in bilateral trading relationships to items which were generally important in the country's external trade. Put differently, emphasis shifted from preparations for bilateral negotiations to preparations for agreements which were multilaterally applied. This does not deny that the pre-1947 agreements were multilaterally applied. Nor does it deny that the scheduled concessions continued to be negotiated bilaterally and item by item until yet further negotiating changes were made in the 1960s. The procedure followed in 1947 and then throughout the 1950s, was one of 'requests' and 'offers'. Here the starting point was requests, still made by principal suppliers or by groups of countries which banded together as principal suppliers. These were addressed to particular trading partners, but copies were distributed by the Secretariat to all members. The replies came in the form of offers to individual trading partners. These offers were sent to the Secretariat, and from there distributed to all members which had made offers. Countries which had made joint requests had to make individual offers if they were to negotiate.[34]

The requests and offers were thus known in advance of actual negotiations which would then start from maximum positions. Some requests would be rejected and some offers withdrawn. Although the actual negotiations took place in private and the final outcome remained uncertain until the negotiations were complete, it was known beforehand what the maximum concessions could be.[35] In a way, this took the negotiations out of politics. In traditional bilateral negotiations, the bargaining usually started with minimum positions which were raised in the course of the negotiations, and this often required reference back to governments. The decision whether to proceed then depended on what political considerations seemed over-riding. For instance, in 1938, the UK Government had to weigh up the political advantages of concluding a trade agreement by which the US Administration laid great store against giving more economic concessions than originally intended.[36] Such problems could no longer arise under the GATT procedure in the 1940s and 1950s, where the final concessions inevitably were below the limits set by the original offers. While no negotiating team could make full use of its tariff-reducing authority, since the final outcome was inevitably less than the maximum, each team acted within authority conferred before the negotiations started. There were then no agonising ratification problems.

As mentioned before, the actual bilateral negotiations continued in private but the range of those negotiations was known to those outside. This facilitated consultations between Commonwealth countries before each negotiation affecting preferences.[37] In general, consultations with other interested parties became customary, and occasionally they would be called to the negotiating table.[38] This was to be important in the negotiations leading to the accession of Japan in 1955. Six countries were persuaded to make concessions to Japan in return for US concessions to them.[39] This was a further development of the trilateral procedures of 1938. Only in 1955 all 'three' parties to the negotiations signed agreements simultaneously.

The accession of a new member was not unprecedented. On earlier occasions, the new industrial members 'paid' for the 1947 concessions by giving more scheduled concessions than they received in the bilateral agreements concluded on accession. But, once admitted, they received unqualified GATT treatment from the older members. It may be added that US negotiators had exhausted over two-thirds of their tariff-reducing authority in 1947, when they wanted to secure the *general* agreement with their American, Commonwealth and European partners; and they did not have so much to give again when others wanted the benefits of the general agreement.[40] When it came to negotiate the accession of Japan, there were several important differences. One was that the US negotiators acted under new tariff-reducing authority conferred in 1954. This was less than that given in 1945. It was not enough to lead to a major all-round tariff reducing initiative, though it sufficed to cope with one major accession and some minor improvements on earlier agreements.[41] Nevertheless, the US wanted to secure the accession of Japan to the general agreement, while others were more reluctant.

A purely bilateral US-Japan trade agreement would not have served the purpose since it would have left Japan free to discriminate between other countries. A negotiation involving the majority of GATT members was not possible at the time. The solution was for the US to induce some other countries to join her in a preliminary negotiation with Japan before the Fourth Round. As already mentioned, this led to the balancing of concessions, where some of what Japan conceded to the US was balanced by some other countries' concessions to Japan which, in turn, was balanced by US concessions to those other countries. These multilateral scheduled concessions were subsequently incorporated into the agreements reached at the Fourth Round (Geneva, 1956).

In order to secure the accession of Japan to the *general* agreement, the US was willing to give twice as much by way of scheduled concessions as she received, just as she had done to secure the general agreement in the first place in 1947. But, in 1956, she had less to give. Her 1956 concessions affected only 7½ per cent of her trade as against close on 80 per cent in 1947, and the overall *ad valorem* equivalent of her tariff reductions was estimated at about 4 per cent in 1956 as against 35 per cent in 1947.[42] Other countries conceded less. For instance, UK tariff cuts affected only about 1 per cent of imports.[43]

Moreover, while in all previous Rounds extension of GATT treatment to new members was unqualified, when it came to admit Japan, fourteen (out of thirty-five) members entered reservations on their own behalf and that of about thirty dependencies.[44] They invoked Article XXXV which entitled them to withhold GATT concessions from a new member until they had negotiated themselves with that member. One of the fourteen was the UK. Although she claimed not to withhold most-favoured-nation treatment from Japan, she continued to apply an earlier bilateral quota agreement to Japanese trade until further negotiation.[45] This did not take place until 1962. Then Japan agreed to impose 'voluntary' restraint on her exports of certain products to the UK, and the UK no longer applied special quotas on Japanese goods. Most other industrial countries 'disinvoked' Article XXXV at about the same time. But its use did not cease until the mid-1970s. For instance, Ireland applied it until 1975, by which time she had joined EC. Former dependencies continued to apply it after attainment of independence, when they became GATT members in their own right. Their special treatment of Japan did not cease until Japan could threaten to withhold from them the generalised preferences she offered developing countries in the 1970s.[46] Even the US could not claim that she treated Japan like any other member of GATT. In 1956, Japan agreed to 'voluntary' restraint of some of her textile exports to the US.[47]

Economically, it makes little difference whether Japan 'voluntarily' restrained her exports or had quotas imposed upon them. Politically, it may have been important to her government to have some say in the control of her trade, despite the domestic difficulties a government faces when it limits its own nationals' activities. Had Japan's export interests remained mainly textiles and steel, her accession to GATT would have had little meaning. Those are price-sensitive decreasing returns activities and their representatives are normally amongst the loudest claimants for protection. The move towards negotiated freer trade did, however, depend on the interest of increasing returns activities in easier access to world markets. Such industries were already important in Japan, in the mid-1950s, and they continued to expand at a faster rate than the traditional ones. In the course of the 1960s, her chief exports were engineering products and there was also marked growth in chemicals.[48] This may have been helped by the accession of Japan to GATT. But the main cause was that she was becoming a mature economy, in the sense of having no spare factors of production, and overcame those problems through buying the technology of the West and engaging more in capital-intensive than labour-intensive activities.[49] This way Japan's commercial interests came to coincide more with those of the earlier industrial members of GATT.

It was mentioned early in this chapter that GATT could not alter any member country's ways but only sketch out a route along which they could move. Japan's accession illustrates this point. GATT did not alter Japan, nor her reluctant partners in GATT. But the Japanese economy moved in directions which made the GATT code of conduct more applicable to her trade in both directions. If initially, some countries were allowed to defer full acceptance of Japan until further negotiations, these negotiations could take place later, along GATT lines, when the Japanese economy had become more like that of the other industrial members.

Nevertheless, GATT results were slowing down. The full acceptance of Japan took several years. Even the scheduled concessions negotiated during the Fourth Round were implemented only with delays, as prescribed by the then new US staging requirements.[50] The sense of urgency which had animated the First Round was gone. Nevertheless, the Fourth Round also lay the foundations for new negotiating procedures. It had been prepared by the first truly multilateral negotiation of scheduled concessions, and this was to be a feature of the negotiations amongst the industrially advanced countries during the Sixth Round.

4. The Second Multilateral Phase

With the accession of Japan, and two years later of Switzerland,[51] GATT embraced all of the industrial market economies. Further progress depended not just on additional US tariff-reducing authority, but also on new ways of negotiating freer trade amongst industrial countries and upon the accession of new members.

Some members of GATT were not content with the universal move towards freer trade at a pace set by the US Congress, and there was a proliferation of regional free trade areas and customs unions in the late 1950s and the 1960s. In those areas, industrial tariffs were reduced by the same percentage amounts across-the-board until they were eliminated. Amongst industrial countries, there were the EC, EFTA and the free trade agreements between Australia and New Zealand and between the UK and Ireland. Some industrialising countries followed this example, and there was a Latin American Free Trade Area, a Central American Common Market, and a free trade area between North Borneo and Sarawak. Most of these arrangements were between countries who were members of GATT. But of the five Central American Common Market countries, only Nicaragua was in GATT. In this case, Nicaragua submitted annual reports to GATT which ensured that even a regional free trade with a majority of non-members would be organised along lines compatible with GATT principles.[52] Nevertheless, if GATT was not to be split up into regional blocs, GATT's universal move towards freer trade had to be reconciled with the regional moves towards free trade in industrial goods.

Industrial goods must be singled out, for the various regional free trade areas either omitted agriculture altogether or, as in EC, coupled industrial free trade with common agricultural protection. Other GATT countries could claim compensation from injury they might suffer from changes in tariff rates which resulted from the new regional groupings.[53] On industrial goods, this meant reconciling universal tariff reductions with regional tariff elimination. These were two moves in the same direction, though at different speeds. If the Fifth and Sixth Rounds are taken together, a fair degree of success was achieved. But there has not yet been much success in reconciling the various forms of agricultural protection of the major GATT members. Agriculture is the prime example of a decreasing returns activity, and one with an especially slow responsiveness of supply to price changes. GATT principles were bent in relation to textiles, another decreasing returns activity, but one where at least some control of supply is feasible. No headway was made in agriculture. The US continued to reserve her agriculture from effective GATT negotiations. Although, in the early 1960s, the EC's common agricultural policy was still in process of being negotiated amongst the member countries, it was effectively made non-negotiable with outsiders. As long as both the US and the EC will not allow effective negotiations about their own agricultural protection, GATT can reconcile only industrial interests.

Free trade areas, in the narrower sense of the term, left constituent countries' external tariffs unchanged and merely suspended the application of import duties on members' trade. There were no changes in any of the tariff rates scheduled in GATT agreements. Third countries might complain of trade diversion and seek the renegotiation of a particular duty, but they could do that at any time under other GATT procedures. As long as import regulations were not more restrictive on formation of the free trade area than before, GATT rules were satisfied.[54] But when the free trade area included provision for the formation of a customs union, with a common external tariff, further problems arose.

Thus, the common external tariff of the EC was arrived at by averaging the previous statutory tariff rates of the member states, and these were sometimes higher than the actual rates applied by some of those countries.[55] The common tariff rates were not necessarily straight arithmetic averages of the former rates, since account had to be taken of different volumes of trade. Invariably, however, this meant that the reduction of one national tariff rate to the common level would be accompanied by an increase in another member's national rate to the common one. Some rates were raised above the levels in individual union member countries' GATT schedules. Since all rates in

GATT schedules had been conceded in at least one trade agreement with another country, that other country was entitled to claim compensation.[56] There could be arguments whether the reduction of tariff rate by one member of the customs union was adequate compensation for an increase in that rate by another. Much of the bargaining during the Fifth Round concerned such arguments between the US and the EC.

The Fifth Round (Geneva, 1960-2) was an attempt to treat the EC as if she were a newly acceding member, although all the EC countries were individual members of GATT. The procedure was similar to the Fourth Round, in so far as there was a preliminary negotiation to deal with the 'accession', followed by an attempt to move further towards freer trade through item-by-item negotiations. Like the Fourth Round, it was made possible through an increase in US tariff-reducing authority, conferred in 1958. Although this was 20 per cent, and so more than the 15 per cent allowed for the Fourth Round or the 15 per cent left over for the Second and Third Rounds taken together, this was authority to negotiate a new accession rather than take a major initiative towards freer trade.

Moreover, the US negotiators' hands were further tied by the peril points procedure, then in vogue in the US, which restricted them more on individual items than overall. In the event, they had to exceed the limits set by the peril points procedure if agreement was to be reached, though they could not exceed their authority under the 1958 Act.[57] One major effect of the peril points procedure was that the US negotiators could not start from maximum positions. As mentioned before, a start from maximum positions had been a major feature of earlier GATT negotiations[58] and had taken those negotiations out of politics. In the Fifth Round, the US negotiators had to refer to the Administration for decisions on items where peril points were involved. Reference back to the home government had been a major feature of pre-GATT bilateral negotiations which started from minimum positions, where the final outcome of a negotiation often depended on a political decision. The Fifth Round did not fully revert to the pre-GATT procedure, but it introduced a range between original minimum and maximum positions. In consequence, success of the Fifth Round was not a foregone conclusion but depended on political decisions relating to individual items in the US. It also depended on the political decision of the EC to be accommodating.

The EC countries had only recently agreed on their common external tariff. This had involved delicate negotiations amongst themselves, since the averaging of member countries' tariff rates is not a matter of simple arithmetic where the size of member countries' markets and volumes of trade vary from item to item. They were reluctant to re-open discussions about too many individual tariff rates. They were making linear across-the-board tariff cuts amongst themselves and offered outsiders a share in this. Their total offer was 20 per cent of their common customs tariff (which was not yet operative). Half of this offer was unconditional and the other half subject to negotiations. Although they had to concede special concessions on individual items, much of what they gave was linear across the board. Other countries continued to make item-by-item concessions. The US gave concessions which were estimated to be worth a 10 per cent overall reduction in the *ad valorem* equivalent of her tariff, on dutiable items, though the actual cuts were concentrated on about 12 per cent of her imports.[59] The UK reduced duties by about one-fifth, but on only 5 per cent of her imports.[60] The percentage of trade in industrial goods affected by these cuts was, of course, higher and the bilateral benefits more even. Nevertheless, the countries which negotiated item by item gave less than the EC which negotiated mainly across the board. Although this included some element of the newly emerging EC 'paying' for international goodwill, the general feeling was that 'the usefulness of item-by-item bargaining hirtherto used in GATT tariff conferences . . . had been largely exhausted' and that 'a linear approach involving tariff cuts across-the-board with a minimum of exceptions might yield better results.'[61]

It will be recalled that the bilateral approach to trade agreements had been exhausted with the UK-US agreement of 1938, when it covered virtually all industrial products. By the 1960s, it was the turn of the simultaneous bilateral approach, when it covered all industrial trading countries. This approach had fulfilled much of its purpose when its wide range had released potential comparative advantage and intra-industry specialisation become the major feature in the growth of world trade. When most of the growth of trade, in both directions, is in the same product ranges, there are no principal suppliers. In consequence, there can be no negotiations through requests from, and offers to, principal suppliers. Interest shifts from the removal of trade barriers on particular products in particular countries, to the removal of trade barriers on the same product groups in all interested countries. Instead of arguing the case for and against protection of product *X* in country *A* or of product *Y* in country *B*, the world of the 1960s began to ask whether and how much product *X* should be protected in all countries. In consequence, the different treatment of products became less important, though it did not cease. The different treatment of countries became more important, though the principles of non-discrimination were not jettisoned between the industrial countries.

Just as simultaneous negotiations entered the picture in 1938 and were to be the main negotiating practice from 1947 to 1962, so linear across-the-board tariff cuts were at hand when the simultaneous bilateral approach had reached the limits of its usefulness. This time the origin of the new approach was in Europe, where all tariffs were falling within the EC and within EFTA in the 1960s, and where most quotas had been abolished in the 1950s. The Fifth Round accepted this contribution from EC, but only at the Sixth Round did all the major industrial countries negotiate along such lines.

The Sixth Round (Geneva 1964-7) started with the advantage of a 50 per cent US tariff-reducing authority and so with the prospect of tariff reductions comparable with those of the First Round. The experience of the Fifth Round had shown that the emergence of the EC had created a new negotiating situation. But across-the-board negotiations and linear tariff cuts could appeal only to countries with an interest in intra-industry specialisation. Countries with less versatile economic structures were not ready for this approach. They considered their apparent bilateral comparative advantage as their only possible comparative advantage. Item-by-item negotiations seemed more suitable to their requirements. In consequence, countries fell into different negotiating groups.

One group consisted of fifteen 'linear countries'. They were the US, the six EC countries, Japan, the UK and most of her EFTA partners.[62] They negotiated the new way amongst themselves. The second group consisted of fourteen 'special arrangement countries'. This was a miscellany of countries, at various stages of development, but all with a concentration of exports on a few items. They included Canada, Ireland and Turkey.[63] The third group consisted of seventeen less developed countries (LDCs) which sought concessions on individual items but were not expected to give anything in return. Finally, there were forty-one non-negotiating members of GATT. All of them were LDCs. They asked for no particular concessions but, like all countries with most-favoured-nation rights, received any concessions others had negotiated amongst themselves.[64]

The linear countries negotiated across-the-board on industrial products. Their initial offers were 50 per cent tariff reductions across the board, but these were subject to exceptions. The 50 per cent offers were maximum offers, in line with GATT tradition. The exceptions meant that some products were either excluded altogether or that offers on individual items were restricted to less than 50 per cent. In effect, the exceptions were minimum offers. The range of bargaining was between the limits of these maximum and minimum offers. This was in line with the US negotiating method during the Fifth Round, and in line with pre-GATT bargaining from minimum positions. The minimum-maximum bargaining had already protracted the Fifth Round which had taken longer to negotiate than any of the first four Rounds. It was one, though not the only, factor in protracting the Sixth Round even more, especially since each negotiating country compiled its own exception list. Details were not published, but it is alleged that some of the smaller countries claimed no exceptions while the EC had a particularly long one.[65] Progress could be made when countries shortened their exception lists and so raised their minimum offers. This was done on a basis of strict reciprocity.[66]

Eventually, the most difficult sectors were isolated from the main stream of negotiations between countries. There were 'sectoral talks' on about 30 per cent of the linear countries' trade in industrial goods. It is reported that these talks not only ranged over the effects of tariff reductions on trade, but also took account of industrial structure, production, consumption and regional issues.[67] The industries covered included chemicals, cotton textiles and iron and steel. In respect of other industrial goods, there were still item-by-item bargains, but these were bargains about the exception lists.

Whatever was achieved in the sectoral talks and in the bargaining about exceptions between the US, the EC, the UK and Japan, was extended to all GATT countries. The industrially more advanced of the intermediate countries thus obtained potential advantages. But, in view of their more specialised actual export trades, they negotiated by the traditional method of requests and offers on individual items. They made relatively few requests and offered correspondingly little. Subsequently they were accused of having been virtually 'free riders' during the Sixth Round.[68] The LDCs were not requested to give concessions and so escaped this accusation.

Overall, the tariff reductions came to about one-third.[69] Industrial countries gave somewhat more on manufactures.[70] The US conceded tariff reductions of 35 per cent overall and 38 per cent on manufactures.[71] This roughly equalled the tariff reductions she had made in the First Round, twenty years earlier, and exceeded what she had given at intervening Rounds. On this occasion, however, the US was not content to receive one scheduled concession for every two given, as she had been at the First Round, but insisted on reciprocity of scheduled concessions with other industrial countries. So did the other industrial countries. The general concessions had already been paid for in earlier Rounds, so that the industrial countries could concentrate on scheduled concessions amongst themselves. The result was that the industrial countries, other than the US, made their biggest tariff cuts this century. Japan headed the list, with 40 per cent reductions. These were her first major tariff cuts since her accession to GATT twelve years earlier when she had conceded less than one-third.[72] The EC reduced tariffs on manufactures by 32 per cent and, since she had already conceded 20 per cent in the Fifth Round, this left her common external tariff on manufactures at around 55 per cent of what had been originally intended only eight years earlier. The UK conceded 34 per cent. In her case, this came to a weighted tariff reduction of 40 per cent in dutiable trade with the US, 37 per cent with the EC and 32 per cent with Japan.[73] It may be noted that these were the largest tariff reductions the UK had made since the trade agreement with the US in 1938, when she had cut tariff rates on a wide range of manufactures by about one quarter.[74]

The largest tariff reductions were made in engineering goods. On machinery and transport equipment, the cuts ranged between 40 and 50 per cent. These were amongst the trades where intra-industry specialisation had made most progress in the 1960s and there was relatively little resistance to tariff cuts. Exceptions were either not claimed or negotiated away in the course of the negotiations on those products. There was just as much, or even more, intra-industry specialisation in chemicals.[75] The US gave nearly full concessions on chemicals. But the UK and the EC felt unable to reciprocate in full, as long as American selling price regulations offset the effects of any US tariff cuts on some items, and the abolition of these regulations did not materialise. None the less, the overall reduction on chemicals still came to 38 per cent. In the case of steel, the main negotiating achievement was the harmonisation of the US, EC and Japanese tariff rates on most items, and some moves in this direction by the UK. There were greater difficulties with textiles, though the incorporation of the Long Term Textile Agreement into the Round made at least a 20 per cent reduction possible.[76] Tariff rates on basic materials were already low but were reduced by 30 per cent. On foods not subject to price support, tariff rates were reduced by 20 per cent but such foods are few in number. There was agreement to renew and revise the already existing International Wheat Agreement. This was essentially an orderly marketing agreement on a product which was reserved from tariff negotiations. The lowest tariff reductions were on beverages and tobacco. These continued to be levied at high rates, mainly for revenue reasons.[77]

In short, the Sixth Round achieved most where intra-industry specialisation had become important. It was moderately successful in reducing tariffs on the more traditional products of the advanced countries, where textiles were supported by an orderly marketing agreement while steel has sometimes been on the brink of one.[78] In general, international economic integration came easiest for the more advanced products.

Since the growth of the world economy depends largely on what happens in its most advanced sectors, any policy which gives that sector easier access to markets is a policy which carries the rest along. When some wanted to go further among themselves, like the EC, the problem was one of co-ordinating moves at different speeds in the same direction, and this was attempted in the Fifth and Sixth Rounds. If agriculture and textiles could not keep pace, special arrangements could be made for them, without slowing down freer trade and intra-industry specialisation in chemicals and engineering. Neither the faster moving countries nor the more adjustable products nor the less adjustable products halted the move towards faster growth of trade than of production. This move was facilitated by GATT which co-ordinated the different speeds at which these sectors moved.

The omission is the countries which could not adjust themselves as fast as the industrial world and took little or no part in advanced intra-industry specialisation. Those countries had become more important in GATT. They had become more important in numbers. As former colonies became independent, they became GATT members in their own right. By the time the Sixth Round was in progress, the majority of GATT members were LDCs. This alone was bound to alter the balance of GATT.

True, the LDCs took little active part in the Sixth Round. All GATT concessions were extended to them, though not all were of direct interest to them. But they were not asked for any scheduled concessions in return. The industrial countries thus 'paid' with scheduled concessions for the LDCs' continued adherence to the *general* agreement.

The general agreement itself was amended. While the Sixth Round was in progress, a special GATT session concerned itself with the problems of its economically less developed members. New Articles were added to GATT.[79] Developed countries would no longer seek reciprocity in trade negotiations with LDCs.[80] Although in practice not so much had been asked of LDCs as of others on former occasions, this was now elevated to a general principle and, as such, applied in the Sixth Round. Developed countries would eliminate customs duties on products of particular export interest to LDCs, and not 'differentiate unreasonably between such products in their primary and processed forms'.[81]

There were other provisions as well, chiefly concerned with development problems, but these were no sooner stated than hived off to other agencies.[82] As pointed out before, it has always been a feature of GATT to accept countries as they are, with their pre-existing laws and economies, and confine itself to the prescription of a future course of conduct in the regulation of foreign trade. References to standards of living or development[83] are statements of the intention of the contracting parties to further certain objectives and that trade policy has a part to play in this. They do not mean that GATT has been turned into a development agency nor that it could act as such. GATT would have to be reconstituted before it could perform such functions.

It is not intended to deal with possible reforms of GATT which may concern the Seventh Round,[84] but to ask why it has not yet been possible to integrate LDCs with the trade policy objectives of GATT. It was not just a question of numbers. Nor was it one of representation of those countries' interests. Nine of the founder members were LDCs and included Brazil, India and Pakistan, so that LDC interests were never unrepresented. But there has been a change in attitudes. The industrial GATT members experienced greater growth of trade than of production, and this was one of the important causes of their prosperity. In the early post-war days it seemed reasonable to think that much of the problems of underdevelopment could be solved through the growth of trade between primary producing LDCs and the major industrial countries, then the US and the UK. Full employment policies in these two countries would ensure growth and the demand for primary commodities. Trade would lead production.

It did in the industrial countries. This was helped by GATT. Trade was also helpful to non-industrial countries. But those that were LDCs often used their own or imported savings to build up their economies in the image of the industrial countries. In important respects, their development followed the pattern of the industrialising countries of the late nineteenth and early twentieth centuries. One of those features was a greater growth of production than of trade. Add to this that world markets were not expanding as rapidly for the major exports of many LDCs as for the exports of the more advanced countries, and the tendencies towards greater reliance on domestic development were re-enforced.

When the LDC's predecessors in industrialisation went through a similar phase, their economies became less interdependent and more rival in the search for raw materials. Any tendencies towards international friction there were on other grounds, were re-enforced. There was no room for anything like GATT or EC.

An exact replay, with a new cast, is unlikely. Today's developing countries have not, or not yet, attained the same degree of rivalry which their predecessors eventually reached by the beginning of this century. But there is rivalry between them, and between them and the traditional industries of advanced countries. The object of that rivalry is to purchase what the most advanced sector has to offer. But that sector is not dependent on outlets in LDCs. As long as its own progress towards freer trade is allowed to continue, it does not resist quotas or subsidies for the traditional sectors in its own country. The LDCs are thus somewhat restricted in their export outlets and driven more upon reliance on domestic growth.

To divide the GATT countries into those whose trade grows more than their production, and those whose production grows more than their trade, divides them into those interested in more integration and those less interested in integration. This distinction does not completely overlap a distinction between developed and developing countries. But it does so sufficiently often, in the circumstances of the 1960s and 1970s, to give meaning for trade policy to the distinction between LDCs and others which GATT embraced in 1965, in accordance with United Nations practice at the time.

Nevertheless, there is risk that this distinction arouses the wrong expectations. Economic structure is not within the competence of GATT and is best left to other agencies. Trade policy is within its competence. Its basic rule is non-discrimination. This means equality, but equality itself can have different meanings in different contexts.

In trade policy, non-discrimination means that there is only one tariff rate in each country for each tariff item. Customs unions are compatible with this definition of non-discrimination, since trade between member countries is classed as domestic trade and there is only one tariff rate per item on foreign trade. If countries' growth of production depends on a greater growth of trade, the principle of non-discrimination has roughly the same meaning for them. Even here there are difficulties, since growth rates differ. For instance, there has been much argument whether the UK should or should not have liberalised trade as much as other industrial countries in the Sixth Round. But this argument is largely about the extension of the meaning of non-discrimination to 'reciprocity'. If all industrial countries are equal under the *general* agreement (non-discrimination), should they or should they not give equal scheduled concessions (reciprocity)? If the answer is that they should, there may even be a case for harmonisation of tariff rates until these ultimately become no more than a toll which is uniformly imposed at all customs frontiers. The argument can be further developed to say that, if countries have different balance of payments performances, and the benefit they derive from trade is thus unequal, they should be allowed to equalise them through variable import surcharges or tariff suspensions. In so far as such arguments occupy legislators and GATT negotiators, they have become arguments about equality of benefits rather than about equality of rights. Equality of rights was the purpose of the GATT principle of non-discrimination. It was recognisable. Once the political decision was taken, it could be administered without further politics. Equality of benefits is always debatable, and its administration always involves trust in statistics and reference to politicians. If 'equality before the GATT' sometimes clashed with equality of benefits for the industrial countries, it was bound to do so even more for the LDCs. The GATT rules suited countries with greater growth of trade than of production. They needed re-interpretation for those countries where this relationship between trade and production could not be taken for granted.

The rule that LDCs need not give any scheduled concessions, in return for any such concessions received, waived reciprocity in tariff negotiations. This was in line with past 'payments' for the acceptance of the *general* agreement and no bending of the general agreement was involved. This cannot be said of the generalised system of preferences which was introduced in the 1970s.

Since the general agreement not to discriminate in trade is an agreement which suits countries whose trade grows faster than their production, a case may be made for bending the rules in favour of countries whose trade would otherwise grow less than their production.

This had already been done in 1955, when the UK was allowed to give tariff preferences to dependent territories in order to subsidise activities which were wholly or largely dependent on the UK market.[85] As long as the preferred supplier was not the only supplier to the country giving the preference, he could get a higher price than his competitors. His production for export was subsidised. By the time the preferred supplier could produce more than the preferential market could absorb, this benefit ceased. By the 1970s, the UK was no longer able to do much this way, since the production of her former dependencies had outgrown her absorptive capacity for most commodities. The EC could help this way, since EC consumption exceeded preferred production of the commodities on which preferences were given. The EC and the other industrial countries introduced generalised preferences on products of interest to all LDCs at various dates between 1971 (EC) and 1976 (US), under a GATT waiver granted for ten years in 1971. In 1975, the EC superimposed a fuller system of preferences to the forty-six countries which signed the Lomé Convention.[86] Where a two-tier system of preferences seemed unacceptable, as in the US, only generalised preferences are given. These are limited to specified quantities on products selected by the giver of the preferences. The quantitative limitation ensures that preferential consumption will always exceed preferred production, so that the preferred producer can get a higher price than non-preferred producers. The same result was ensured in the Lomé Convention which gave unlimited preferences only on products where EC consumption exceeds the overseas associates' production. In either case, there is some subsidisation of production for export and thus a greater chance that LDC trade will grow by more than LDC production. To the extent to which a system of limited generalised preferences can attain this target, LDCs may become more interested in equality before the GATT. A temporary bending of the rules will then have helped towards the attainment of the long-term objectives of the GATT.

Nevertheless, a subsidised increase in trade between industrialised countries and LDCs is more likely to be along the lines of inter-industry specialisation than of intra-industry specialisation. If so, the LDCs' interest in GATT is likely to remain more muted than that of the industrialised countries. The LDCs' development prospects through trade will in any case remain a function of what happens in the industrial world. While the industrial world remains divided into separate tariff areas, and while each of these areas offers its own generalised preferences, the LDCs may be pulled in different directions.[87]

At the time of writing, it is not impossible to visualise a world where the US, the EC and Japan use flexible tariffs and flexible exchange rates as instruments of macro-economic policies for short-term national ends, coupled with preferences to LDCs to subsidise the availability of supplies. This would not be the world of the first six Rounds which was concerned with more equality of rights. At best it would be a world with some rules about how to flout this equality. The outcome of the Seventh and subsequent Rounds should be judged according to whether they can help to avoid such situations by making the international equality of commercial rights more secure. Issues must not be confused. Benefits concern production opportunities and welfare. This must be dealt with by means of investment, fiscal and monetary policies. GATT's concern however is neither more nor less than the equalisation of trading rights. The purpose of general GATT concessions is to give the same rights to all foreign traders, and that of scheduled concessions is to make the rights of foreign traders more like those of domestic ones.

Notes

1. On the functions of the various international economic organisations see J.H. Richards, *International Economic Institutions*, Holt, Rinehart and Winston Ltd., London 1970, especially Chapters 7 and 8.
2. *Report on the Geneva Tariff Negotiations*, Cmd. 7258, 1947, Protocol of Provisional Application of the General Agreement on Tariffs and Trade, I (b) for the original members. *Report on the Annecy Tariff Negotiations*, Cmd. 7792, Protocol of Application, I (a) for acceding members. See also later Protocols.
3. Exchange of Letters, 30 October 1947, Cmd. 7258, Appendix C, paras. 6 and 8.
4. Article XXVIII. See also Gerard Curzon, *Multilateral Commercial Diplomacy*, Michael Joseph, London, 1965, p.115.
5. Article XIX.
6. H.J. Tasca, *The Reciprocal Trade Policy of the United States,* University of Pennsylvania Press, Philadelphia, 1938. See also note 26 to Chapter 3.
7. Wilbur F. Monroe, *International Trade Policy in Transition,* D.C. Heath, London, 1975, p.11.
8. Stanley Hornbeck, *The Most-Favored-Nation Clause in Commercial Treaties,* University of Wisconsin Bulletin, Vol.6, p.342; quoted by R.C. Snyder, *The Most-Favored Nation Clause,* King's Crown Press, New York, 1948, p.211.
9. R.C. Snyder, ibid., p.244.
10. See Chapter 3, Section A3.
11. US Tariff Commission, *Operation of the Trade Agreements Program*, First Report, p.29, and H. Tasca, *Reciprocal Trade Policy,*p.164.
12. US Tariff Commission, ibid., p.29.
13. Richard Kottman, *Reciprocity and the North Atlantic Triangle, 1932-38*, Cornell University Press, Ithaca, N.Y., 1968, e.g. p.121, and H.J. Tasca, *Reciprocal Trade Policy,* e.g. p.53.

14. Ibid.
15. For a recent account of the history of Imperial preference, see Ian M. Drummond, *British Economic Policy and the Empire, 1919-39,* Geo. Allen and Unwin, London 1972. For earlier works, see e.g. F.C. Benham, *Britain under Protection,* Macmillan, London 1940; W.K. Hancock, *Survey of British Commonwealth Affairs*, Vol.II, Oxford University Press, 1940.
16. Cmd. 7258, Appendix C, para. 5; *Canada-West Indies Trade Agreement,* 1925, West Indian 214.
17. *Trade Agreement between the UK and the US, 1938*, Cmd. 5882, Foreword.
18. Cmd. 5882, Articles 2, 21 and 22.
19. Ibid., Schedule I. Note that Part II of that schedule reserves preferential margins for articles with sugar content, and also held out the promise of consideration of a reduction in the tobacco preference on expiry of then current obligations in 1942.
20. Schedule II relating to Newfoundland was the one exception. There were none in Schedule III relating to colonies and protectorates.
21. Cmd. 5882, Articles 7-10 and 15, and Exchange of Notes No.1.
22. US Tariff Commission, *Operation of the Trade Agreements Program*, 1st Report, p.19; and *Historical Statistics of the US*, series U 15-20.
23. Twenty-three countries were represented. They are listed in Cmd. 7258, Appendix A. These countries included two customs unions, Benelux and Syria-Lebanon, so that the number of negotiating units was less than the number of countries.
24. For an example, see pp.91-2 on the changes in the escape clause.
25. US Tariff Commission, *Operation of the Trade Agreements Program,* 25th Report, p.43.
26. Ibid., p.44.
27. US Tariff Commission, *Operation of the Trade Agreements Program,* 19th Report, p.239 puts the average at 35 per cent.
28. Except 1920. See *Historical Statistics of the US*, Series U 15-20.
29. US Tariff Commission, 19th Report, Table 3, p.238. The measure is the value of trade affected.
30. Derived from Cmd. 7258, paras 8-16, and totals of trade in London and Cambridge Economic Service, *The British Economy, Key Statistics,* Table K. Based on trade in 1938.
31. US Tariff Commission, *Operation of the Trade Agreements Program*, 1st Report, p.23. Based on trade in 1939.
32. US Tariff Commission, *Operation of the Trade Agreements Program*, 3rd Report, pp.7-8; 5th Report, p.10; 19th Report, Table 3, p.238. Note that in Table 3 of the 19th Report, there is an arithmetical error in the column relating to US concessions as per cent of imports. On the basis of other information given in that Table, the percentages should read:

First Round	77.9 (and not 77.5)
Second Round	3.5 (and not 0.3)
Third Round	7.2 (and not 0.7)
Fourth Round	7.4 (and not 0.7)
Fifth Round	11.6 (given correctly)
Sixth Round	45.6 (given correctly)

33. For details of UK concessions see *Report on the Annecy Tariff Negotiations,* Cmd. 7792, pp.6 and 8; and *Report on the Torquay Tariff Negotiations,* Cmd. 8228, Section II.
34. G. Curzon, *Multilateral Commercial Diplomacy*, pp.72-3.

35. Ibid., p.74.
36. For details see e.g. Ian M. Drummond, *British Economic Policy*, and Richard N. Kottman, *Reciprocity*.
37. This point was stressed in every Report by H.M. Government on GATT negotiations. See e.g. Cmnd. 3347, para. 52.
38. G. Curzon, *Multilateral Commercial Diplomacy*, p.75.
39. The six other countries were Canada, Denmark, Finland, Italy, Norway and Sweden. Cf. US Tariff Commission, *Operation of the Trade Agreements Program*, 8th Report, pp.84-5.
40. See note 33.
41. See p.103.
42. S.D. Metzger, *Trade Agreements and the Kennedy Round*, p.17, and notes 27 and 33 to the present chapter.
43. The total UK concessions related to 3 per cent of exports, but two-thirds of these were bindings of existing rates. See *Report on the Geneva Tariff Negotiations, 1956*, Cmd. 9779, paras. 5-8 and *Key Statistics*, loc. cit.
44. US Tariff Commission, *Operation of the Trade Agreements Program*, 8th Report, p.85, note 8.
45. *Statement of H.M. Government on the Question of Japan's Accession to the Agreement*, April 1955, Cmd. 9449.
46. European Commission, *9th Report on the Activities of the Communities*, Brussels, 1976, p.219; Gerard and Victoria Curzon, 'The Management of Trade Relations in the GATT, in Andrew Shonfield (ed.), *International Economic Relations in the Western World, 1959-71*, O.U.P. for Royal Institute of International Affairs, 1976, pp.264 and 282 (note 45).
47. See p.99.
48. GATT, *Japan's Economic Expansion and Foreign Trade, 1955 to 1970*, GATT Studies in International Trade, No.2, Geneva 1971, pp.19-22.
49. Ibid. p.9; and Chapter 5, section 2 of this book.
50. See pp.103-4.
51. Provisionally in 1958, permanently in 1962. Cf. *Report on the Geneva Tariff Negotiations, 1960-2*, Cmnd. 1804, Appendix, Final Act, para. 2(e) and Protocol of 16 July 1962.
52. US Tariff Commission, *Operation of the Trade Agreements Program*, 14th Report, pp.45 and 48.
53. GATT Article XXIV (6).
54. Article XXIV (5) (b).
55. Lawrence B. Krause, *European Economic Integration and the United States*, Brookings Institution, Washington 1968, p.51 and footnote.
56. Article XXIV (6).
57. US Tariff Commission, op.cit., p.21.
58. See note 35.
59. S.D. Metzger, *Trade Agreements*, p.17 and Note 32.
60. Cmnd. 1804, paras. 9 and 12.
61. *The Kennedy Round of Tariff Negotiations, 1964-7*, Cmnd. 3347, para. 2.
62. US Tariff Commission, *Operation of the Trade Agreements Program*, 19th Report, p.170. The linear EFTA countries were Austria, Denmark, Finland (an associate), Norway, Sweden and Switzerland. The exception was Portugal.
63. The other intermediate countries were Australia, Czechoslovakia, Greece, Iceland, Israel, Portugal, South Africa, Spain, Yugoslavia. See US Tariff Commission, ibid.
64. Nine of the forty-one started but did not complete negotiations. Thirty-two never participated. Cf. US Tariff Commission, ibid., p.173.
65. G. and V. Curzon, *Management of Trade Relations*, p.183.

66. Ibid., p.185.
67. Ibid. and op. cit. there.
68. See p.114.
69. Cmnd. 3347, para. 10, puts it as 'well over 30 per cent' on industrial goods. The US Tariff Commission, op.cit., p.250, estimated the overall cuts as 36 per cent.
70. Standard International Trade Classification 5-8.
71. US Tariff Commission, op.cit., pp.238-9 (but see Note 32 re Table 3) and Table 4, p.259.
72. Ibid., Table 4: and 8th Report, p.93.
73. Cmnd. 3347, para 16. Weighted by trade.
74. *The Economist*, 19 November 1938, Supplement on the Trade Agreement, p.5. Note that these tariff cuts were on manufactures mainly of interest to the US but they were extended to all countries with most-favoured-foreign-nation rights.
75. For a ranking of products according to the degree of intra-industry specialisation, see Herbert G. Grubel and P.J. Lloyd, *Intra-Industry Trade*, London, Macmillan, 1975, Tables 3.1 and 3.2. For details of tariff cuts, see US Tariff Commission, op.cit., 19th Report, pp.249-63, and Cmnd. 3347, paras 10-26.
76. On ASP and textiles, see pp.86-7.
77. US Tariff Commission, op.cit., p.250.
78. See pp. 98-103. There is a possibility of an orderly marketing agreement on steel between the US and Japan, coupled with US quotas on imports from other sources, at the time of writing.
79. Contracting Parties to the GATT; *Introduction of Part IV of the General Agreement*, Basic Instruments and Selected Documents, Thirteenth Supplement, Second Special Session of the Twenty-second Session, Geneva, July, 1965.
80. Article XXXVI (8).
81. Article XXVII (1) (a).
82. Articles XXXVI (6) and (7), and XXXVIII (2) (b) mention international lending agencies, agencies of the UN, and UN Conference on Trade and Development.
83. Articles I and XXXVI.
84. On such issues, see e.g. David Robertson, 'Multilateral Trade Negotiations', *National Westminster Bank Quarterly Review*, February 1973.
85. Cmd. 9413, Document 4, paras. 1 (a) and 2 (a).
86. ACP-EEC Convention of Lomé, Cmnd. 6220, 1975.
87. For a detailed summary of preferences in force in 1975, cf. Bettina Hürni: 'Die bestehenden Systeme von Präferenzzöllen zugunsten von Entwicklungsländern', *Aussenwirtschaft*, June 1975.

5 THE RESPONSE: EUROPEAN COMMUNITIES; JAPAN; PRIMARY PRODUCERS

1. The European Communities

(i) The Levels of Rights

Not content with most-favoured-nation rights, Europeans* carried the search for equality a stage further. By mid-1977, trade within Europe was free of tariffs, European enterprises could establish themselves and Europeans could be employed anywhere in the EC area. If this has not made Europeans equally at home anywhere in the EC, it has at any rate made them each other's equals in every EC country.

In its early phase, European integration was largely a response to US initiatives. GATT, dating from 1947, was intended to lead to a world of non-discriminatory trading but Europe's war-ravaged economies were then in no position to trade much. US financial aid was offered and accepted. At the European end, it was administered by the Organisation for European Economic Co-operation (OEEC). This consisted of representatives of seventeen European governments and started operations in 1948. Its immediate task was to allocate US funds to assist the growth of European production. In order to avoid wasteful duplication, some arrangements had to be made to facilitate trade between the aided countries. At the time, quantitative controls of trade were so widespread in Europe that any tariff concessions negotiated under GATT were of secondary importance. OEEC dealt with the problem by gradually freeing trade between aided countries from quantitative controls. When recovery had gone far enough that Europe could face US competition, trade with non-European countries was also freed from such controls. By the end of the 1950s, most trades in industrial goods were liberalised in this way. OEEC's task was done.[1]

OEEC had led from aiding production to the liberalisation of trade. It was in the latter field that it was to leave its most enduring mark. For through liberalising intra-European trade first, it established the principle of the priority of European over international rights in Europe. During the OEEC phase, this was a priority in time and not yet

* Throughout this chapter, 'Europeans' means nationals of EC countries and European countries associated with EC in the 1970s.

a priority of a permanent nature. What was first given to Europe was subsequently given to all. When that was done, European countries' trade restrictions were mainly by tariff, as in the US. Since GATT rules allowed for only two levels of rights, the choice was either to let European trading rights relapse to the level of international rights or raise them to the level of national ones. Europe chose the latter. Tariffs were removed on intra-European trade. Although the 10 per cent tariff reductions made in 1959 were extended to all most-favoured nations, this was not repeated. What was given to all in that year, was subsequently given to Europeans only. This phase of intra-European tariff reductions lasted until 1977, when tariffs ceased between the nine countries of the enlarged Community. During this phase, trade policy led. Effects on production and production policies followed.

This approach had been preceded by Benelux, a customs union between Belgium, the Netherlands and Luxembourg, which came into operation in 1948. Ten years later, the three countries were ready to sign a treaty of economic union,[2] though this was overtaken by the formation of the European Economic Community (EEC). Its significance was mainly that it pointed the way towards the trade-led integration which was to be the most effective form of integration in the post-war period. So far in this book, the term integration has been consistently used in this sense. Unless qualified, it will contintue to be so used. But it will have to be qualified in relation to various attempts at Europe-building. The original OEEC idea of leading through production to trade continues to have its adherents. That idea's most important manifestation to date has been functional integration.

This was attempted in the European Coal and Steel Community (ECSC) which came into operation in 1952, the European Atomic Energy Community (Euratom) which came into force at the same time as EEC, and later in some of the activities of the EEC of which the Common Customs Tariff and the Common Agricultural Policy (CAP) have attracted most attention. Although each of the functional integration schemes included provision for the establishment of a common market, this was not their sole or major point. The main purpose of Euratom was to promote research and ensure the dissemination of technical information.[3] ECSC was also concerned with research, but the emphasis was on common rules of competition. There was also provision for intervention in quantities of production and, on occasions, in prices.[4] In CAP, an attempt was made to simulate a price competitive market. In such a market the interaction of demand

and supply determines price, and price determines consumption and production. CAP prices are determined by political considerations and in the hope that this will result in politically acceptable effects on consumption and production. In case the hope does not materialise, there is provision for direct intervention in the market and for subsidisation. Although it has sometimes favoured consumers,[5] the principal purpose was to regulate production. In general, functional integration means common rules of production to which trade must adjust itself. Any internal integration which may result is production-led.

Inevitably this somewhat confuses the issue of the level of rights. Functional integration establishes special internal rights for certain sectors. Because this internal discrimination is by activity and not by nationality, it is still possible to have one level of European rights and another for most-favoured-nation rights for each product. The GATT rule of non-discrimination between most-favoured nations can be adhered to. But, as will be shown in subsection (ii) (c), some forms of functional integration can make it virtually impossible to negotiate any narrowing between European and most-favoured-nation rights.

The Common Customs Tariff has some of the characteristics of functional integration. It separates EC production conditions from those elsewhere. Through giving different rates of protection to different items, it creates a number of different levels of internal rights. At the time of its introduction, the expectation was that internal free trade would lead to the equalisation of product prices within EC. A distinctive common price level would emerge for each product within EC, different from that without. The external tariff would ensure the separation of EC prices from those elsewhere. Had this expectation been fulfilled, there would have been a kind of functional integration for every product. The tariff could then have been described as a form of functional integration. Nevertheless, the description does not altogether fit. There were no rules of production written into the tariff. Protection was given to so many items that no clear special rights emerged. The differences in the rates of protection given to individual items were less marked than those in much of pre-war tariff legislation. Above all, there appears to have been no equalisation of product prices in the EC. Instead there came differentiation in production. In other words, instead of trade adjusting itself to the prices of the lowest cost producer of given products, production was adjusted to the demands of trade and there was no discernible effect on prices. This point will be considered at greater length in section (iii) (e). Here let it suffice to say that internal integration was largely trade-led. Externally, the Common Customs Tariff was used as an instrument of bargaining in GATT negotiations, and these narrowed the difference between European and most-favoured-nation rights. Through internal free trade and external tariff reductions, the Common Customs Tariff was effectively used as an instrument of trade-led integration.

When the EEC, ECSC and Euratom were merged into one organisation, the European Communities (EC), in 1967, the new organisation comprised elements of trade-led and functional integration policies. Of the three constituent Communities, EEC was the most influential. Its trade-led integration policies covered virtually all tradeable industrial activities, where no functional integration stood in the way. Moreover, although the Treaty of Rome which established the EEC[6] provided for rules of production as well as for trade, it was specific on how trade within the Community was to be freed but left implementation of the production rules to be worked out later and separate from the tariff. Some of the problems of relating rules of trade and production will be considered later in this chapter. Here let it suffice to say that the EC owes much of its influence to the trade-led integration of the EEC.*

The principal instrument of the EC's trade-led integration policy was the Common Customs Tariff, which could be used that way as long as functional integration was largely confined to non-industrial activities. Externally, the tariff enabled the EC to take some international initiatives. The creation of a common market with a common tariff was in itself an international initiative. It gave Europeans trading rights they never had before, and more than the US Administration could offer under the legislation then in force. So as not to lose influence over the move towards freer world trade, the US offered further negotiations in the Trade Agreements Extension Act of 1958 and the Trade Expansion Act of 1962. These would narrow the difference between national and international trading rights in the US, and between European and international trading rights in EC. In the early 1960s, the enlargement of the EC to include the UK was under negotiation, and the US offered complete tariff-free trade in industrial goods in which the US and the enlarged EC together would account for most of world trade. Had this become effective, the

* Strictly speaking, all references to events before 1967 should use the letters EEC, and all references after that date EC. For the sake of convenience, EC will be used throughout the remainder of this chapter.

priority of European over international rights in Europe would have been a mere priority in time, as during the OEEC phase, and European integration would have been a stepping stone towards a North Atlantic free trade area. Any further move towards European integration would have been confined to functional integration. As it was, trade-led integration in industrial products continued to go further in Europe than internationally. But the difference between national (or European) and international trading rights was further narrowed in GATT negotiations. When the enlargement of the EC did materialise in the 1970s, the US responded with a further offer of negotiations under the terms of her Trade Act of 1974, although this did not repeat the free trade offer. Thus, as long as EC could offer Europeans more rights than they could get elsewhere, EC gained an initiative in shaping the *Pax Americana* towards a *Pax Atlantica.* Through giving Europeans more than GATT rights, it created a demand for more GATT rights. During the OEEC phase, Europe just responded to US initiatives. During the second phase of integration, EC-US relations became a dialogue.

EC gained this influence partly because of the commercial importance of the member states. Smaller customs unions of the post-war period, such as the Central American Common Market, could not exert more than local influence. But at least as important as EC's economic size was that the Common Customs Tariff clearly delineated the difference between European and most-favoured-nation rights. The difference was definable and, therefore, negotiable. Although a free trade area also equates area rights with national ones and the effects on trade may be no less favourable,[7] it makes no such clear distinction between the two levels of rights.

For instance, the European Free Trade Association (EFTA) was formed in 1959,[8] comprising seven European countries which did not then join the EC. Like the EC, EFTA conformed to the GATT rule that there should be only two levels of trading rights in each country. In EFTA, this was done through exempting intra-area trade in industrial goods from national tariffs. The latter continued to be applied to non-area trade. The outside world accepted EFTA but, on the whole, did not respond to it. One reason may have been that the value of EFTA trade was only about two-thirds of the value of EC trade, but this still was a sizeable amount of trade. More important was the absence of a common external tariff. Although there were only two levels of trading rights within each EFTA country, there were as many national and most-favoured-nation rights in EFTA as there were

EFTA countries. There was no clear delineation between EFTA and most-favoured-nation rights. Trade negotiations continued to be in the hands of individual governments. EFTA never became a negotiating unit. It did not aspire to become one. There was no need to respond to EFTA.

The main difference between EC and EFTA was that EC became an international negotiating identity and EFTA did not. This does not mean to say that EFTA limped behind EC in all respects. As far as the freeing of trade was concerned, EFTA led to somewhat quicker results. Formed only two years after the signature of the Treaty of Rome, EFTA started to reduce tariffs a year later than EC and completed it a year earlier.[9] EFTA concentrated on this one issue. No time was spent on writing a new tariff. Functional integration was not attempted. The special problems of agriculture were, as far as possible, dealt with through bilateral trade agreements.[10] Where no such agreements were concluded, national agricultural policies continued as before. The free movement of workers and the right of the establishment were recognised as essential if free trade was not to be frustrated. But these were rights to be applied for and granted by national authorities, and not automatic rights as in EC.[11] Restrictive practices were to be dealt with as and when necessary. There was no attempt to write common rules of competition.[12] Day-to-day administration was entrusted to a GATT-style Secretariat. But there was provision for political directive by the Council of Ministers, as in EC. In the event the EFTA Council appears to have been most effective when it came to the acceleration of tariff reductions and the admission to associated membership of a few countries which also sought European free trade without loss of national negotiating identity.[13] Given the target of regional free trade, the EFTA approach was simpler. Nevertheless in the 1970s EC carried the day. EFTA countries either joined EC or became associated with it. Through the clear delineation of European rights, EC became a negotiating unit and so could exert more influence over the course of international economic relations than a free trade area can do. EC had acquired an identity. Or, to use international jargon, EC had become an instrumentality.

(ii) Integration and Harmonisation

(a) Integration Effects. By the mid-1970s, EC had an identity but not yet a personality. Externally, EC was recognised as a negotiating unit by countries to whom tariffs mattered as a means of delineating

the levels of rights, such as the US and Japan, though still largely ignored by countries which controlled trade by other means, such as the USSR. Internally, the existence of EC seemed assured through votes cast in national parliaments and in referenda – even if few could have defined what precisely Europe meant to them. At the risk of some over-simplification it may be said that its external relations gave EC its identity, but only internal developments can give it the character of a distinctive personality. At the risk of still further oversimplification, it may be added that the internal developments must be such as to improve the opportunities of production of goods and services.

Trade-led integration policies are at an end when the last trade barriers have been removed. Integration effects may continue, but the policy impetus may be lost unless there are opportunities for widening the area of integration. At the time of writing, several Mediterranean countries are queueing up for admission. They are European and so have a right to negotiate for admission, though not an automatic right to admission.[14] They are not yet as industrialised as present members. Thus, their joining will probably open opportunities for inter-industry rather than intra-industry specialisation between their industries and those of present members. They will also have to adjust their agriculture to the requirements of CAP. The immediate prospects for further intra-industry specialisation seem greatest between the EC of Nine and the US and Japan.

Here economic and political realities diverge. Non-European powers have no right to negotiate admission under the Treaty of Rome. Complete free trade between EC and non-members would mean the end of the EC customs union. EC would lose its identity. EC-US-Japan relations remain a GATT issue. Success in GATT can still further technological opportunities and failure might drive Europe inwards. But as long as the GATT achievements are not reversed, and as long as free trade within EC continues, integration effects can continue even when the original integration policies are over.

Free trade normally leads to more trade, and more trade leads to trade-induced effects on production. Where production techniques are given, these effects are thought to be predictable on the basis of investigations into relative costs in member countries.[15] Predictable or not, they can last for only a few years. Subsequently, production and trade may settle at somewhat higher levels than before, but the integration effects on growth are over. The result may include a shift in the location of production from higher cost to lower cost areas, without any change in the nature of production. Had European integration led to such results and no others, Europe would have enjoyed once and for all trade gains but its character would have been left unchanged. But where production techniques are not given, an increase in trading opportunities can alter the character of European production. There can be fuller utilisation of the opportunities provided by industrial innovations which would not pay so well in more restricted markets. There can be increased interdependence. As long as both free trade and technological innovations continue, there need be no time limit to integration effects.[16] Integration effects can outlast integration policies for as long as new increasing returns activities are possible.

(b) Equality of Opportunities over Time. Integration policies lead to equality of rights and integration to more opportunities. What happens to opportunities may be uneven over time or between sectors and between countries. For instance, equality of trading rights can more easily lead to new production opportunities in times of prosperity than in times of depression. Although the Treaty of Rome recognised the possibility of cyclical disturbances, it had no more to say on the subject than that this would be a matter for common concern.[17]

When the depression came, in the 1970s, the EC Commission found itself in a position resembling that of national Departments of Trade. It was concerned. It could expect to be consulted. But the major economic policy weapons used at the time to combat the depression were fiscal and monetary, and these were firmly in the hands of the national authorities. EC had few independent sources of revenue and blueprints for monetary integration were shelved. EC's authority did not go much beyond integration policies. These were under strain.

In times of depression, fewer new production opportunities could be taken. Hence, the free trade between the original six members and the freeing of trade with the three new members could not lead to the hoped for integration effects on production. Now, an integration policy which is not followed by production effects, is an external affairs policy in danger of losing domestic support. If it was argued in Chapter 1 that domestic growth without appropriate growth of trade puts undue pressure on world resources and sours international economic relations, it is equally true that a growth of trade without appropriate domestic economic growth also has its risks. In short, the target of integration policy should be to ensure a situation where trade leads production *and* production can follow trade. The latter condition is lacking in times of depression. Neither EC nor GATT nor any other instrument of integration policy could cope with this problem. Their chief task was to survive until economic recovery came. They did.

(c) Equality of Opportunities Between Sectors through Protection for Producers. Although not endowed with powers to deal with differences in production opportunities over time, functional integration schemes give EC clearly defined powers to influence some sectors' production opportunities relative to others. These schemes have some common features. Invariably they give special protection which is administered by special agencies. Euratom was an attempt to hasten the arrival of the nuclear age before the market was ready for it. But Euratom was too starved of funds to be as effective as may have been hoped.[18] ECSC and CAP set out to regulate production of traditional activities which cannot easily adjust themselves to changing market conditions. Whether this was done mainly through intervention in quantities (ECSC) or prices (CAP), the intention was to protect producers from the vagaries of the market. It may be that in the absence of common protection, cartels would have re-emerged in steel and national protection would have continued in coal and agriculture. Whatever the economic merits of the case, at least some European governments would not have agreed to a common free trade market in industrial goods without common protected markets for agriculture, coal and steel. The practical policy issue was not whether these activities should be protected but how they should be protected. The result was that these three groups received special treatment. In effect, agriculture, coal and steel receive internal protection relative to other activities. Whether this does or does not exactly compensate them for their special adjustment problems, is another question.

Once there is internal protection, it is unlikely that free competition from abroad will be tolerated. In the case of agriculture, EC member governments were not even content to leave protection from outside competition to the Common Customs Tariff. They added a levy system which, in effect, is a second and more impenetrable tariff wall. CAP regulations lay down minimum import prices, usually known as threshold or sluice-gate prices. If a consignment is offered at a price below the relevant threshold price, EC imposed a levy equal to the difference between the offer and the threshold price. The purpose is producer protection which is further assured through internal intervention.* The threshold prices are negotiated between member governments and can be revised each year. Thus the levy system is internally negotiable. In this sense, it is flexible. It is also variable since the incidence varies from consignment to consignment. Altogether it is one of those tariff systems which is considered a domestic issue, of which outsiders are not expected to complain as long as it is non-discriminatory.[20] The claim of non-discrimination can be upheld as long as all imports are treated alike irrespective of origin. Nevertheless, outsiders are faced with a second tariff which is virtually non-negotiable as far as they are concerned. True, tariff rates on agricultural commodities in the Common Customs Tariff can be bound or reduced in trade negotiations. But this has little meaning when the appropriate threshold prices can be raised autonomously.

The CAP levy system has more in common with the sort of thinking which lay behind US tariff legislation of the 1920s than with trade-led integration. One possible interpretation is that CAP-assisted structural reorganisation of EC agriculture will eventually make it more adjustable to changing market conditions and less dependent on protection. If so, CAP may move slowly towards production-led integration and later to trade-led integration, the way OEEC did quickly in relation to industrial goods. This is an idealistic long-run interpretation. It does not fit the performance of CAP during its first ten years, and least of all its attitude towards trade with non-members. Although trade between EC countries was encouraged, national self-sufficiencies increased, and trade with non-members was discouraged. Agricultural production was to be protected as it was or as it might respond to internally decided measures. There could be no response to external trade. Whatever the case for and against this particular form of

---

* Although details vary from commodity to commodity, the general object of intervention is to limit price fluctuations to a range between certain maximum and minimum levels. The idea was not EC's. It was tried in International Wheat Agreements in the 1950s. The EC variant of this method of price control works roughly as follows. The threshold price is related to, but not identical with, an internal target or guide price. There is also an intervention price which is fixed at a lower level. If the market price rises above the threshold price, imports should keep the price down to that level – though they have not always done so. If the market price falls below the intervention price, national agencies in EC are instructed to accumulate stock, though they can do this only if storage facilities are available. When stocks cannot be increased or are likely to deteriorate, the surpluses are disposed of in world markets at whatever prices they can fetch. EC finances the loss. Sums earmarked for this purpose cannot be allocated to structural reorganisation of agriculture, which should be the second major form of intervention and be financed out of the proceeds of the levies.[19]

protection may have been when it came into operation in 1967, it could not lead to trade-led integration with the outside world. CAP may have given EC some personality but rather a withdrawn one, to which there could be no response.

This contrasts with the EC's more friendly traits in most industrial trade. In fairness, it should be added that this was no special feature of EC. No major country allowed trade-led integration in agriculture during the third quarter of the century. At the risk of some repetition of points made in Chapter 1, a few words about the difference in attitude towards agriculture and manufacturing industry may not be out of place in the present context.

One major reason for this difference in attitudes was that the technological progress of the time affected manufacturing and agriculture in different ways. Technological progress in manufacturing frequently led to opportunities for intra-industry specialisation, with production under increasing returns conditions of products with a short market life. When trade became freer, such opportunities could be taken. The result was trade-led integration, where trade grows more than the production of manufactures and encourages the growth of production of manufactures. The same opportunities are not open to trade in agricultural commodities. There are limits to such trade. Its growth cannot for long exceed the growth of manufacturing. Agricultural basic materials are wanted mainly by manufacturing industries. The volume of trade in such materials thus cannot for long exceed the growth of the relevant manufacturing industries. If the latter find ways of saving on materials, the trade in such materials grows correspondingly less. Demand for internationally traded food tends to grow with increases in urban populations. This too is largely tied to the growth of manufacturing. In short, trade in agricultural commodities cannot exceed the growth of manufacturing. Moreover, the market life of agricultural and other primary products is still unlimited as far as one can see. Technological progress then means more production of the same goods, and possibly more standardised and gradeable products. Decreasing returns on capital employed can be staved off but never averted. Agricultural trade is limited by the demand restraint of the growth of manufacturing and the supply restraint of decreasing returns. As shown in Chapter 1, it would be best integrated through free markets, but that would leave it behind manufacturing which has reached a higher stage of integration. If manufacturing responds to trade-led integration and agricultural production were left to respond to a competitive free market economy, agriculture would limp behind. There might then not be enough food for industrial areas. Intervention is necessary unless and until it becomes possible to gear agricultural production more closely to particular uses and users.

Agriculture is an extreme case. At the other extreme are the manufacturing activities which can most easily adjust themselves to trade-led integration. In between are numerous manufacturing and mining activities with varying abilities to adjust themselves. Coal and steel came low in that ability. But when coal and steel first came under the aegis of the High Authority established under the ECSC treaty in 1951, these two activities were thought of as commanding heights of the economies of member states. The treaty could then be seen as an exercise in European peacemaking through the fusion of essential interests.[21] In the first few years of ECSC both coal and steel were growth activities. The political aspiration seemed supported by economic events. But from the mid-1950s until the energy crisis of the 1970s, the demand for coal was adversely affected by the increasing availability of other sources of energy. The High Authority found itself engaged in organising an orderly retreat from coal through organising job creation schemes in coal mining areas, authorising national subsidies and the like.[22] Only in the mid-1970s were attempts made to halt the decline and assist the stabilisation (but not an increase) in coal production for the next ten years.[23] In steel, output doubled in the 1950s, but the industry began to face problems of excess capacity in the 1960s and suffered more than most during the depression of the 1970s. The EC response was largely to control output. In retrospect, the ECSC part of EC has turned out to be mainly protectionist. But it was less protectionist than CAP. Tariff rates on ECSC products were negotiable. Although there was secondary protection through internal intervention, there was no impenetrable second tariff. There were also significant differences in the way the two were financed. ECSC received its finance from levies on producers as well as through borrowing and grants from member governments, so that it contained an element of self-help.[24] CAP finance depended on import levies which were imposed to raise market prices and contributions of member governments. Others paid for CAP. ECSC and CAP were the only forms of functional integration entrusted to EC, though EC became party to the various international textile arrangements of the 1960s and 1970s.[25] This was a form of quota protection, where member states' quotas of the 1960s became EC quotas in the 1970s.[26] But here EC acted in its purely international role. There was no problem of a common financial burden. All costly aids were left to member states, and EC's task was confined to supervision, ensuring that any such aids did not frustrate intra-EC free trade. That was part of the policy of harmonisation where, at least to date, production rules were subordinate to trade-led integration. This will be considered in the next subsection. Here we examine what functional integration can achieve.

Suppose it is true that agriculture is less adjustable than coal and steel, and the latter less adjustable than textiles, and textiles less so than activities which receive only tariff protection or none. If so, the relative degrees of protection given to those various activities were at any rate in the right order. This neither condones nor condemns any of the details. These were worked out separately and at different rates for each of the three protected groups. So far there does not seem to have been any attempt to agree on the economic circumstances in which special protection is to be given for a time, instead of giving permanent special treatment to a few. Should the latter attitude continue, common EC policies for a few specially selected activities would lead to new forms of discrimination. In place of discrimination by nationality would emerge discrimination between activities.[27]

(d) Equalisation of Opportunities through Harmonisation. Integration means change and therefore the disturbance of the existing state of affairs. Where integration policy goes only some of the way, as in GATT, any unforeseen unfavourable effects can be corrected through renegotiation of trade concessions. Where integration policy goes all the way, as in EC, there can be no renegotiation once the trade barriers are down. Any corrective mechanism becomes an issue of internal policy. Although the risk of widely different effects on production is minimised as long as only countries with similar economies are in EC, some divergences in production effects are bound to occur. This becomes more likely when member states have different commercial laws, pursue independent fiscal and monetary policies, or simply when they interpret Community policies in different ways. EC's corrective mechanism is known as harmonisation. How far this should go is EC's major internal policy issue.

Some hold the view that harmonisation should be a mere corrective, to be used only when the freeing of trade from customs duties does not by itself lead to one market area. For instance, as late as the mid-1970s, when the Common Customs Tariff had been applied to the external trade of the original six members for more than a decade and a half, there were still differences in customs laws and procedures of the member countries. It still mattered into which member country goods from outside EC were first imported since the common rules were sometimes differently interpreted by the various national customs authorities. Internal controls of intra-EC trade continued. If the main reason was that agricultural trade was subject to monetary compensation at internal frontiers in order to ensure a common price level in the face of fluctuating exchange rates, the result was that all trade could be held up at those frontiers. Even if it were not for the complexities of CAP and all trade were in industrial goods, as long as member countries want to collect national trade statistics, the customs posts remain. Since these posts are administered nationally, differences in law and procedures continue. Despite progress towards the harmonisation of internal controls and procedures, the Commission's report for 1975 includes the statement that 'it is high time the customs union became fully established'.[28] Can this be achieved until there is a common customs service and the internal customs posts disappear? Would the loss of statistics outweigh the gain of undisturbed trade?

To others, including the EC Commission, harmonisation means more than the tidying up of administrative problems created by integration policies. At one time, the Commission expressed the view that there should be 'a single market having the characteristics of a domestic market'.[29] If this meant that Europeans were to be equally at home anywhere in EC, rules relating to production conditions had to be harmonised. The question remains how much harmonisation is necessary for that purpose. In 1973, the Commission wrote that 'laws are only aligned when essential to the creation of the common internal market: and then only to the degree necessary to fulfil that goal.'[30] Two years later it wrote that 'there seems to be no reason for applying different rules to identical or similar situations in the absence of special circumstances'.[31] Although written with special reference to company law, it could just as well have been written with reference to patent rights, competition policy and virtually anything which affects production opportunities. Such harmonisation may be an aid to integration. But carried to the extreme of establishing uniformity for its own sake, it goes beyond the requirements of trade-led integration and may even impede it.

Not surprisingly, there is much controversy about how far integration should go. Trade-led integration depends on the removal of restraints. Because it prevents national governments from discriminating between Europeans, this is sometimes referred to as negative integration.[32] If everything is negative that limits the actions of governments, the description is correct. But, without wishing to enter into a terminological dispute, it seems only fair to add that without compliance with the European Commandment not to steal fellow Europeans' profits or wages, trade-led integration could not become effective. If this is negative, then positive integration would be the power to enforce specific common rules which prescribe how exactly economic affairs are to be conducted. Here again, national governments are restrained. Only in this case, the relevant authority is delegated to EC. The extreme examples of this approach to date are to be found in functional integration. In between these two extremes there is a range of interventions which are designed mainly to ensure that the increased opportunities of trade-led integration are neither frustrated nor abused.

Seen this way, the purpose of harmonisation is to make trade-led integration work. The effects on commercial activities can be positive or negative, and the net result will vary from case to case. For instance, the removal of technical barriers to trade, such as different national safety standards for motor cars, means that some national governments' incompatible positive laws must be altered or altogether removed. In consequence, there can be more commercial activities. National governments have however been somewhat reluctant to alter their laws. In the mid-1970s, the Commission reported an average time lag of four years between the issue of its directives on safety standards to the member governments and implementation by those governments in their own ways.[33] This does not take account of the time taken to prepare the directives and to have them approved by the European Parliament. Whether through frustration or excessive zeal, the Commission sometimes carried harmonisation rather far. Could not trade associations or municipalities concern themselves with the safety of electrically operated lifts and could not the definition of marmalade be left to housewives?[34]

Technical barriers to trade were not the only obstacles to trade which were left after the removal of tariffs. Other obstacles to a truly common market were met in a variety of ways. Amongst the most notable were the gradual emergence of a common policy relating to competition between firms, the elaboration of a European company law, the establishment of a European Patents Office, and much else down to the mutual recognition of medical and law degrees taken in European universities.[35] The last mentioned is a clear indication that Community law had become an important subject. Altogether, once the economic arguments for removing trade barriers had carried the day within the European context, the lawyers moved in. They nibbled at incompatible national laws. When they had done so long enough, a body of Community law emerged.

With the final removal of tariff barriers amongst the Nine in 1977, trade-led integration effects need not cease but the policy impetus will be lost unless integration policies can be pursued in other spheres. Any internal policies are almost inevitably production-led, at least in the initial stages. They involve expenditure, if only to supervise the way they work. It is therefore not just coincidence that the Treaty provisions for direct elections to a European Parliament were activated around that time.[36] However circumscribed the powers of that Parliament may be,[37] it will at least be able to supervise the Commission's expenditure which is financed out of the latter's 'own resources'. In 1977, these consisted of customs duties and levies. From 1978, this should also include a share of value added tax imposed in member countries.[38] Should the Parliament want to extend EC activities into fields such as regional and social policies, while member governments do not wish to make a contribution, there will be a temptation to raise levies, which can be done without breach of current trade agreements, and import duties when current trade agreements expire. Although to date GATT agreements have been extended though sometimes renegotiated before expiry, they are for three years at a time. They could be denounced.[39] Whether such temptation will be resisted is likely to depend on the relative priority attached to the trade-led integration effects of past policies and new policies pursued for internal reasons. The temptation will however remain strong as long as EC depends on a limited number of indirect taxes.

Even limited fiscal policies are bound to have some impact on the monetary situation. It thus seems likely that the moment EC pursues an active fiscal policy, proposals for monetary integration will become more immediately relevant than when they were first mooted.[40] Like fiscal integration, monetary integration would be initially an internal issue. But, unlike fiscal integration, it would soon have direct international implications and affect relations with the outside world. Once there is one set of monetary rules applicable within EC and another for the exchange of the European currency into other currencies, discrimination between the various non-member countries can be avoided as long as there are two (and only two) clearly defined levels of rights. For Europeans the new level of rights must be 'net rights.'[41] Otherwise they will not support the change from national to European rights. For non-Europeans, their level of rights must be negotiable. Otherwise they will resent the change. If these conditions are satisfied, new European rights can be created beyond the present commercial rights, and they may have to be created if, for instance, trading rights are not to be frustrated through exchange controls and exchange depreciations. The policy impetus can then be maintained without risk of worsening international relations. As the number of policies increases, the need to harmonise them also increases. But this will be harmonisation of several new rights rather than the harmonisation of one new right with a multitude of national rules.

(iii) Expectation and Performance

(a) Interdependence. Whatever EC's future, to date it has left its mark mainly in trade. From the time of its formation in 1958 until 1972, the trade between the six members (intra-EC trade) grew at an annual rate of 15 per cent and their trade with the outside world (extra-EC trade) at an annual rate of 8½ per cent. Since world trade also grew at an annual rate of 8½ per cent and world trade includes EC trade, the EC countries made a more than appropriate contribution to the growth of trade.[42] Subsequent developments were complicated by the enlargement of the EC, which meant a period of tariff reductions between old and new members from 1973 to 1977, when trade between the old members was already tariff-free, and amongst the new members Denmark and the UK were already in a free trade area while Ireland and the UK were in the process of forming one. This alone would make the interpretation of trade developments difficult until 1978, when the transition period is scheduled to be over. Moreover, all this was overshadowed by the world depression. For what the data to 1975 are worth, they suggest the following. By value, world trade grew sharply in 1973 and 1974 but only moderately in 1975. By volume, its growth was marked in 1973, moderate in 1974 and negative in 1975. Against this background, EC trade of the Nine grew at about the same rate as world trade in 1973 but less in 1974 and 1975. Extra-EC trade grew somewhat less than intra-EC trade in 1973, but more in the following two years. In 1975, intra-EC trade fell slightly by value and more so by volume, the first setback in the growth of intra-EC trade since 1967 and the first marked one

during the life of EC. The setback must not be exaggerated. In 1972 and 1973, intra-EC trade of the Nine accounted for 52 per cent of EC trade. In the next two years it was still 49 per cent and this proportion started to rise again in 1975.[43]

The growth of trade, however substantial, is not an adequate indication of the EC countries' contribution towards world interdependence. Clear results emerge where the growth of trade is related to the growth of gross domestic production. This relationship is known as 'trade ratio.'[44] In 1960, the trade ratio of intra-EC trade of the Six came to 5.4 per cent for both imports and exports. Then it rose each year, except in 1967, to reach 9.4 per cent for imports and 9.5 per cent for exports in 1972. The most marked[45] increases occurred in 1968 and 1969, which was at or just after the end of the transition period. There were no marked divergences between the import and export trade ratios in any year. This continued even during the depression. The intra-trade ratios reached slightly over 11 per cent in 1974. Although there was a setback to 10 per cent in 1975, it was still above 1973 or earlier levels.[46] All this suggested substantial trade creation in EC.

The trade ratios for the extra-EC trade of the Six fell from 10.3 per cent in 1960 to 8.8 per cent for imports and 9.5 per cent for exports in 1972. This indicates trade diversion in extra-EC trade. It will be noted that less trade diversion is indicated in extra-EC trade than the trade creation noted in intra-EC trade. There were further differences between developments in extra- and intra-EC trade. Extra-EC trade fluctuated more, and this was more noticeable in exports than in imports.[47] If these fluctuations are smoothed out,[48] a steady movement towards greater intra-EC interdependence is confirmed, but the conclusions relating to the somewhat reduced interdependence with the outside world must be modified. The trade ratio in extra-EC imports fell until the mid-1960s and then stabilised.[49] It would seem that the trade diversion effects were largely over by the end of the transition period. In extra-EC exports, trade diversion seems to have been most marked in the early 1960s. From the mid-1960s onwards, the extra-EC trade ratio rose again and in the second half of the decade was higher than at the beginning.[50]

The general experience of outside suppliers to EC was shared by the three countries which were to accede in 1973. The EC import ratio for their goods fell from 1.4 per cent in 1960 to 1.2 per cent in 1963. It recovered to around 1.3 per cent by 1965 and then stayed at that level until 1971. Subsequently it rose to 1.9 per cent in 1974, and even during the setback of 1975 was 1.7 per cent. By then however the three countries had acceded and it seems best to consider the Europe of the Nine. In 1972, the last year before the three countries' accession, the intra-EC trade ratios of the Six and the Nine were sufficiently close so as not to break the continuity of the argument.[51] Both intra-trade ratios of the Nine were at 9.6 per cent in 1972. Both rose to 12 per cent in 1974. In 1975 they were still 11 per cent despite the trade depression of that year. The extra-EC imports trade ratios of the Six and the Nine were also close at around 8.8 per cent in 1972. By 1974, that ratio had risen to around 13½ per cent and then fell back to 11½ per cent in 1975. This indicates that EC trade suffered more outside than inside EC, but even intra-EC imports had a worse setback than EC gross domestic product. In extra-EC exports, where the Six had a 9.5 per cent trade ratio in 1972, the Nine had one of only 8.8, and the Six continued to have a higher extra-EC export ratio than the Nine. The setback of the Nine in 1975 was however less marked in extra-EC exports than in imports.[52] While it is too early to assess the effects of the trade depression, it is possible to say that the setback to EC interdependence in 1975 was not so severe as to offset earlier increases in interdependence. This applies to the Nine since 1972 as well as to the Six. Further, since a growth of intra-EC trade ratios can be taken as an indication of increased interdependence and the extra-EC trade ratios did not fall proportionately and recovered, the net effects of EC to date were to increase international interdependence.

(b) Trade Creation and Trade Diversion. The increases in member countries' interdependence vindicated the faith of the founders of the European Communities in economic integration as a tool of peace-making,[53] but it seems to have surprised some economists. When the subject was first mooted as a serious policy issue in post-war Europe, the freeing of trade was still discussed in terms of inter-industry specialisation. The GATT tariff negotiations of the time were conducted with this end in mind.[54] A customs union which carried tariff reductions to their logical conclusion through tariff elimination within one area, was analysed in similar terms. The most influential writing on the subject, at that time, explained customs union in terms of the re-location of industries.[55] Within the union, the abolition of trade barriers would lead to the expansion of particular industries in the areas where their costs of production were lowest and to contraction where their costs were highest. Any

shift in the location of industries from high to low cost areas would lead to trade creation, since the low cost area would now supply the whole market. There would be 'creative destruction'.[56] To the present day, customs union tends to be favoured by those who seek change and opposed by those who want to see no change in their country's economic structure.[57] The appropriate adjustments may be most difficult for a country at a lower stage of development and a less versatile economic structure than that of its customs union partners.[58] Such a country might suffer an undue share of the destructive element in creative destruction, while a more versatile partner would reap most of the benefits of the creative element.

Those afraid of the destructive element were joined in opposition to customs union by some who thought in terms of worldwide free trade. The latter stressed the point that a customs union would lead to trade diversion as well as trade creation.[59] Trade diversion would occur when a country imports from a higher cost producer after union than before union. Before the union, the source of supply was the lowest cost producer in the world. After the formation of the union, the source of supply might be the lowest cost producer in the union. The result is not certain. The union partner's costs may be as low as anybody's. Even if it is not, trade diversion will occur only if the union's protection at least offsets an outsider's cost advantage. Although this point can be exaggerated, it is most unlikely that a customs union can be formed which does not involve at least some trade diversion. The issue is whether trade creation exceeds trade diversion. If it does, then there is a net improvement in the allocation of world resources through the net shift from higher to lower cost production. Implicit in the writings of the early post-war period and before was the assumption that lower cost production would lead to lower prices. Many writers still accept this view. Where production functions are given, they are right to do so.

According to such writings, a customs union will be most beneficial or least harmful if the union leads to a reduction of member countries' tariffs, and if member countries' economies are sufficiently diversified and versatile that the creative effects can outweigh the destructive ones in each of the member countries. Both aspects of EC have frequently been examined. The results vary according to the assumptions made and the methods of calculation. But they seem to agree on two points. One is that the trade creative effects of EC, during its first decade, were greatest in Italy and France, the two countries with the highest national tariffs before alignment with the lower

Common Customs Tariff, so that there was freer trade with non-member countries as well as free trade with members. The other is that trade creation exceeded trade diversion.[60]

But the nature of trade creation was not as anticipated. According to the early post-war writings, member countries would specialise in different industries. In consequence, the composition of their exports to other EC countries was expected to become increasingly different. In fact, it became increasingly alike.[61] Net trade balances in individual products became less. This had already been a characteristic of Benelux in the 1950s.[62] It came to be repeated on an EC scale in the 1960s and 1970s. Integration did not so much alter the location of industries as the nature of industries.

(c) Intra- and Inter-Industry Specialisation. The change in the nature of industries occurred where the scope for intra-industry specialisation was greatest. In the early years of EC integration, this was most marked in machinery and transport equipment. By the end of the 1960s it became even more marked in chemicals.[63] As far as consumer goods were concerned, the effect was concentrated on consumer durables, such as motor cars and domestic appliances, and noticeable also in certain textiles. Generally, the growth of intra-EC trade was confined to a limited number of items, affecting perhaps one quarter of the trade in consumer goods.[64] In activities where there was less immediate scope for intra-industry specialisation, the effects were less marked.

It has been argued that trade creation in EC was largely the result of intra-industry specialisation in manufacturing.[65] Add to this that intra-industry specialisation is suitable only for increasing returns activities which, in turn, require new production functions. It follows that any extrapolations of past trends will 'forecast' results below performance. If some economists have persistently understated the possible effects of integration, the reason is not just professional caution. All extrapolations must at least start with the assumption of given production functions.[66] That some of their estimates came out well below subsequent performance was largely due to intra-industry specialisation in some activities. They were not necessarily so far out for other activities.

The key point is that full use can be made of freer trade only where there are opportunities for intra-industry specialisation, and that the damage done by trade restrictions is that they frustrate such specialisation in modern industry. The latter point was made about half a century ago, in another context and long before European integration was on the agenda.[67] It was argued that the greater effectiveness of US than of other industries at the time was due to the larger size of her market, that the art of selling had become the search for finding markets for potential (not actual) products, and that economic progress depends upon the progressive specialisation of industries by which increasing returns are realised.[68] This writing foreshadowed the path US and later European industries were to follow. All that was lacking to make it a blueprint for integration policies was reference to the international policy means through which the realisation of increasing returns could be facilitated, and the term intra-industry specialisation which did not appear in the literature until the 1960s. There was no specific reference to prices, though the statement that markets had to be sought should have acted as a warning against the expectation of old-style price-competitive trading in goods produced under increasing returns.

Prices will be considered further in subsection (e). Here let reference be made to yet one more test of the effects of free trade on inter- and intra-industry specialisation. So far, the argument has tried to relate theoretical expectations to actual performance, but has not been able to compare European experience with the experience of similar economies which did not pursue any integration policies. The only study at hand is one of the relative experience of Northern Ireland and the Republic of Ireland.[69] The two economies' manufacturing sectors were found to be similar in all respects but one. The exception was that Northern Ireland has remained part of the UK customs area throughout, while the Republic resorted to high protection in the 1930s. The latter's protection was not abandoned until 1966, when free trade with the UK was to be restored in stages for most manufactured goods by 1975.[70] This was eventually overtaken by both countries' accession to EC. It should be added that the bulk of the trade of both Northern Ireland and the Republic of Ireland is with the UK, and that there were no foreign exchange problems in UK-Irish trade. The investigator found Northern Ireland the more specialised economy. Her industries exported a higher proportion of their output and so participated more in inter-industry specialisation. But they also imported more like goods, so that the trade balance in those products was less. Hence there was also more intra-industry specialisation. When tariffs were lowered under the UK-Republic of Ireland free trade agreement, the difference between the two Irish economies narrowed by the early 1970s, and narrowed more in intra-

than in inter-industry trade.[71] While there may have been special factors at work in the two economies which led to this result, and while these two economies are not altogether representative of EC economies, they provide a test case for the finding that integration alters the nature, rather than the location of industries.

(d) The Trade Balance. Inter-industry trade leads to a widening of the trade balance (exports minus imports) in each product relative to the value of total trade (exports plus imports) in that product. But intra-trade leads to a narrowing of the trade balance in each product relative to the value of total trade in that product. If then the overall effect of industrial free trade is more growth of intra- than of inter-industry trade, there is a tendency for the overall trade balance between any two industrial free trade countries to narrow.

Of course, there are other influences at work which also affect the trade balance between any two countries. Even if other influences are ignored, the freeing of trade may lead to both inter- and intra-trade responses. Moreover, inter- and intra-industry effects do not come about with equal ease or with equal speed. Generally, inter-industry trade involves no change in technology, while intra-industry trade does. For this reason alone, the more immediate response to freer trade is likely to be an inter-industry response with a widening of the trade balance between the two or more countries, while intra-trade and the narrowing of the trade balance come later. This point will now be examined in more detail. An attempt must also be made to find out what sort of country will experience the initial improvement of its trade balance.

When there are spare resources in one country, its responses to new inter-trade opportunities may be almost immediate. Even where there are no spare resources to start with, new inter-trade opportunities imply the contraction of some activites as well as the expansion of others. The contracting ones then release factors which may be used by the expanding ones. Without too much exaggeration, it could then be said that an inter-trade response provides its own spare resources. Such a transfer of resources will normally be the easier, the less technologically advanced the relevant activities are. In any case, in order to utilise inter-trade opportunities, there must be quantitative growth of production in the expanding activity. It is not so necessary to rethink and reorganise the nature of that activity. By contrast, the opening of frontiers to intra-trade is unlikely to show early results. More time is needed to effect the appropriate technological and organisational changes which alter the nature of industrial activities. The intra-trade response is likely to take longer than the inter-trade response.

The short-run (inter-trade) effect of freer trade in industrial goods on the trade balance is a widening of that balance in individual products. Added together, this may lead to a widening of the trade balance relative to total trade between the two countries. This result is not certain. If the two countries are of equal size, at the same stage of development and respond equally quickly, the overall trade balance between the two countries may remain unchanged. But if one country has more spare resources for its expanding activity or more easily transferable resources than the other, the trade balance is likely to move in favour of the former. A technologically less advanced country is likely to have relatively fewer specific factors, and therefore relatively more transferable ones. If then trade is freed between a technologically less advanced country and a technologically more advanced country, the trade balance will at first move in favour of the technologically less advanced one. This short-run outcome is likely to persist until intra-trade effects come into play. By then, the overall trade balance between the two countries will tend to become less relative to the value of total trade between them. The reason is that intra-trade is essentially reciprocal.

For an example it will be useful to look at the overall trade balance between the UK and the Republic of Ireland. The two countries were in monetary union, so that their bilateral commercial relationship was not affected by exchange controls and currency realignments. There was no language barrier, and there were fewer of the differences in laws and tastes which often divide economies. The commercial barrier between them was mainly a tariff barrier.

Soon after the first tariff reductions, the trade balance between the two countries widened, relative to the value of the total trade between them. That balance had averaged around 3 per cent of the value of total trade in 1962-5, which was before the free trade agreement. It widened to around 5 per cent in 1967-70, when the first tariff reductions were made. Then it fell to one half of one per cent in 1971 and 1972, the last two years before the two countries' accession to EC and before the depression.[72] The industrially less advanced country, Ireland, could take relatively quick advantage of the increased opportunities for inter-industry trade. The trade balance widened and turned in Ireland's favour. The industrially more advanced country, the UK, depended more on intra-industry trade, and this took more time. When it was effective, the trade balance approached zero. Since the UK was more advanced in intra-industry trade than any other major country at that time, one wonders whether her accession to EC will be followed by a similar sequence of balance of trade effects.

For other examples, it seems best to look at the experience of the original six members of EC. Take the case of Germany. Although she was not free from currency realignments, her trade was freer from exchange and administrative controls than the trade of her partners. At least in a one-sided way, there were fewer obstacles to the working of changes in tariffs than in other EC countries. Also to be noted is that, at the time of the formation of EC, Germany was less advanced in intra-industry trade than France and the Benelux countries. For this reason alone, there should have been more similarity with Irish than with UK experience. Perhaps it should be added that, in 1959-60, German trade with EC was more balanced than her trade with the rest of the world. Her trade balance with EC was equivalent to 5 per cent of the value of her total trade with EC, that with the rest of the world 7 per cent. In the first few years of falling trade barriers in EC, her trade balance (as a percentage of total trade with EC) widened. It peaked in her favour in 1963 when it was 14 per cent. At the same time, her trade balance with the rest of the world narrowed to 1 per cent. Subsequently the process was reversed. By 1970-2, her trade balance with EC averaged 2 per cent of the value of her EC trade (and was in deficit). Her (surplus) balance with the rest of the world came to 13 per cent of the total value of trade with the rest of the world.[73] By itself, the German experience might be interpreted as one of trade diversion. But its resemblance to Irish experience in relation to the UK, suggests an alternative interpretation. It is that the country, which initially, is less advanced in intra-industry trade derives a short-term advantage from freer trade in the form of an improved trade balance with a partner country or countries. If however that country has opportunities for increased participation in intra-industry trade, the balance of freed trade will eventually tend towards zero. As in the Irish case, the tendencies towards intra-industry trade began to affect the trade balance about three years after the first tariff cuts. But it took longer to attain near balance in freed trade between

Germany and EC than between Ireland and the UK.

An examination of the trade balances of the other EC countries [74] also showed tendencies towards balance in trade with EC. The nature and the speed of adjustment varied from country to country and in one case, France, other influences caused a clear break in the movement. Details are as follows.

The Netherlands showed the quickest result and Belgium-Luxembourg the slowest. In 1959-61, the Netherlands trade balance with EC averaged about 8 per cent of the value of total trade with EC and the imbalance was rising. In the next three years it was down to 4 per cent. Although it rose again in the mid-1960s, the 1959-61 level was not reattained in any three-year period. In the late 1960s, the balance fell further. By 1970-2, it averaged less than 3 per cent.[75] The Belgian trade balance with EC widened from less than 2 per cent in 1959-61 to a peak of 9 per cent in 1970. In 1971-2, it was down to less than 3 per cent. The Italian balance with EC rose from 8 per cent in 1959-61 to 11 per cent in 1963-5 and then fell back to 2 per cent in 1970-2. The tendency towards balance asserted itself, whether the movement was via an increased deficit (the Netherlands) or surplus (Belgium) or a movement from deficit via surplus to near balance (Italy).

The most complex case was that of France. There was a clear break in the continuity of the movement in 1967. Initially, the French EC balance moved fairly quickly. It rose from 5 per cent of the value of total French EC trade in 1959-60 to 7 per cent in 1961-2. Then it fell back to average 2 per cent in 1963-6. The initial rise in the French surplus with EC, followed by near balance, in those years, seems a 'perfect' example of a country which was relatively well placed to take immediate advantage of some new inter-trade opportunities and early advantage of new intra-trade opportunities. But the French balance of trade with the rest of the world deteriorated (from a surplus equivalent to 4 per cent of the value of total trade with the rest of the world in 1959-61 to a deficit of 5 per cent in 1962-6). Measures taken to improve the overall trade balance helped to reduce the deficit with the rest of the world to near balance. But one effect was that the deficit was diverted from the rest of the world to the EC. In 1967-9, the French deficit with EC was equivalent to 9 per cent of the value of French EC trade. It fell back to 3 per cent in 1970-2. Near balance in French EC trade was restored. But the balance with the rest of the world was even less, with 2 per cent.

The French case shows that a country's general trade problems may over-ride (and break the continuity of) any tendencies towards trade balance with customs union partners. It is too early to say whether the depression of the mid-1970s will have similar effects. It is also too early to say how the accession of the UK, Denmark and Ireland will affect the position. All that can be said is that, wherever free trade opens up opportunities for intra-industry trade and these opportunities are taken, there will be tendencies towards near balance of trade.

This was the case amongst the original six EC countries. In different ways and at different speeds, each member country had attained near balance in its EC trade. In 1971-2, that balance came to 3 per cent or less of each member country's total EC trade. Each case, taken by itself, could be interpreted as accidental or due to a variety of other causes. But this 'accident' happened to each of the member countries, about ten years after the initial intra-EC tariff reductions and within four years of complete tariff-free trade.

Since the trade balance is a major obstacle to monetary co-operation between countries, its near elimination paved the way for serious consideration of monetary union as the next step in European integration. The project was shelved during the depression. Should the tendencies towards trade balance reassert themselves in the EC trade of the Nine once the depression is over, interest in the subject may revive.

(e) Prices. Where intra-industry trade is more important than inter-industry trade, the freeing of trade affects the nature rather than the location of industries, and trade balances in individual products narrow. This is the opposite of what one would expect under inter-industry trade. It would therefore be surprising if the effects of free intra-industry trade on prices were the same as under free inter-industry trade. When freer trade leads to inter-industry specialisation, there is a tendency towards product price equalisation. The shift in production to the lowest cost area allows for the production of a larger quantity of the same goods at a lower cost. Different people produce the same, and they do it better. Unimpeded competitive trading in such products ensures that product prices will tend towards equality throughout one common market.

Where intra-industry specialisation predominates, there is no such tendency towards product price equalisation. One price per product prevails only in the sense that each producer is concerned with only one sub-product which is unique in quality and price. The major change through intra-industry specialisation comes through improved quality and increased variety of goods. This is made possible through further specialisation which allows for longer production runs for goods produced under increasing returns on capital employed. Unit costs fall. The same people produce different goods. They do so to mutual advantage. Their earnings rise. There will be a tendency towards equalisation of increments of factor earnings. If this is a form of price equalisation, it is an equalisation of marginal changes in factor prices in the activities which participate in intra-industry specialisation. Since it is impossible to get sufficiently detailed data to prove or disprove the point, the following must concentrate on what happened to product prices paid by consumers and then be content with indirect evidence relating to factor prices. Where 'price' is mentioned without qualification, it will mean price paid by consumers.

Already in the first half of the 1960s, the Commission noticed that 'on the whole, the common market seems to have had less effect on prices than on the volume of supplies made available to consumers.[76] Since this observation dates from a time when the customs union of the original Six was still in the transition period, it could still be expected that disparities between prices in the various member countries would at least narrow once the customs union was complete and had been in force for a few more years. Yet even in the early 1970s, when these conditions were satisfied, it was reported that 'consumer prices still vary widely from country to country even if imports of the product in question account for a sizeable share of the total consumption'.[77] Various reasons were suggested. Tax rates varied from country to country. But although prices net of tax showed lesser disparities for some products, they showed larger ones for others.[78] Cross-frontier wholesale trade still met insurmountable administrative formalities at the border,[79] so that there was no effective cross-frontier competition in trades where independent wholesaling is still important. In other trades, where EC rules on competition gave dealers the opportunity to import directly, in branded products 'dealers obtain their supplies of these products on the national market, i.e. from the producer's regular general importer'.[80] Last, not least, the efficiency of the distribution system varied from country to country and its rationalisation made uneven progress.[81] From 1972 onwards, fluctuating exchange rates made it impossible to make meaningful comparisons of retail prices in member countries.

This test of the effectiveness of EC must wait until exchange rates stabilise again.

A similar inquiry was made by EFTA.[82] Here too it was found easier to point to an increase in the volume of intra-area trade than to any clear effect on prices. Although the EFTA study seemed more confident than the EC ones that the tariff reductions had a damping effect on prices, it was not possible to quantify the results. The expected product price equalisation remained elusive. The reason may be that the inquiries were made too early or that other distortions of competition overshadowed the results. But even if other distortions can be overcome, price disparities will not cease where they 'are primarily attributable to decisions taken by producers and only partly to the differences found in distribution costs and dealers' mark-ups or taxation'.[83]

These results may have disappointed those who thought integration would lead to inter-industry specialisation and product price equalisation. But, in EC, 'trade creation has resulted largely from intra-industry specialisation in manufacturing'.[84] In consequence, it was effective in activities where either quality or model competition prevails and product price equalisation is not acceptable.[85] Any tendencies there are towards price equalisation must be towards the equalisation of marginal factor prices. This is another way of saying that there are tendencies towards the equalisation of changes in factor rewards. The distribution of such rewards between interest, dividends, retained profits, salaries and wages, is subject to a number of influences which may vary from country to country and even from firm to firm. The problems of distribution to particular factors can be evaded through taking them all together. This still leaves the question of how far a particular change in factor rewards should be attributed to intra-industry specialisation, especially where firms are multi-product firms and not all of their activities are affected by such specialisation or not to the same extent.

To the best of the writer's knowledge, no one has yet overcome those difficulties. The direct evidence leads to only two firm conclusions. One is negative, namely that product price equalisation cannot be expected where integration comes mainly through intra-industry specialisation. The other conclusion is positive and asserts that this form of specialisation is undertaken for mutual gain of producers. This leads to the presumption that there will be tendencies towards equality of the marginal increment to producers' earnings.

Further support of the last point depends on indirect evidence. One is provided by a study of changes in average earnings in manufacturing in thirty-five countries, including the EC countries, in 1956-65.[86] Although that period ends early for the present purpose, it covers years when integration made progress and international comparisons were not yet vitiated by currency disorders. The investigators found that average earnings in manufacturing tended to grow at approximately the same rate in all industrial countries. That rate corresponded approximately to the rate of productivity growth in the most rapidly advancing sectors.[87] Earnings increases in that sector reflected increases in real values created. Other sectors which wanted to keep their factors had to pay them more than before. But where such increases did not reflect higher real values created, the difference had to be passed on in the form of higher prices. Thus, where the growth sector was relatively large, it was easier to contain the rate of inflation without risk of unemployment than in countries where it was smaller. Since the growth sector roughly coincided with the sector which offered most scope for intra-industry specialisation and EC facilitated intra-industry specialisation, EC can claim to have had some damping effect on prices. But this is not the same as equalisation of product prices. The process was one of equal increments of earnings through intra-industry specialisation. Where the effect did not become too diluted through increased pay in sectors which did not create additional real value, the real effects predominated. All this assumes that the lessons of 1956-65 are still relevant, and that integration policies which encourage such tendencies are not frustrated by national policies.

For further indirect evidence, it may be useful to digress briefly into economic theory. As pointed out before, traditional trade theory assumed both decreasing returns activities and inter-industry specialisation, and showed how free trade would lead to product price equalisation. A major post-war contribution was the theory of factor price equalisation. Written at a time when the same assumptions still seemed valid, it pointed out that free trade would lead to factor as well as product price equalisation. Although contested at the time, it proved to be another economic writing ahead of its time. In the following decades, the assumptions of decreasing returns and inter-industry specialisation became less and less tenable in relation to the industrial countries' trade. The appropriate assumptions became increasing returns and intra-industry specialisation. If there still were tendencies towards product price equalisation, they are not discernible in most trade in industrial goods. If there are tendencies towards the equalisation of prices, they are in the equalisation of changes in factor rewards.[88]

If so, the European customs union is a producers' union. The same can be said of the whole integration movement of which European integration was the part that went furthest. Any direct benefits to consumers lie in improved quality and increased variety, rather than lower price. Nevertheless, real incomes were raised. For real incomes can rise when earnings rise relative to prices and not only when prices fall relative to incomes. Under increasing returns conditions, the emphasis must be on the former. Consumers are not deprived. For, in general, 'capacity to buy depends on capacity to produce.'[89]

2. Japan

Since capacity to produce determines capacity to buy, the capacity to produce medium and high technology goods has come to be a precondition for the attainment of the highest possible living standards. The US led the way. At first she did so nationally but in the third quarter of the century her trade agreements allowed for international intra-industry specialisation. Europe responded by carrying integration policy further than the US was willing to go. A short period of production-led post-war recovery was followed by trade-led integration in industrial activities. By contrast, Japan's response was a lagged response. Until the 1970s, Japan could be described as a 'catching-up country'[90] where, in matters of trade and trade policy, most things seemed to happen somewhat later than in Western industrial countries. Only then was she getting ready for full participation in intra-industry specialisation.

This does not deny her post-war economic achievements. In the 1950s, she was the poorest amongst industrial countries. By 1966, her income per head exceeded that of Ireland and, by 1973, that of the UK. In the mid-1970s, it came to about five-sixths of the EC average.[91] By then, her gross national product was exceeded only by the US and the USSR, and she was second only to the US as a trading country. In 1973, her new role was symbolised when she hosted the opening session of the Seventh (Tokyo) Round of GATT negotiations, and one of the major questions before that Round was how to further the economic integration of Japan with the Western industrial world.

Nevertheless, Japan's trading structure in the early 1970s resembled that of other industrial countries in the 1950s. Three-quarters of her imports were primary commodities, as in the US, the UK and Germany two decades earlier.[92] Most of her exports were manufactures, as in the UK and Germany and, to a lesser extent, the US. In other words, Japan had reached a trading structure similar to that of some other industrial countries just before intra-industry specialisation raised the share of manufactures in their imports. Subject to some exceptions, Japan's trade relations were still of the inter-industry specialisation kind. It would seem that this point did not escape the notice of the Japanese authorities. They expected a reorientation of the Japanese economy, in the 1970s, from one with 'natural-resource-consuming' industries to 'brain-intensive' industries. It was also thought that there would be greater reliance on exports which competed on quality rather than on price.[93] Since Japan is not well endowed with natural resources, the envisaged shift would reduce her import dependence. But goods which compete on quality are most suitable for intra-industry specialisation and this implies at least a possibility of more balanced trade in manufactures.

One reason why Japan's long-term policy-makers could prepare for intra-industry specialisation was that they had other countries' experience to draw on. Although they were as ill prepared as others for the depression of the 1970s, which put a temporary halt to intra-industry specialisation, the long-term strategy of catching up appears to have been left intact. Another reason was that Japan's import structure of the early 1970s had only just been attained, and so could not seem to be a normal state of affairs as it seemed in the UK in the 1950s. In the UK, such an import structure had prevailed throughout the first six decades of the present century, under free trade and various regimes of protection. When it began to change in the late 1950s, UK industry had evidently made or was making the appropriate technological adjustments. But the authorities and commercial interests seemed to be taken unawares and unready for the necessary policy and marketing adjustments.[94] In Japan, the import structure underwent two major long-term changes in the course of the century, and both were the result of policy changes. At the turn of the century, most of Japan's imports were manufactures but, in the 1930s, only one-quarter were.[95] The post-war trend was the other way. At the time of Japan's accession to GATT, in 1955, manufactures accounted for only 10 per cent of her imports. Subsequently, imports of manufactures grew by more than other imports. By 1970, their share was again about one quarter and still rising.[96]

The fall in the share of manufactures in total imports, from the 1900s to the 1930s, was encouraged by tariff policy. Following the example of continental European powers, Japan abandoned a low tariff for protection in 1899. This was followed by several upward revisions made between then and the 1930s.[97] By the end of that period, Japan had caught up in the sense that she had become another textile and heavy engineering country. She had become less interested in supplies from the outside world's industrial sector and more dependent on imported basic materials. Although the nature and sources of her imports changed, her import dependence did not. The ratio of imports to her gross domestic product (GDP), fluctuated around 13 per cent throughout that period.[98] None of this gave her export success in the sense of making the outside world demand more of her goods relative to her output. The ratio of exports to GDP fluctuated around 11 or 11½ per cent during that period.[99] The growth of trade in either direction remained closely linked to the growth of domestic production. It was supply-determined.[100] Since Japan's production grew more than the world's and her products were not superior to those already available from other sources, she could gain markets only at unfavourable prices, to the detriment of the standard of living in Japan and of employment elsewhere.[101] This was neither the first nor the last case in economic history of production-led growth leading to international difficulties. But it attracted special attention since Japan was ready to add significantly to the supply of traditional goods just at a time when those industries were suffering from stagnation and depression.

The post-war development was entirely different, though it was not a clear case of trade-led integration either. To start with, neither the export nor the import trade ratio to GDP regained their pre-war level. Nor did they move in the same direction once the post-war reconstruction problems were over. In 1947, production was low, and the import and export trade ratios around 1 per cent. By 1955, production had increased nearly seven-fold, and the import trade ratio to over 10 per cent. Then that ratio steadied with a downward trend. The average for 1955-9 was 11 per cent and that for 1969-73 under 9 per cent. The export trade ratio was 8 per cent in 1955, averaged around 9 per cent in 1955-9, and 8½ per cent in the first half of the 1960s. Then it recovered to nearly 10 per cent in the late 1960s and early 1970s.[102] Thus, the export trade ratio shows an increase in interdependence between Japan and the world from the late 1960s onwards, but the import trade ratio does not.

There are several reasons for the different showing of the import and export trade ratios. One is that Japan was a late-comer to the removal of trade barriers. Although on accession to GATT she lowered her tariff by nearly one third, this was her first major tariff cut this century. Other GATT countries had acted earlier. A new tariff law, of 1961, brought the Japanese tariff in line with international nomenclature, but it retained high protection on manufactures. Whittled down by 40 per cent in the Kennedy Round, it still remained higher than the tariffs of other major industrial countries. It needed a 20 per cent unilateral tariff reduction, in 1972, to bring the Japanese tariff in line with the rates prevailing in those countries.[103] Further unilateral tariff reductions were prepared in 1977, with a view to reducing the trade surplus. Of the earlier tariff changes, only the accession to GATT was followed by a noticeable increase in the import trade ratio and for two years this stood at between 12 and 14 per cent. But this was not maintained. One reason was that other trade controls, including quotas, continued to be used for balance of payments and protectionist reasons. In the abolition of quotas too, Japan was somewhat late. In Europe, virtually all quotas on industrial goods had disappeared by the end of the 1950s. Japan began to dismantle quotas in the early 1960s, so as to qualify for status as a country which protects industrial goods mainly by tariff. But the process was not completed until the 1970s.[104]

Of at least equal significance was the change in the structure of Japanese industry. Engineering industries became more important and textiles less so, and this meant more reliance on domestic value added and less on imported materials. This alone would have kept the import trade ratio down. The change did not come about by accident. It depended on the import of technology.

A country can import technology by importing high technology products, by allowing the establishment of foreign firms, or by purchasing licences to make use of foreign technology. In the early post-war period, most imported manufactures were producer goods. The total was limited by a shortage of foreign exchange, most of which was earmarked for basic materials for existing industries. When import controls were eased, an increasing variety of manufactures were admitted, including consumer goods such as textiles. In short, direct imports were not the main way through which Japan gained access to the achievements of higher technology. Nor was the establishment of foreign firms. Foreign firms were not given full rights of establishment until 1973, and even then a few activities were excluded.

Previously, full foreign ownership was only allowed in industries in which Japan was already strong. Generally, liberalisation of foreign establishment tended to follow the growing strength of the various sectors of the economy.[105] By the 1970s, Japanese industry had largely caught up and Japanese firms had begun to establish branches overseas. Although in the early 1970s the number of Japanese firms operating in the US was still only one-tenth of the number of US firms operating in Japan,[106] an outward spread of the Japanese economy had begun, mainly but not solely to the US.[107] This illustrates the point that reciprocal rights of establishment are more easily given when the countries concerned are at a similar stage of economic development than when there is a wide technological gap. True, where the technological gap is so wide that modern technology is inaccessible without the establishment of foreign firms, the latter may yet be welcome. But this other extreme did not apply to Japan at any time during the post-war period. What Japan had in the early 1950s was low technology industry. The catching up policy was to raise the level of technology in Japanese-owned industry.

This was facilitated by licensing. In the early 1950s, Western firms did not take too much interest in the Japanese market. Japanese firms took the initiative in negotiating technology contracts. Since these involved expenditure of foreign exchange, they were controlled by the authorities. At first, only new producer goods and processes for existing industries were approved, but this was widened in the late 1950s to include the requirements of new industries. In the course of the 1960s, the controls were eased further until automatic approval was given for such contracts, unless they involved exceptionally large expenditure or related to strategic goods. US and other foreign firms were willing to supply their know-how under licence, since the technology gap was sufficiently wide and their own R & D facilities so superior that they sold only yesterday's knowledge.[108] This was often developed further in Japan, at least initially with a view to immediate returns. Japanese industrialists could thus advance their technology, at a cost of royalty payments but at a saving of R & D expenditure. While some Japanese firms developed high technology entirely unaided, licensing contracts speeded up the progress of others.[109] With the narrowing and closing of the technology gap, the phase of one-sided technology contracts is now largely over.

Although some of the new products were first developed for the export market, a special kind of demonstration effect seemed to operate. What sold well in the US was wanted in Japan, and the home market absorbed between 80 and 90 per cent of licensed output.[110] This was in line with a general characteristic of the Japanese economy until the mid-1960s, when Japanese producers were reported to prefer selling in the protected home market whenever they could.[111] Innovations may have been developed on the basis of foreign technology and foreign tastes, but with a view to domestic opportunities. The process has been described as one of 'supply-oriented exports'[112] which corresponds to production-led growth.

The situation changed in the mid-1960s, about the time when Japan's own R & D efforts became more marked. From then onwards, exports grew more than GDP. Exports of electrical consumer durables and motor cars did particularly well, and these are industries with higher ranking in intra-industry specialisation than textiles. It should be noted that these goods were imported from Japan mainly by countries which also produced and exported them. So that their products be accepted there, Japanese exporters became 'increasingly more inclined to adjust their prices to those prevailing in their main markets'.[113] These were moves towards Japanese participation in intra-industry specialisation. At the time, however, they were rather one-sided. There were some Japanese imports of goods which she exported, but this was less marked than in other industrial countries.[114]

Because of the depression of the 1970s, it is not yet possible to say whether this is another instance of Japan being somewhat late. Perhaps her earlier purchases of foreign technology delayed the time when it would be a choice of buying from abroad goods produced with specialised foreign technology or going without. The technology purchases were largely in engineering. In chemicals, where growth came later than in engineering, Japan ranked top in intra-industry specialisation.[115] More certain is that intra-industry specialisation depends on reciprocal access to markets. As shown before, it was not until the 1970s that the incidence of the Japanese tariff on manufactures was in line with the tariffs of other industrial countries. Moreover, if Japan was late in reducing trade barriers on products suitable for intra-industry specialisation, other countries imposed restraints on Japan's traditional exports. Some of these restraints were discussed in earlier chapters[116] and there is no need to repeat the details. Suffice it to say that the result of Japanese import controls was to make the composition of Japanese imports more traditional, and the result of other countries' restraints on Japanese exports was to make the composition of her export trades less traditional. The combined effect was one-sided, stultified intra-industry specialisation in trade between Japan and other industrial countries, and especially the US. The chief problem in Japanese-Western commercial relations was not the trade balance, which was a symptom rather than a cause of the one-sided nature of the relationship in the early 1970s, but the nature of the trade.

3. Primary Producers

(i) Imbalanced Integration

The imbalance in Japanese trade in the 1970s was one between exports of manufactures which could be integrated into the world of the *Pax Americana* and imports of primary commodities which could not. This was a case of partial integration. In manufactures, Japanese enterprises caught up through studying markets which were more advanced than their home market. As a rule, economic missions were sent to investigate market conditions before commercial missions went out to sell.[117] Exports could then be produced for particular uses, and sometimes also users, in the importing countries. Production and markets were integrated. Inevitably some actual and potential rivals in importing countries were discomforted and sought protection. But, if and when they got it, GATT machinery was available to ensure that such protection was temporary and that there was time to renegotiate and reconsider. It would appear that Japanese exporters were sometimes slow in adjusting to changing prices in importing countries but that the complaints frequently subsided if and when they did.[118] The difficulties were the greater, the less the use and user of a product could be specified. Through moving away from such products as far and as fast as feasible, Japan contributed to reduction of possible friction. By the mid-1970s, Japanese textiles had ceased to be a 'threat' to importing countries. Though there were difficulties in steel and a few other products, complaints appear to have been less frequent in trades in newer and more brain-intensive products. No such moves towards integration occurred in the Japanese import trade. Most imports were primary commodities where, by definition, neither use nor user can be identified at the point of production. The nature of these products was not, and could not be, determined by specific Japanese requirements as compared with the requirements elsewhere. Nor could their price. In short most Japanese exports could be produced and sold for specific uses in particular markets but most Japanese imports were not specially produced for Japan. This imbalance was of special importance in Japan's trade relations with the US, her principal export market for manufactures and principal supplier of primary commodities. In the course of the 1960s, the bilateral trade balance between the two countries turned from one of US surplus to one of Japanese surplus, as Japan became increasingly able to produce more for the US market, but the US did not so specifically produce for Japan. In the course of the 1970s, however, Japan's imbalanced trade structure made her vulnerable to sharp rises in import prices caused by events elsewhere.

This is not the only example of a country whose exports and imports were unevenly integrated. Such imbalance also caused special problems in the UK, though in different ways. The share of primary commodities in UK imports fell from about three quarters in the 1950s (or any earlier decade this century) to less than half by the early 1970s. Despite the dramatic fall in this ratio, it remained somewhat higher than in most other industrial countries. This share will probably fall further, as dependence on imported oil becomes less, as domestic food production grows, and as intra-industry specialisation raises both imports and exports of manufactures. In the 1970s, however, the UK was still more vulnerable to changes in primary commodities prices than most industrial countries. Moreover, unlike Japan which also exported mainly manufactures, the UK did not take full advantage of the opportunities for integrated trading in manufactures. True, her growing imports of manufactures were increasingly produced for special uses in the UK and priced accordingly. But her growing exports of manufactures to industrial countries, which could and should have been marketed in similar ways, all too often were not.[119] Delays in UK accession to EC may have been a reason for the slow adjustment to new marketing techniques, but the UK had full GATT rights long before Japan.

The ECs position, in relation to balanced integration, is difficult to evaluate. Total intra-EC trade always appears 'in balance', whether overall or in relation to particular products, as long as imports and exports are valued in the same way. It is so by definition, since one member country's imports are another member country's exports. But if the total external trade of the six original EC countries is added together, the position in the early 1970s was that primary commodities accounted for less than two-fifths of imports (which was less than in the UK and Japan) and somewhat less than one-fifth of exports (which was more than in the UK and Japan). If however intra-EC trade of the Six is excluded, somewhat over half of imports were primary commodities (or more than in the UK and less than in

Japan).[120]

Of the major industrial countries, only the US had no such imbalance in the early 1970s. About one third of both her imports and exports were primary commodities.[121] The share of US trade which could not be integrated into the world of the *Pax Americana* was thus about the same on both sides of the trade balance. This too had its problems, compared with both the situation in the US's own recent past and that in other industrial countries. Twenty years earlier, primary commodities had accounted for close on half of her total imports and less than a quarter of exports.[122] The direction of the change in imports was in the same direction as in European industrial countries. But the change in exports, though less marked, was in the opposite direction to that in Europe and Japan. The US had started the post-war period as the dominant exporter of R & D intensive manufactures which can be produced for particular uses and users. When others became increasingly able to respond, her trade balance in such products narrowed. In short, a relatively high dependence on exports of primary commodities and a narrowing lead in manufactures contributed to US trading difficulties in the early 1970s, despite the even balance in the relative importance of primary commodities and manufactures in her foreign trade at that time.

A balance between primary commodities and manufactures does not, by itself, prove an equal degree of integration in imports and exports. It merely indicates such a possibility in the circumstances of the third quarter of the century. As the case of the UK shows, integration opportunities are not always taken. As the case of the US shows, relative integration opportunities for one country may become less, at least temporarily, simply because it was ahead at the beginning of whatever period is taken into consideration. Moreover, integration opportunities vary from manufactured product to manufactured product and even from transaction to transaction. Nevertheless, a division of the trade balance into manufactures and primary commodities roughly coincides with the division of goods on which trade barriers have and have not been effectively reduced in the third quarter of the century. This, in turn, roughly coincides with a division into goods where trade-led integration could and could not operate.

(ii) Imbalanced Integration and Relative Trading Performance

The omission of primary commodities from the integration movement of the third quarter of the century affected the relative trading position of the various industrial countries as well as the relations between the industrial and primary producing worlds.

Japan and the UK may be taken as examples of how two industrial countries were affected. Both exported mainly manufactures. Both were net importers of primary commodities. Thus both sold, or could have sold, their exports on quality and at prices prevailing in the various importing markets. Their imports of primary commodities, however, were not produced to their specific requirements. These imports could have been bought by any other importing country. Import prices of such commodities were world prices, whether determined by the market or controlled by exporting countries for reasons of their own. Unless special arrangements could be made with particular suppliers, changes in the unit prices paid by the two importing countries would normally result from the same causes.[123]

Throughout the third quarter of the century, Japan was one of the fastest growing industrial economies and the UK one of the slowest. At the same time, Japan's imports continued to be mainly primary commodities while the UK's did not. For both reasons Japan put more additional pressure on the world's primary commodities supplies than the UK. But the unit prices Japan had to pay for such imports were not determined by the interaction of her own demand with world supplies. They were determined by world demand and world supplies. Since world demand rose less than Japanese demand, Japan benefited from not having to pay as much as her own demand conditions warranted. The opposite applied in the UK, which had to pay more than her own demand warranted. Although this was not the only influence on the two countries' import prices, it contributed to the stability of Japanese import prices in most of the post-war period to 1972, and to the rise in UK import prices. The subsequent supply restraints in some primary commodity trades, however, affected Japan's import prices somewhat more than the UK's.[124]

This reads like a variation of the theme of Chapter 1, that different growth rates can cause difficulties in the relations between industrial countries which compete for the same supplies. In the early twentieth-century days of inter-industry trade, this could be a major cause of friction. The way to contain it, then, was overseas investment to increase supplies of primary commodities and the UK's unilateral free trade in manufactures provided an additional safety valve. In the days of intra-industry trade in the third quarter of the century, competition for supplies continued to create problems but were secondary to the problems of access to the markets for R & D intensive products in other industrial countries. Measures to increase supplies were still important, and failure to ensure supplies caused difficulties in the 1970s. Yet even when viewing the situation at a time when some of those difficulties still persist, the freeing of trade between the industrial countries remains the most effective way of containing possible friction between those countries. If the UK and Japan are again taken as examples, difficulties arose because UK traders did not take up all the integration opportunities open to them and Japan was slow in providing them. Although this had its bilateral aspects, the remedy was and remains multilateral. It was a question of developing new UK marketing techniques in selling to all industrial countries and liberalising Japanese imports from all sources.

Imbalanced integration elsewhere reflected the same kind of problems, though usually in less extreme form. In the course of the third quarter of the century, the US appears to have become slower in making full use of her industrial integration opportunities. Both the US and the EC remained unwilling to provide full integration opportunities through going all the way to free trade. Nevertheless the risk of early twentieth-century-style rivalries between the industrial countries could be averted as long as trade barriers were not raised and further negotiations towards yet freer trade could still proceed. Perhaps the strongest evidence of how far the pacification of the industrial world has gone under the *Pax Americana* came during the so-called oil crisis of the 1970s. Then, all industrial countries experienced difficulties with supplies of primary commodities. Although intra-industry trade could not expand at the accustomed rate while attention was fastened on problems which had arisen in trade with primary producers, no new frictions arose between the industrial trading countries which could not be resolved within the existing framework. GATT remained intact and the enlargement of EC was confirmed.

(iii) The Omission of the Primary Producers

If the 1970s revealed the strength of the *Pax Americana* as a *Pax* between industrial countries, it also revealed its weakness. This was inadequate integration between the industrial and the primary producing worlds which was then coming to a head. Though dramatised by political events and usually referred to as the oil crisis, it can also be thought of as the culmination of an imbalance in world economic integration which had concentrated on one sector only.

For a long time, this seemed to present no problem. Occasional supply restraints were short-lived and seemed attributable to ephemeral causes. Trade in primary commodities was closely correlated to what happened in manufacturing. Between 1948 and 1970, the quantum of production of manufactures rose 3.3 fold and international trade in primary commodities, at constant prices, 3.2 fold.[125] That trade was carried along by a prosperous industrial world, at a ratio of approximately 1:1. Although it is accident that the two growth rates came so close between the two years, the average of year-by-year changes gives a similar result. A higher rate of growth of trade in primary commodities, relative to manufacturing, is inconceivable for any length of time, since it would mean that the industrial world is accumulating unwanted stocks. A lower growth rate of such trade is conceivable. In the first half of the century, it tended to be 0.8 for any 1 point change in manufacturing. Thus, in the third quarter of the century, international trade in primary commodities grew as much as can be expected and more than earlier this century. With some justification it could be said that whatever was good for manufacturing was good for primary producers. All the same, the primary producing world was just carried along. It had no direct part in the decision taking of an integrating industrial world to which it was geared. Primary producers could not give the world economy purpose and direction. The industrial world did.

The industrial world's influence over the primary producing one did not only extend over its trade, but also over the quality and quantity of its production. It provided the tools, such as agricultural machinery, fertilisers, oil-rigs and so on. The technological progress of the time made primary production increasingly dependent on industrial supplies, while manufacturing became relatively less dependent on supplies of primary commodities. The industrial world's influence over primary production was of course shared with the primary producers themselves. But influence over production is not the same as influence over trade. Years of political or weather disturbances apart, the course of trade in primary commodities remained closely associated with the course of manufacturing and not with the course of primary production. Taking the change from 1948 to 1970 once more as representative of that period, while trade in primary commodities rose 3.2 fold (in line with the growth of manufacturing), primary production grew only 1.8 fold.[126]

A greater growth of trade than of production also occurred in manufacturing. In fact, the ratios of the growth of trade to growth of production were similar in these two sectors of the world economy.

From 1948 to 1970, international trade in manufactures at constant prices, grew 6.4 fold and the quantum of manufactures produced 3.3 fold, which gives a ratio of 1.9:1. In primary commodities, where trade expanded 3.2 fold and production 1.8 fold, the ratio was 1.8:1. In both cases, trade grew nearly twice as much as production.

In manufactures, this was largely due to intra-industry trade. But there was no equivalent scope for intra-trade in primary commodities. In manufacturing, there were two tendencies at work. One was that intra-industry trade encouraged the growth of R & D intensive activities which meant less input of primary commodities relative to other factors. The other tendency was that, with rising prosperity, the industrial countries were able to maintain a steady ratio of imported primary commodities to industrial production. True, the position varied from commodity to commodity. For instance, international trade in fuels rose 5.3 fold and of all other primary commodities 2.8 times. Since the production of manufactures grew 3.3 fold, the fuel trades grew 1.6 times as much but other primary commodities trades, taken together, only 0.8 times as much. It will be noted that the growth of the fuel trades was less than that of international trade in manufactures, and that the ratio of the growth of trade of other primary commodities to the growth of manufacturing continued to be the same as it had been earlier this century. Further disaggregation would show other differences. For the present purpose, however, it is enough to say that, overall, there was primary commodities saving but no saving of internationally traded ones. What appears to have happened was that the industrial countries 'saved' primary commodities by producing *relatively* fewer at home and compensated any shortfall through increased imports. The most notable instance was that the industrial countries let their coal production stagnate or decline and imported more oil. Although an illustration of inadequate integration, this point will not be pursued here. It would carry the present argument too far away from its main point, which is that the industrial integration of the industrial countries was not, or was not adequately, accompanied by integration of industrial with primary producing activities *within* those countries.

The locus of imbalanced integration between manufacturing and primary production was in the industrial countries. These countries were not only the world's main producers of manufactures. They also produced more primary commodities than the rest of the world combined[127] and more than entered international trade. Whether primary production grew enough relative to manufacturing thus depended foremost on what happened in those countries. There is no one right ratio. If, from 1948 to 1970, world primary production grew at only slightly more than half the rate at which manufacturing grew, this gave no cause for concern at the time. Difficulties arose only when the growth of manufacturing became relatively less qualitative than before. More purely quantitative growth would require near equivalent growth of inputs, including primary commodities.

Such problems arose in the early 1970s. After growth rates of 7 or 8 per cent in 1968 and 1969, industrial production rose by only 2 per cent in 1970 and 1971.[128] That was not enough to maintain employment in those countries. Worried by rising unemployment, governments sought to avert an incipient slump through accelerated inflation. They succeeded in so far as industrial production rose by 7 and 10 per cent in 1972 and 1973 respectively. But much of this represented revival and re-employment rather than new growth. For whatever reason, qualitative growth had slowed down and the recovery inevitably started with re-employment of factors in their former occupations. In other words, growth was relatively more quantitative than before. It depended relatively more on the availability of traditional inputs and therefore more on increased availability of primary commodities. This was not forthcoming. From 1970 to 1973, the growth of primary production was less than one third of that of manufacturing.[129]

It would appear that even without special aggravating factors, the industrial world was moving towards a primary commodities supply restraint. One escape from such a restraint would have been more qualitative R & D based growth. For whatever reason, there was not enough of that kind of growth at the time. Trade policy alone cannot create such growth though the reduction of trade barriers can facilitate it. Had it been politically possible to over-ride the staging requirements in the implementation of the tariff cuts agreed during the Kennedy Round or to speed up the negotiations for the enlargement of the EC, trade could have been freed somewhat earlier. But it is doubtful whether either could have had the necessary immediate impact on qualitative growth.

There were however several aggravating circumstances with immediate impact. One was the accelerated inflation which the various countries deliberately pursued in the hope that this would improve their domestic employment situations. To make this possible, fixed exchange rates were abandoned. Whatever else the policies of the time may or may not have achieved, they increased demand for primary commodities needed for quantitative growth. Since monetary expansion does not, by itself, increase domestic supplies of primary commodities, pressure on international supplies intensified. The result was a scramble for primary commodities. In the course of 1972/3, and before the oil crisis, quoted future prices of agricultural commodities and some minerals doubled.[130] Although these quoted prices moved ahead of actual prices in 1973, unit values of internationally traded agricultural commodities rose by nearly half and those of minerals by about one third.[131] Such sharp increases were without precedent in any peacetime year of the twentieth century.[132] More was to follow in 1974 when the rise in prices was aggravated, but not originated, by the oil crisis.

That crisis should not be allowed to obscure the events which were already leading the industrial world towards a primary commodities supply restraint. Input costs rose. Industrialists found it increasingly difficult to afford the primary commodities needed to maintain the volume of production at a level which could have kept their labour force as fully employed as before. Unemployment re-appeared. The countries which had inflated most and let their exchange rates drop most, were the countries with the greatest difficulties in this respect. But all had acted in the expectation that quantitative growth was possible and that international supplies of primary commodities would always be available in 'the market'.

Not all the difficulties of the time can be attributed to this attempt by industrial countries to accelerate quantitative growth in disregard of international supplies of primary commodities. Adverse weather conditions in 1971-2 led to poor grain harvests in the Northern hemisphere. In order to compensate for domestic shortfalls, some countries entered the international market and purchased from others who had less than usual to dispose of. The industrial countries were unable to contain the resultant rise in grain prices, though they themselves were the principal producers. If they could not contain grain prices, they were even more vulnerable to oil prices. In the third quarter of the century, the industrial world had allowed itself to become dependent on imported fuels, and especially imported oil. Towards the end of 1973 an artificial restraint on supplies coupled with a sharp increase in prices was imposed by non-industrial oil-producing countries. The industrial world had no immediate response.

This is not the place to add to the already voluminous literature on the oil crisis. Here it must suffice to say that it was only the most dramatic of a series of events which limited the possibilities of purely quantitative industrial expansion, and only the most extreme case of lack of integration between manufacturing and primary production within the industrial world. To let control of the chief source of industrial fuels temporarily go outside the industrial world was of course compatible with the principles of inter-industry specialisation. These principles no longer explain what was happening in the relations between industrial countries which came to be governed by intra-industry trade. The latter means an eventual narrowing of the trade balance in individual products. But inter-industry trade means a widening of the trade balance in individual products. The combination of the two tendencies means that, even in the absence of special crises, an integrating industrial world is liable to run into imbalance with its suppliers.

This is a variant of the relatively quicker inter- than intra-trade response to new opportunities, discussed with reference to European countries on pp. 181-6. There are some differences. Here, the 'country' which is less advanced in intra-trade is the primary producing world or a sector of that world. New opportunities are not so much trade-led as led by industrial production. Primary producers can and do respond to inter-trade opportunities. But to date, they have had next to no intra-trade opportunities. The reasons will be discussed in Chapter 6. Here the question is whether this situation results in a long-run tendency towards industrial deficit with the primary producing world or whether this tendency is likely to be offset by other influences.

According to the preceding argument, industrial growth provides new trading opportunities for primary producers, and this would turn the balance of trade in the primary producers' favour unless and until there is an intra-trade response. Since no such response could come from primary producers, there was a tendency at work towards long-run balance of trade deficit of the industrial sector. But this tended to be offset by other influences.

One way of avoiding a deficit is to buy less. Although industrial growth usually meant an absolute increase in purchases of primary commodities, it tended to be accompanied by increases in productivity. Less inputs were needed per unit of output. The way this affected primary producers is shown by another secular trend, namely the lesser growth of international trade in primary commodities than of output of manufactures. There was a relative fall in demand for primary commodities.

This relative fall in demand may have obscured the need to ensure a growth of primary production in line with the requirements of industrial production. Put differently, there was no such direct link between supply and demand in primary commodities trades, or any inter-trades, as has emerged in the more closely integrated intra-trades. By the early 1970s, primary production grew relatively slowly, and this was aggravated by harvest failures and artificial restraint in oil output. No conceivable increase in industrial productivity could have offset these supply restraints. One consequence was that, for a time, the industrial world went into deficit with its inter-trade partners. The escape from this deficit would be industrial recovery. In the second half of the century, this can only mean more intra-trade and more valuable manufactures for all trade.

An alternative escape from imbalance between the industrial and the primary producing worlds, might be for the industrial world to pay less attention to its intra-trade. This escape would counter some of the major achievements of the third quarter of the century. Trade-led industrial growth and the improvement in international commercial relations would be in jeopardy. Instead, there might be more stability, in the sense of producing the same goods over longer periods of time. Even if this were a desirable objective, nobody seems to know how to bring it about. Attention has already been drawn to how the policy-makers of the 1970s sought to protect existing employment by means designed to offset a deficiency in demand, and how this led to relatively more demand for primary commodities at a time of supply restraints. This strengthened the hands of those primary producers who questioned the *Pax Americana*.

Yet the answer is not in their hands. Any attempt to hold the industrial world to ransom must eventually rebound. If the industrial world buys relatively more primary commodities but absolutely less, primary producers may be hurt. For the industrial world provides most of their markets. It is however not necessary to seek a negative solution to the problem of unequal integration of industrial and primary producing interests and to any imbalance of trade between the two sectors. While it would not be possible to develop intra-trade in primary commodities the way this has been done in manufactures, it seems possible to apply to primary commodities trades at least one of the features of intra-trade. This is to gear production to particular uses and users. An example of what can be done that way is provided by the trade in tropical timber. In that trade, it has been found that direct sales to specific users of semi-finished products mean more stable prices than those obtained in 'commodity timber' sold through the market mechanism.[133] While this does not do away with agents and importers, direct contact with the end-user is becoming increasingly important.[134] This is compatible with the points made in relation to intra-industry trade. Competition, if this is still the right word, is not so much on price as on meeting the quality required by the end-user. This development manifested itself first in the most advanced manufactured goods, and, thanks to freer trade, was to be a major cause of industrial prosperity in the third quarter of the century.

Applied to primary commodities, there would have to be more specialisation in primary production. There would also have to be more direct links between primary producers and industrial producers, the main users of traded primary commodities. In the twentieth century world today, there has been a direct relationship between industrial production and trade in primary commodities. But periods of exceptional supply restraint apart, there has been no direct relationship between primary production and trade. Isolated instances apart, there has been no direct link between primary and industrial producers. To establish such links would not lead to intra-trade the way it has developed between industrial producers. The products are too different and so are the conditions under which they are produced. There would however be less isolation of primary producers from decision-taking in and for the world economy.

The section must not conclude on this note, for there seem to be no immediate prospects of major developments in this direction. The lead would have to come from the principal primary producers. For most commodities, these are the major industrial countries. Their policy to date has been internal protection for agriculture and some other primary producing interests. Thus, they isolated their own primary producers from the mainstream of domestic developments, though their freer trade policies allowed international integration in most manufactures. As long as such attitudes continue, there is little or no prospect of international economic integration for primary producers. If the nature of the goods and technological factors make it difficult to integrate primary producers into the *Pax Americana*, policy considerations continue to make it virtually impossible.

Notes

1. Organisation for European Economic Co-operation, *A Decade of Co-operation* OEEC, Paris, 1958, Chapter III.
2. Ibid, p.63.
3. *Treaty establishing the European Atomic Energy Community*, Treaty Series No.1 (1973) – Part II, Cmnd. 5179, pp.162-94, especially Article 2.
4. *Treaty establishing the European Coal and Steel Community*, Paris, 1951; William Diebold, Jr., *The Schuman Plan*, Frederick A. Praeger, New York, 1959, esp. pp.79-81; A.E. Walsh and John Paxton, *Into Europe*, Hutchinson, London, 1973, Chapter 16.
5. For instance, export levies were imposed in years when EC cereal prices were below world prices.
6. Cmnd., 5179 – II, pp.1-160.
7. EFTA, *The Trade Effects of EFTA and the EEC, 1959-1967,* Geneva, 1972, p.45 claims that more new trade could be attributed to EFTA than to EEC.
8. *European Free Trade Association* (Convention of Stockholm), Cmnd.906, 1959.
9. EC took from 1959 to 1968, EFTA from 1960 to 1967. Both accelerated their schedules of tariff reductions.
10. F.V. Meyer, *The Seven*, Barrie & Rockliff, London, 1960, pp.113-7.
11. Compare Article 16 of Cmnd. 906 with Part II, Title III of Cmnd. 5179 – II.
12. Cmnd. 906, Article 15 and Cmnd. 5179-II, Part III, Title I.
13. Finland and Iceland became associates of EFTA. Ireland confined herself to a free trade agreement with the UK (Cmnd. 2858, 1965).
14. Cmnd. 5179-II, Treaty of Rome, Article 237.
15. Cf. e.g. John Williamson, 'Trade and Economic Growth' in John Pinder (ed.), *The Economics of Europe*, Charles Knight & Co., London, 1971.
16. This goes further than the scale effects studied by Christopher Layton, *The Benefits of Scale for Industry*, in J. Pinder, ibid.
17. Treaty of Rome, Article 103.
18. John Pinder, 'Positive Integration and Negative Integration,' *World Today*, 1968, reprinted in M. Hodges (ed.), *European Integration*, Penguin, London, 1972, p.139.
19. For a brief outline of the working of CAP see e.g. A.E. Walsh and John Paxton, *Into Europe*, Chapter 8; or Dennis Swann, *The Economics of the Common Market*, Penguin, London, 1975, Chapter 6.
20. See p.68.
21. ECSC Treaty, Preamble.
22. A.E. Walsh and J. Paxton, *Into Europe*, pp.158-9.
23. EC Commission, *Ninth General Report on the Activities of the European Communities in 1975*, Brussels 1976, p.200.
24. A.E. Walsh and J. Paxton, *Into Europe,* pp.158-9, 168; and EC, *Ninth General Report*, pp.172-4.
25. See pp.98-102.
26. Compare EC First General Report, 1967, p.385: 'EEC *Member States* made substantial concessions' with Fifth General Report, 1971: '*The Community* declared its readiness to conclude . . . agreements' (italics mine).
27. This is a variant or elaboration of a theme suggested by Theo Peeters and Wolfgang Hager, 'The Community and the Changing World Order' in M. Kohnstamm and W. Hager (eds.), *A Nation Writ Large*, London, Macmillan, 1973, p.25. There attention is drawn to the growth of domestic interventionist policies at a time of a move towards international *laissez-faire.*
28. EC, *Ninth General Report,* Brussels, 1976, p.52.

29. EEC Commission, *Eighth General Report on the Activities of the Community, 1.4.1964-31.3.1965*, Brussels, 1965, p.27.
30. EC, *Seventh General Report*, Brussels, 1974, p.122.
31. EC, *Ninth General Report,* Brussels, 1976, p.74.
32. John Pinder, 'Positive Integration and Negative Integration', *World Today*, 1968.
33. EC, *Ninth General Report*, p.62.
34. Ibid., pp.65 and 141.
35. The recognition of medical qualifications became effective in 1976, that of lawyers was then still under consideration. See EC, *Tenth General Report*, Brussels 1977, pp.209-10.
36. Treaty of Rome, Article 138 (3).
37. For instance, it can dismiss the Commission but only member governments can appoint a new one. See Articles 144, 157-8.
38. Following uniform assessment of VAT from 1977 onwards, this is to replace member contributions to the EC budget. See EC, *Tenth General Report*, p.19.
39. See Chapter 4, Section 1.
40. EC, *Fourth General Report*, 1970, secs. 76-80 and relevant sections in later General Reports.
41. I.e. the worth of new rights exceeds the burden of new obligations.
42. George M. Taber, *Patterns and Prospects of Common Market Trade,* Peter Owen, London, 1974, p.17.
43. For details see Eurostat, *Foreign Trade, 1958-74* and *Monthly General Statistics Bulletin*, 11-1976. Luxembourg 1977.
44. OECD, *Policy Perspectives for International Trade and Economic Relations*, (Rey Report) Paris 1972, esp. Table 2. Note that the Rey Report relates trade to GNP while the ratios shown here relate to GDP.
45. 'Marked' increases or divergences means changes of 0.5 per cent a year or more.
46. Derived from Eurostat, *National Accounts Yearbook*, 1976, Table A3 and opa. cit. in note 43.
47. Average deviations from a five-year moving average, compiled from data for 1960-74, were: for intra-EC imports 0.23, intra-EC exports 0.16, extra-EC imports 0.36 and extra-EC exports 0.41 for 1962-70.
48. By a five-year moving average.
49. From 9.6 in 1960-4 to 9.0 in 1964-8, and then remained at 9.2 for 1965-9 to 1968-72.
50. From 9.2 in 1960-4 to 8.75 in 1962-6. Subsequently it rose in every five-year period. It equalled or exceeded 1960-4 in 1966-70. In 1968-72 it was 9.5.
51. 9.4 for imports and 9.5 for exports of the Six, and 9.6 for both imports and exports of the Nine.
52. In exports from 11.8 to 11.2 compared with from 13.5 to 11.6 for imports.
53. See e.g. note 21.
54. See pp.135 and 138.
55. Jacob Viner, *The Customs Union Issue*, Stevens & Sons, London, 1950, Chapter 4, esp. pp.43-51.
56. This term was not used by Viner. It is taken from Joseph Schumpeter, *Business Cycles*, McGraw Hill, London, 1939.
57. Maurice Peston, *The Philosophy of Major Change*, in J. Pinder (ed.), *Economics of Europe*, esp. pp.216-17.
58. J. Viner, *Customs Union Issue,* pp.69-71; J.M. Fleming, 'On making the best of balance of payments restrictions on imports', *Economic Journal,* March 1951.

59. J. Viner, ibid.
60. See e.g. Bela Balassa, 'Trade Creation and Trade Diversion in the European Common Market', *Manchester School*, May 1974, M.E. Kreinin, 'Effects of the EEC on Imports of Manufactures', *Economic Journal*, September 1972; EFTA *The Trade Effects of EFTA and the EEC, 1959-1967.*
61. B. Balassa, ibid., p.120; Christopher Saunders, *From Free Trade to Integration in Western Europe*, Chatham House – PEP European Series No.22, London, 1975, p.25.
62. EEC, *Fourth General Report*, Brussels, 1961, p.86.
63. See e.g. EEC, *Fifth General Report*, Brussels, 1962, p.99 and *Tenth General Report*, Brussels, 1967, p.137.
64. EEC, *Tenth General Report*, p.140.
65. B. Balassa, 'Trade Creation', p.127.
66. For a cautious approach see e.g. H.G. Johnson, 'The Gains from Freer Trade with Europe', *Manchester School*, September 1968.
67. Allyn A. Young, 'Increasing Returns and Economic Progress', *Economic Journal*, December 1928.
68. Ibid., pp.532, 535, 539.
69. Dermot McAleese, 'Do Tariffs Matter?', *Oxford Economic Papers*, March 1977; and 'Industrial Specialisation and Trade in Two Small Economies', *Economic and Social Review*, January 1976.
70. *Agreement establishing a Free Trade Area between the UK and the Republic of Ireland*, Cmnd. 2858.
71. Dermot McAleese, 'Do Tariffs Matter?' and 'Industrial Specialisation'.
72. Derived from *Monthly Digest of Statistics.*
73. Derived from OECD, *Market Surveys*, Series C.
74. Ibid.
75. Although it was as high as 5.9 per cent in 1971, it was 1.3 per cent in 1970 and 0.7 per cent in 1972.
76. EEC, *Seventh General Report*, Brussels, 1964, p.105.
77. EC, *Sixth General Report*, Brussels, 1973, pp.89-90.
78. EC, *Fifth General Report*, Brussels, 1972, pp.129-35.
79. EC, *Sixth General Report*, Brussels, 1973, p.90.
80. Ibid.
81. Ibid., pp.88-90.
82. David Robertson, 'The Effects of EFTA Tariff dismantling on Prices', *EFTA Bulletin*, November 1966, pp.5-7.
83. EC, *Fourth General Report*, 1971, p.246.
84. B. Balassa, 'Trade Creation', p.246.
85. See Chapter 2, Section 2.
86. H.A. Turner and D.A.S. Jackson, 'On the Determination of the General Wage Level -- A World Analysis', *Economic Journal*, December 1970.
87. Ibid., pp.832 and 845.
88. P.A. Samuelson, 'International Trade and the Equalisation of Factor Prices', *Economic Journal*, June 1948. Much of the subsequent criticism was based on the ground that the theory would not apply under conditions of increasing returns with inter-industry specialisation. A restatement of the theory under conditions of increasing returns with intra-industry specialisation still seems to await its author.
89. Allyn Young, 'Increasing Returns', 533.
90. Kiyoshi Kojima, *Japan and a New World Economic Order*, Croom Helm, London, 1977, p.31.
91. Eurostat, *National Accounts, 1960-75*, Table A4.
92. GATT, *Japan's Economic Expansion and Foreign Trade, 1955-70*, Studies in

International Trade, No.2, Geneva 1971, p.14.
93. Japanese White Paper on International Trade and Industry, 1971 quoted by Terutomo Ozawa, *Japan's Technological Challenge to the West, 1950-74*, M.I.T. Press, Cambridge, Mass., 1974, pp.11-12.
94. See pp.57-9.
95. Derived from Kazushi Ohkawa and Henry Rokovsky, *Japanese Economic Growth,* Oxford University Press, 1973, note 2 on p.173 and Basic Statistical Table 13.
96. GATT, *Japan's Economic Expansion,* pp.14 and 18.
97. K. Kojima, *Japan*, pp.23-4.
98. Averages for 1905-13 and 1930-7 come to about 12½ per cent, and for 1920-9 to about 13½ per cent. Derived from K. Ohkawa and H. Rokovsky, *Japanese Economic Growth*, Basic Statistical Tables 1 and 13.
99. Averages for 1905-13 11 per cent and for both 1920-9 and 1930-9 11½ per cent. Derived from Ohkawa and Rokovsky, ibid.
100. Ibid., p.174.
101. Ibid., p.173 and W. Arthur Lewis, *Economic Survey, 1919-39*, Allen & Unwin, London, 1949, Chapter IX.
102. Five-year averages. Data to 1963 derived from Ohkawa and Rokovsky and from 1964 onwards from *International Financial Statistics,* tables on Japan, rows 70, 71 and 99b.
103. See p.150, and K. Kojima, *Japan*, pp.24-7.
104. K. Kojima, ibid., pp.27-8.
105. For details see T. Ozawa, *Japan's Technological Challenge,* pp.57-62, and K. Kojima, *Japan,* pp.35-6.
106. Robert Scalapino, *American-Japanese Relations in a Changing Era,* the Washington Papers No.2, Centre for Strategic and International Studies, Georgetown University, Washington, D.C. The Library Press, New York, 1972, p.51.
107. For details, see GATT, *Japan's Economic Expansion,* Table 14.
108. T. Ozawa, *Japan's Technological Challenge*, pp.20-9.
109. John K. Emmerson, *Arms, Yen and Power*, Dunellen, New York, 1971, pp.313-15.
110. T. Ozawa, *Japan's Technological Challenge,* pp.32-3 and 47.
111. Leon Hollerman, 'Recent Difficulties in Japan's Economic Development', *Banca Nazionale del Lavoro*, March 1969, p.71.
112. Ibid., p.72.
113. GATT, *Japan's Economic Expansion,* p.42.
114. For details see ibid., pp.27-8.
115. Herbert G. Grubel and P.J. Lloyd, *Intra-Industry Trade,* Macmillan, London, 1975.
116. See pp.98-103, 142-4.
117. William E. Bryant, *Japanese Private Economic Diplomacy,* Praeger, New York, 1975, p.50.
118. Statement based on press reports in 1976 and the first half of 1977.
119. See pp.57-9.
120. Averages for 1970-3, derived from Eurostat, *Monthly Trade Bulletin*, Special Number 1958-75, Tables 1 and 7; and OECD.
121. Averages for 1970-3, f.o.b. derived from UN, *Statistical Yearbook, 1975*, Tables, 150-1, and IMF, *International Financial Statistics,* US table, line 71.v., came to 33 per cent for imports and 30 per cent for exports.
122. Averages for 1950-3, for crude materials and crude foodstuffs, as shown in *Historical Statistics of the US*, Series U 61-3 and 67-9.

123. Differences in transport and distribution costs can be regarded as a near constant from one year to the next.
124. Import unit value indices (1972 = 100) for 1958, 1968, 1972 and 1974 were for Japan: 104, 101, 100, 199 respectively and for the UK 72, 85, 100, 193, respectively. Derived from UN, *Statistical Yearbook,* Table 155.
125. UN, ibid., Table 14.
126. Ibid.
127. Hugh Corbet, *Raw Materials,* International Issues No.1, Trade Policy Research Centre, London, 1975, pp.7-8.
128. UN, *Statistical Yearbook.*
129. Ibid.
130. For details see e.g. Futures Price Index of 27 Markets, as shown in *Commodity Yearbooks, 1975* and *1976*, Commodity Research Bureau, New York, pp.11 and 4 respectively; and Metallgesellschaft A.G., *Metal Statistics, 1965-75*, Frankfurt am Main, 1976, pp.324-62.
131. *UN Monthly Bulletin of Statistics,* September 1976, Selected Series of World Statistics.
132. J.S. Chard and F.V. Meyer, 'Fluctuations in Food Import prices and Balance of Payments', *The Bankers' Magazine,* June 1972.
133. Donald Moore and Malcolm Cheslyn, 'Overseas Marketing of Tropical Timber', *International Trade Forum,* July-September 1974, p.5.
134. Ibid., p.6.

6 INTRA-TRADE AND INTERNATIONAL TRADE POLICY

1. Intra- and Inter-Trades under Free Trade

Internal protection means that foreign economic policy remains a domestic issue. Decided upon unilaterally, it is virtually non-negotiable. Effects on foreign countries are incidental. Those countries are not expected to complain as long as they are treated alike. Before 1934, this was the US attitude towards all protection. Tariff rates were set according to domestic requirements. The same attitude prevailed elsewhere. For instance, the UK decided unilaterally whether to be free trade or protectionist. Trade agreements softened these attitudes. Once trade barriers became negotiable, the various national foreign economic policies became intertwined. An international trade policy emerged. In place of domestic policies with international implications came the integration of the various domestic policies into an international one.

Old attitudes lingered however. The change came only gradually. The preceding chapters have pointed to certain landmarks in the history of trade policy. Yet it is not possible to say precisely when international considerations were given sufficient weight relative to domestic ones, to justify the term 'international trade policy'. But it can be said that the change has taken place in industrial products and has not taken place in temperate zone agricultural commodities. True there were some reductions on tariff rates on some agricultural commodities. But these were virtually meaningless where national authorities continued to intervene in quantities and prices. To this day, US agricultural legislation has priority over trade agreements legislation. Quantities of relevant imports can still be unilaterally determined in order to ensure that imports do not frustrate domestic production plans. The EC tries to regulate agricultural production through intervention in prices. It wants no disturbance of such prices through outside influences. In different ways, both the US and the EC want production-led, rather than trade-led developments in their agriculture. So does Japan. GATT-style negotiations can lead to only limited results for such commodities.[1] Perhaps an OEEC-type of approach would be more suitable. But this has not been attempted.

Yet even if all obstacles to the freeing of agricultural trade had been overcome, the results could not have been as dramatic as they were in manufactures. The main effect of freer trade in manufactures was the growth of intra-industry trade. Freer trade is a precondition for intra-trade. But it is not a sufficient condition. Some further conditions have to be satisfied as well.

The basic condition appears to be a short market life of the product *relative* to the length of the R & D stage. Implied is production under increasing returns to scale. This leads to a second condition, namely increased specialisation between producing units within each product range. Implied here is that trade can grow by more than production, and that such trade reduces and does not cause the risk of a supply restraint. A third condition is that the use and the user of the product can be identified at the point of production. Implied is production of specific goods. These conditions can be satisfied and lead to intra-trade only when trade is free or becoming freer. They are not necessarily satisfied when trade is free and becoming freer. In the third quarter of the century, most manufactures satisfied one or more of these conditions. Only few primary commodities satisfied the third condition and none all three. The remaining pages of this book will be concerned with the trade policy implications of these conditions, starting with the implications for primary commodities.

Primary commodities cannot satisfy the basic condition of a short market life relative to the R & D stage. Virtually every primary commodity which is currently available is likely to be wanted for as long as one can see. This does not mean absence of R & D. In fact, R & D has led to major technological feats in various primary producing activities. One example, in the third quarter of the century, was a marked increase in temperate zone agricultural output despite a substantial decrease in the labour force. But when the market life of a commodity seems endless, even an R & D stage of, say, one or two decades, is short relative to the subsequent market life of the commodity concerned. The basic condition for intra-trade is not satisfied. It may be added that, in all cases, where market life is long relative to the R & D stage, there is no such compelling need to recoup R & D costs quickly as there is in the case of products with a short market life. In other words, in the case of commodities with a long market life, intra-trade is not necessary.

Such commodities continue to be produced long enough that production gets past the increasing returns stage. Hence most of such production takes place under conditions of decreasing returns to scale. Although technological progress can be expected to lead to improved grading, the overall effect is not product differentiation but standardisation. Produce from different farms become perfect substitutes, and production methods become more alike. This is incompatible with the second condition for intra-trade. In such circumstances, intra-trade becomes less possible.

As the commodities produced by numerous suppliers are perfect substitutes and there are numerous consumers, such commodities continue to be sold through intermediaries, be they private merchants or state agencies. Although some primary production can be geared to specific uses, in the third quarter of the century this was exceptional. Generally, the uses and users of primary commodities are unknown at the farmgate or pit-head. Thus the third condition for intra-trade remains unsatisfied in all major primary commodities trades.

Since the conditions for intra-trade do not apply in primary commodities trades, these trades must remain inter-trades even under free trade. In consequence, these trades operate under certain demand and supply restraints which can be overcome in intra-trade but not in inter-trades. Take the demand restraint first. As shown in the preceding section, the demand for internationally traded primary commodities is largely industrial demand, and the growth of such trades has remained closely correlated to the growth of manufacturing. This demand restraint could not be overcome even where there was free trade, as in basic materials. True, there were some import duties, but they were usually low and in most cases imposed for revenue reasons. For the sake of their domestic manufacturing interests, importing countries seldom impeded the growth of such trades. Even in the inter-war years, there had been relatively few restrictions on such trades. After the war, importing countries freed such trades as soon as they could. In most cases, traditional markets functioned again in the 1950s. At least within this range of commodities, a *Pax Britannica* style of unilateral free trade was restored. Free trade allowed those trades to grow towards the limit set by the growth of industrial production.

This contrasts with the position of manufactures, where the conditions for intra-trade were given. There, free trade could lead to a greater growth of trade than of industrial production. Since firms specialised in a smaller number of products within their possible range and bought in the rest from other firms at home or abroad, trade could grow by more than production. Since each could specialise more and have longer production runs in goods manufactured under conditions of increasing returns, production became more profitable. In consequence, production grew by more than it could otherwise have done. The contractual freeing of trade between industrial countries made trade-led growth possible. Where trade is a cause of increased production, it pushes back any possible supply restraint. This too cannot be taken for granted in inter-trades.

Inter-trades are trades where most production takes place under conditions of decreasing returns. A price competitive free market then gives producers an adequate return to keep capital intact but not enough to finance expansion of their activities. At the beginning of the century, the funds for expansion could be provided by freely functioning capital markets. Producers could then buy or hire the factors they needed for further production. By the third quarter of the century, however, capital markets no longer functioned so freely. Moreover, for at least some primary production, additional factors were not available. The chief example is temperate zone agriculture. No major new land areas could have been made available for such agriculture. It was not even possible to retain the bulk of the labour force. The growth of output depended on R & D. This has to be financed.

Again, there were opportunities for manufactures through intra-trade which are not available to inter-trades. Where intra-trade led to the growth of increasing returns activities, the nature of pricing changed. In quality, model or improvement competition, it became possible to charge enough for the product that sales proceeds could make a contribution towards the R & D costs incurred by industry. This does not mean to say that industrial R & D became self-financing. Much of the R cost was borne by universities and other public or professional bodies. But the D costs are usually a charge on the industries concerned. The multilateral abolition of trade barriers led to intra-trade and increasing returns, so that the market price could make a contribution to D costs. Free trade helped towards the self-finance of industrial progress.

It could not do so for temperate zone agriculture. Under free trade, there would have been relatively more cross-frontier trade than there was. It is not certain, however, that there would have been more trade in absolute terms, for the free market price obtainable in an inter-trade, with production under conditions of decreasing returns to scale, could not have been high enough to make a contribution to D costs. In consequence, there would have been less growth of production. Since an increasingly urbanised world wanted additional supplies of temperate zone agricultural commodities, some way had to be found to cover the D costs of agriculture. The ways chosen by the US and the EC raised prices above free market levels. Ideally, the difference should cover the D costs. Whether or not this ideal has been attained, the point is that the problem of temperate zone agriculture is in the first place a problem of production rather than a problem of trade. Any national, Community or international action must then concentrate on production-led growth. It would seem that agriculture could be more responsive to an OEEC style production-led approach than to a GATT style trade-led one. Yet all international policy must ensure equal or greater growth of trade than of production. If this condition is not satisfied, the policy cannot remain international for long, since domestic considerations will almost certainly predominate.

2. Maintaining the Momentum towards Free Trade

(i) Products

Freer trade without agriculture is an incomplete freer trade. But without closer links between producers and users of agricultural commodities, none of the conditions for intra-trade apply. In the absence of unforeseen developments, agriculture must remain less responsive to freer trade than manufacturing. Moreover, freer agricultural trade cannot affect its own production and other trade as much as freer manufactures trade does. One implication is that, at least for some time to come, agriculture is likely to remain the most protected sector. This further implies that farmers are likely to be least affected by the international move towards equality of commercial rights. By definition, the protected have a special status. They are nobody else's equals.

This is not an argument for discrimination by activities in place of discrimination by nationality. It is mere recognition of the effects of discrimination in favour of certain activities through internal protection. An inevitable consequence of such discrimination is that those in the favoured activity are not the equals of others at home nor the equals of those in like activities abroad. Again, this is not an argument in favour of less equality for those in one activity or group of activities compared with others. Much of the argument of this book has been concerned with the importance of the move towards commercial equality of rights, both on economic grounds and for the sake of improved international relations. But it has also been asserted that international trade policy must fit economic facts. It is not always possible to do everything at once, nor is it always possible to obtain identical results simply by applying the same policy in all circumstances.

At the time of the opening of the Seventh (Tokyo) Round of GATT negotiations, the major industrial countries' tariffs on finished manufactures still averaged about 8½ per cent *ad valorem.*[2] This was a major inroad into the profitability of exporting. While tariffs were not the sole cause of the difference in profitability of home and export sales, their removal could go a long way to eliminate that difference.[3] There was still room for meaningful tariff reductions. Moreover, tariff reductions on manufactures can have more far-reaching effects than other tariff cuts. The reasons for this assertion will now be briefly restated.

The reciprocal freeing of trade has proved to be most effective where the conditions for intra-trade are satisfied. As shown in the preceding section, these conditions are a short market life of the product relative to the R & D stage, increased specialisation within industries, and the possibility of identifying use and user of the product at the point of production. The respective implications of these conditions are production with increasing returns on capital employed, the greater growth of trade than of production, and the production of specific goods. Although these points are inter-related, in a consideration of international trade policy the crucial point is the greater growth of trade than of production.

Only in intra-trades can a greater growth of trade than of production be sustained. So it was in manufactures, in the third quarter of the century. Technological opportunities to improve industrial production became economic opportunities through freer trade. That made specialisation possible. Firms specialised more in production, but still wanted to satisfy their customers over the whole range of products within their competence. In order to do so, they had to buy in what they did not produce themselves but continued to sell, and they could afford to buy in more because they supplied their specialities to other firms. The further such specialisation went, the more could the growth of trade exceed the growth of production. Because trade made production more profitable, the volume of industrial production was raised. There was a direct link between the growth of trade and of production. In other words, there was trade-led growth. The growth of industrial production, in turn, raised the demand for internationally traded primary commodities. Although the link between the growth of trade in manufactures and the growth of trade in primary commodities was indirect, the growth of the latter could still be attributed to the growth of the former. At this point, the discernible effects of the growth of trade in manufactures ceased. Throughout this century, trade in primary commodities has normally been more closely correlated to what happened in industrial production than in their own production. And, so far, it has not been possible to integrate industrial and primary production the way industrial production came to be integrated in intra-trades.

As long as such circumstances prevail, international trade policy is most effective if it concentrates on trade in manufactures. It must be assumed that positive growth of the world economy will continue to depend foremost on trade policy relating to manufactures, at any rate for the rest of this century. As long as tariffs still reduce the profitability of such trade, it remains possible to give the world economy a further stimulus through tariff cuts on manufactured goods. But the argument must not be so rigid as to exclude the unforeseen. Nor must it give the impression that the results can suit all countries or all types of manufactures to the same extent.

Intra-trade itself was an unforeseen result of the multilateral reduction of trade barriers. Until the 1950s, these reductions were negotiated bilaterally on the basis of apparent comparative advantage between two countries. Each country sought concessions on its major exports, in the hope that these industries would expand. And each country gave concessions on its major imports, in the fear that its import-competing industries would contract. The balance of advantage was thought to be that the expansion of the industries in which the country's comparative advantage lay would outweigh the loss of industries in which the country had a comparative disadvantage. In most cases, events turned out differently. By the time a large number of concessions had been bilaterally negotiated and multilaterally applied, trade barriers on most products had been reduced. Bilateral comparative advantage ceased to be relevant. Comparative advantage with the whole trading world became relevant. This did not work through the growth of one industry here and its destruction there. Instead, there came specialisation within industries, altering the nature of industrial activities rather than their location. Comparative advantage in technology within industries became decisive. It depended on having partners within those industries who would exploit other technological advances relevant to such industries. Such trade was essentially reciprocal between an industry in one country and its partners in all other countries which also allowed freer trade. In consequence, the industrial countries experienced simultaneous growth of imports and exports of goods under the same tariff heading. Any further reduction of trade barriers had to take account of this development. Negotiating interest of the major industrial countries shifted from the item-by-item approach to the linear across-the-board approach.

Carried to its logical conclusion, the latter approach should lead to complete free trade between industrial countries. In the 1960s, it was used this way by the EC and other regional free trade schemes. Their move to regional free trade was effected in several linear across-the-board tariff cuts. This went beyond the needs of intra-trades, though it was in those trades that free trade was to become most effective. In GATT, it was not possible to go so far. US legislation limited the possible extent of the tariff reductions, and this constraint continues. It was not possible to include all products. Nor were those included selected on the basis of any intra-trade criterion. It was not even possible to negotiate identical tariff cuts for all of the groups included. Nevertheless, there was a move towards 'reciprocity' which went some way towards meeting the needs of intra-trade.

Across-the-board tariff reductions were an international trade policy response to the rise in intra-trades. It is not yet clear whether further policy adjustments will follow. Perhaps the only way is the one by which industrial countries edge somewhat closer towards free trade in a large number of industrial goods whenever US trade agreements legislation allows a new GATT Round. It may be doubted however whether there can be many more GATT Rounds. For negotiating purposes, tariffs are now low, at least compared with what they were in the 1930s. None of the major commercial powers has so far shown willingness to abandon tariffs altogether. And tariffs are an important source of revenue for fiscally less developed countries. Attention has shifted to non-tariff barriers. Since this involves harmonisation of laws besides tariff law, progress along such lines will be determined by political rather than economic considerations.

Whatever the *ad valorem* equivalent of tariff rates for negotiating purposes, it is always higher for trading purposes. For the former, it is estimated relative to the value of the goods, for the latter relative to the profitability of transactions. If further tariff reductions can no longer be achieved in such dramatic ways as in the 1940s and 1960s, there is still a case for making international trade less unprofitable relative to domestic trade. If this can no longer be done through negotiations which embrace all industrial products, perhaps a new product approach may be possible. This is not a novel idea. The ECSC and the US-Canadian agreement concerning automotive products provided free trade for a limited range of goods. The across-the-board approach itself split up GATT negotiations into sectors. Perhaps this points to freer trade for some products than for others.

Should such an approach be accepted, products would have to be graded according to their responsiveness to intra-trade. In the 1960s and 1970s, products at or near the top of a list of responsive products would have included chemicals and certain engineering products. At or near the bottom of the list, being closest to inter-trades, would have been most paper and textile products. Primary commodities, being pure inter-trades, would not have been included. In such circumstances, reciprocal tariff reductions would have most impact if they concentrated on products at or near the top of the list. This is a medium- or long-term argument. It will be recalled that inter-trade effects may show more quickly than intra-trade ones, though the inter-trade ones have less effect as time goes by. The effects which international trade negotiators seek depends on the time scale they have in mind as well as on the industrial structure of the countries they represent.

The choice between quick and more lasting effects is virtually the same as that between relatively minor and major effects. Suppose the negotiators opt for quick results. They then remove tariffs first and/or most on products near the bottom of the list. Tariff reductions normally increase the volume of trade which, in turn, raises production. This is a once-and-for-all increase in trade. In manufactures, reciprocal tariff reductions usually lead to at least some specialisation which increases the demand for trade, and increased trade further raises the profitability and volume of production. In all such cases, there is trade-led growth. But the greater growth of trade than of production is not the same in all products. Trade-led growth, if measured by how much more trade grows than production, is likely to be greater in the products near the top of the list than in those near the bottom. The argument returns to the point that the impact of tariff reductions is likely to be the greater the more intra-trade responsive the product.

This is not a new principle but reflects the outcome of the Sixth (Kennedy) Round. For instance, tariff rates on chemicals were reduced by nearly twice as much as those on textiles. The lesser tariff reductions on textiles were agreed only because they were accompanied by a revised orderly marketing agreement. In effect this meant tariff reductions for all but quota restraint on some. It is not intended go into detail, but it may be useful to point in general terms to differences between intra- and inter-trade relationships which can lead to discrimination between countries.

(ii) LDCs

As far as trade between Western industrial countries was concerned, the reduction in textile tariffs presented no special problems. There was some intra-textiles trade and this was encouraged by the tariff cuts. There was no need for quotas. Virtually none were applied in trade between those countries. Matters were more complex in relation with some Asian countries. The issue that is singled out for consideration is the effect of the growth of inter-trading by LDCs on their commercial relations with the advanced industrial countries.

By the 1960s, it had become customary for the advanced industrial countries to extend all tariff concessions to the LDCs without asking for any concessions in return. Effectively, the industrial countries made unilateral tariff concessions to the LDCs. The result was a one-sided growth of trade. This included what, taken by itself, is the least attractive feature of inter-trade, namely that the growth of an industry in one geographical area comes at the expense of the same industry in another. Such a situation is liable to occur when trade does *not* grow by more than production. In such circumstances, trade does not grow in response to demand. Instead it is the means by which production in excess of a country's home requirements displaces production elsewhere. Such growth is production-led – which is another way of saying that it may cause international difficulties.

The last point must not be exaggerated, especially as long as only one group of products is involved and especially one with a relatively low intra-trade responsiveness. But as long as trade is freed by one side only, the same sort of situation is liable to occur in other products. Generally, one-sided free trade can encourage inter-trade and not intra-trade in particular products. If the advanced industrial countries then defend their established interests through the imposition of quotas, one-sided free trade gives way to bilateral protectionism. The alternative would be for LDCs to lower their tariff rates on products of which they have become net exporters. They are no longer LDCs in respect of those products. This way they could become participants in intra-trade. Then it would be in their interest to renounce special privileges and seek equality.

(iii) Industrial Countries

The industrialising LDCs' interests are only beginning to shift from an item-by-item (or 'cloth-for-wine') inter-trade interest in international trade to an across-the-board (or 'cloth-for-cloth') intra-trade one in particular products. By contrast the most advanced industrial countries' interest has generally become an across-the-board one. In exceptional cases, they revert to an item-by-item approach. These exceptions tend to include cases where they meet inter-trade style quantitative (price) competition from industrialising countries. One policy issue, in the relations between industrialised and industrialising countries, is the reconciliation of inter-trade to intra-trade attitudes. This involves a change from a 'beat your rival' to a 'join your partner' mentality. Not the least of the problems involved will be to know exactly when to make this adjustment.

This will not be easy, though future participants in intra-trading will at least know what to expect. The older industrial countries did not. As pointed out more than once in this book, intra-trade was not planned. It developed at a time of growing international goodwill amongst the industrial countries, when the appropriate technological opportunities were available and the reduction of trade barriers made it possible to take those opportunities. At first, the tariff reductions were intended to facilitate inter-trade. By the time they covered a wide range of products, their effects were felt across the board, whichever way they were negotiated. Negotiating procedure followed the facts. Yet the full implications were not recognised for some time.

The country which was probably hurt most by the slow recognition of the significance of intra-trade was the UK. She led in such trade. If intra-trade is taken as an index of technological advancement, the UK should have done particularly well in trade and production. She did not. Now, a technogical lead in trade does not necessarily imply such a lead in production. What it does imply is an apparent comparative advantage in trades which, at the time, best satisfied the conditions for intra-trade. While this leaves open the question of where the UK stood in relation to other countries' technology, such a comparative advantage was possible only in one of the high technology countries. In all those countries, the technology for intra-traded products ran ahead of economics. Although international trade policy followed the needs of intra-trades, other economic policies often continued as if this was still a world of inter-trades. Of course the inter-trades had not disappeared and, in the early post-war years, they were still the more important ones. But the intra-trades grew more. Perhaps there was no policy or business decision which could have served both kinds of trades equally well. But the needs of the growing sector were unknown. Intra-trade had gone on for some time before it was recognised. It took some years before the implications were thought out, and even longer before the findings became widely known. Recognition of intra-trade was probably no slower in the UK than elsewhere. But just because the country led in intra-trade, the gap between technological opportunities and economic interpretation was particularly wide.

It does not follow that earlier recognition of intra-trade could have solved all of the UK's post-war trading problems. But it could have affected the responses to these problems if, for instance, some of the changes in the balance of trade had been interpreted with intra- as well as inter-trade in mind. Thus, case studies of the effects of intra-European free trade have indicated a tendency for inter-trade effects to be quicker than intra-trade effects. If it is legitimate to apply these findings to the UK's post-war trading experience, the following interpretation emerges. It is that the freeing of trade initially weakens the balance of trade of the technologically more advanced country, and the UK was the technologically more advanced country in relation to most countries. Subsequently, the intra-trade effects assert themselves and there is a tendency towards balanced trade. The end result is an increase in real output in both countries. But before this stage is reached, there is a net transfer of goods from the less advanced to the more advanced country, and of money from the more advanced to the less advanced country. This is the purchase price of widening the area of intra-trade. In the absence of monetary union between the trading countries, this can add to the balance of payments difficulties of the more advanced country, though only for a time.

Had this interpretation been known and accepted, the responses to the UK's recurrent trading problems would have been different from what they were. These responses were based on inter-trade theory, so that a deterioration in the trade balance was attributed to 'inefficiency'. Remedial measures were designed to improve the performance of the inter-trades in what was thought to be a price competitive world. It is not inconceivable that such measures improved the performance of inter-trades and held back the intra-trades. If so, the national product grew less than it might have done, there was less of an initial deficit after the freeing of trade but also less of a subsequent movement towards trade balance. On either the inter- or intra-trade interpretation, there was different efficiency. But only on the inter-trade interpretation did this necessarily mean lesser efficiency in the UK.

The UK's was an extreme case of the problems created by intra-trade or rather by the late recognition of the nature and significance of such trade. But it was not an unique case. Most, if not all, advanced industrial countries must have made some such unintended 'payment' for this effect of the freeing of trade. But for a country with average technology in trade, payments and receipts would have cancelled out. In so far as there was a payment, it was a payment after the event. The first effects of freer trade were inter-trade effects and these favoured the technologically 'small' country. This is compatible with received international trade theory which explains inter-trade. The intra-trade effects take longer to materialise and favour the 'large' and the 'small' country alike, at least in their balance of trade effects. There seems to be the equivalent of an entrance fee, and this has to be paid by the large country. None of this is meant to suggest that intra-trade is against the interest of the large country. A large country which cannot or will not pay the entrance fee, deprives itself of full commercial utilisation of what technological advantages it may have.

Again, it is not suggested that it is unusual for a 'large' country to 'pay' others for acceptance of its ways. But usually this is made in advance of implementation of a policy. Examples from trade policy include the willingness of the US to give more scheduled concessions than she received in return for other countries' acceptance of her business ethics of non-discrimination. Or the willingness of all industrial countries to give special tariff favours to LDCs, in the expectation that the latter will observe non-discrimination. Since it was thought that tariff reductions would lead to an increase in inter-trade, one-sided tariff reductions also meant a worsening of the large country's balance of trade.

When the US made such 'advance payment' to other industrial countries in order to ensure their adhesion to GATT, her negotiators could only have expected to 'buy' more inter-trade. In effect, she got intra-trade as well. The intention was to gain easier access to foreign markets for her exports. These included products of her increasing returns industries. Such products had specific uses and short market lives relative to their R & D stage. They already satisfied two of the conditions for intra-trade. The third condition, specialisation within industries, was made possible on an international scale through tariff reductions on items within the same product range. This is, of course, rationalisation after the event. To repeat, intra-trade was not foreseen at the time when the first major tariff reductions were made.

Intra-trade was an outcome of freer trade policy which underwrote the intention of the policy makers. It made trade-led growth possible and so furthered integration. International economic relations tend to be easier with trade-led growth than with production-led growth. In the former case, an increase in trade leads to a growth of domestic production. In the latter, growth depends on success in a scramble for factors. Almost inevitably this implies different attitudes towards other producers. Where growth is trade-led, you join your partners and respect their values, including their prices. Where growth is production-led, you try to beat your rivals and undercut their prices, which means that you interfere with their values. It need hardly be said that mutual respect of values eases commercial relations.

The cause of the freer trade policy was a mixture of motives which included the desire to underwrite peace through commerce, free trade theory which indicated that this was a suitable means towards that end, and the wish to provide wider markets for increasing returns activities. Common to the motives was equality: equality of the right to live, equality of the right to work (without having the proceeds of one's work taxed away in a discriminatory manner), and equality of the right to innovate (without obstruction through artificial narrowness of markets). If it was not possible to equate national and foreign rights, at least it was possible to put all foreign rights (or lack of rights) on an equal basis through most-favoured-nation treaties, and to narrow the difference between national and most-favoured-nation rights through scheduled concessions. The end was equality of rights, the means the freer trade policy, and the economic outcome intra-trade.

It is important to make this distinction between ends, means and commercial outcome, if the lessons of the third quarter of the century are to be good guidelines to future action. If policy concentrates on intra-trade, it concentrates on the unpredictable outcome of the combination of freer trade and technological progress. Since the results of tomorrow's R & D cannot be known, they are not definable and therefore not negotiable. Freer trade is negotiable, but all that is needed there is that present policies continue. There may be a case for seeking more international co-operation in problems which intra-trade has either created or not solved. For instance, the likely short-run balance of trade effects of intra-trade may call for more international monetary co-operation. But the long-run ones seem to make this less necessary.

If policy concentrates on further freeing of trade, it will meet with the obstacle of its own success. Trade in industrial goods cannot be freed further in EC. In GATT, tariff reductions have not yet reached their economic limit. But, unless at least the US, the EC and Japan should be willing to adopt complete free trade, GATT must be close to the political limit of what it can do. It may be that some progress can be made in reducing non-tariff barriers to trade. If so, non-tariff law will become negotiable.

Should the movement towards the equality of rights have to depend solely on international trade policy in the years to come, it may soon die of atrophy. The policy impetus would be lost. That would be almost inevitable. If trade policy stands still, while numerous national policies continue, it could only be a question of time before the active policies encroach upon the inactive one. If the movement towards equality is to continue, it must be given new impetus in a definable and negotiable way. Monetary integration is a possibility, but there may be others.

Whatever means are chosen, they should support and not replace what has been achieved. In the third quarter of the century, international trade policy provided the link between technological progress and political aspirations. Freer trade was, and will continue to be, an essential first step towards equality. Nevertheless, freer trade is only a means towards that end and not an end in itself.

Notes

1. For an account of the prospects in the late 1970s, see e.g. T.E. Josling, *Agriculture in the Tokyo Round Negotiations,* Thames Essays, Trade Policy Research Centre, London, 1977.
2. Estimate by K. Kojima, *Japan and a New World Economic Order*, Croom Helm,

London, 1977, p.125, based on GATT and Japanese data.

3. Note that according to one of the estimates of J.D. Gribbin; *The Profitability of UK Exports*, Government Economic Service Occasional Paper No.1, HMSO, p.6, the difference between profitability of UK home and export sales also came to 8½ per cent. That these results were identical is accident, but that they were close is unlikely to be mere accident.

INDEX

For Product Safety Concerns and Information please contact our EU representative GPSR@taylorandfrancis.com
Taylor & Francis Verlag GmbH, Kaufingerstraße 24, 80331 München, Germany

www.ingramcontent.com/pod-product-compliance
Lightning Source LLC
LaVergne TN
LVHW010629300926
849162LV00001B/99
9781138099692